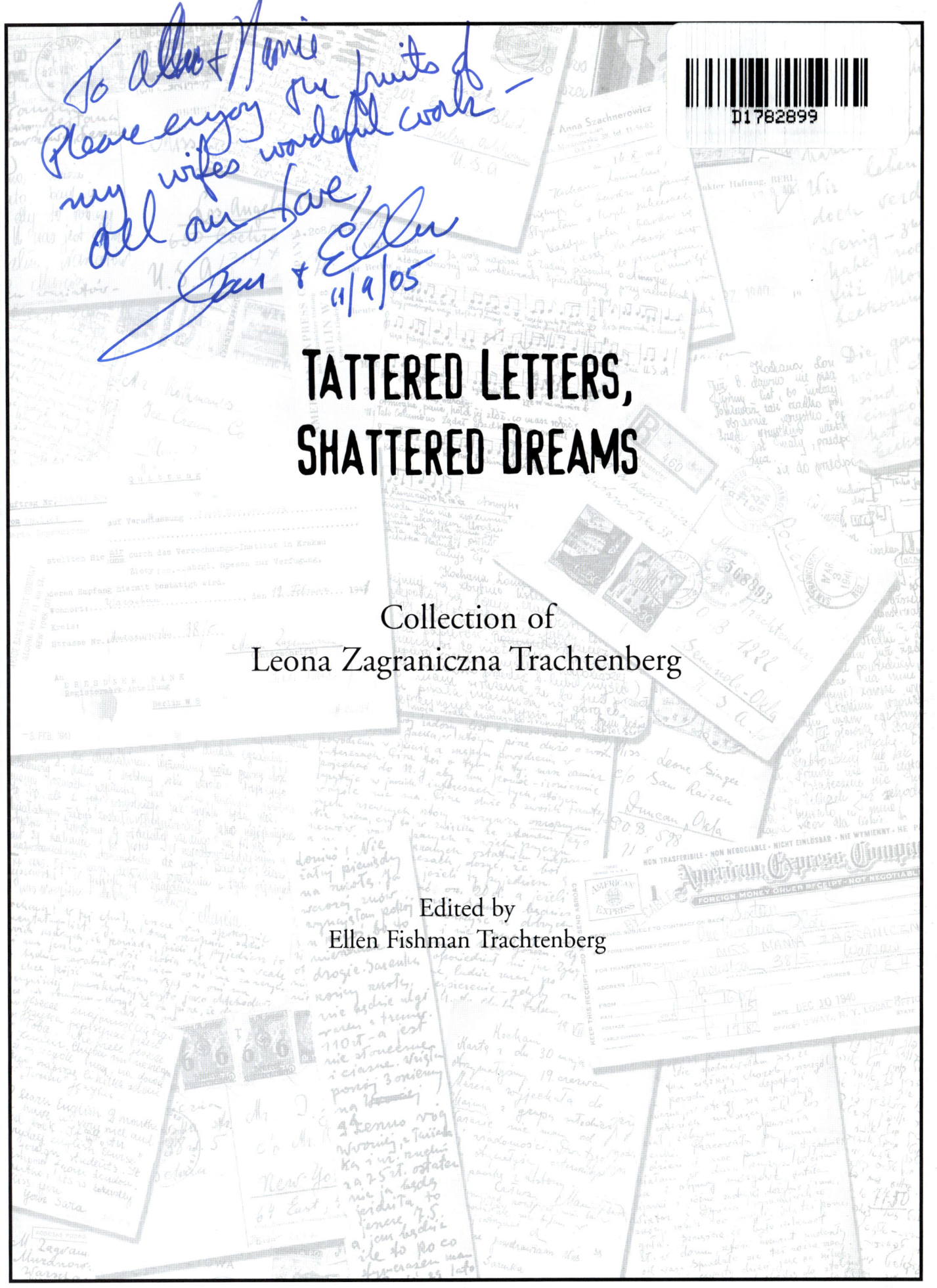

TATTERED LETTERS, SHATTERED DREAMS

Collection of
Leona Zagraniczna Trachtenberg

Edited by
Ellen Fishman Trachtenberg

Copyright © 2005 by Ellen Fishman Trachtenberg

All rights reserved.

Designed by: Jodi Braham, Pictor Design Studio

This book may not be reproduced or quoted in whole or in part by any means whatsoever without written permission.

Printed in the United States in association with
Holocaust Museum Houston
Houston, Texas

ISBN: 0-9659781-9-2

LCCN: 2005928188

DEDICATION

This book is dedicated to the family members who experienced man's inhumanity to man firsthand and especially in memory of Mania, Sarenka and Tamara.

Their own words, written over sixty years ago, allow us to experience their incredible spirits, their love of life, their hopes and dreams. Through these personal letters, we were finally able to "meet" our loved ones, to spend time with them and to love them. Their words and spirit have entered our hearts and we will pass them on to our children, grandchildren, and our future generations.

Mania and Jacob's legacy lives on...

In their grandchildren...
Leonard Wolf Trachtenberg (of blessed memory)
Daniel Stephen Trachtenberg
Marcia Trachtenberg Strongwater

In their great-grandchildren...
Alan Randall Trachtenberg
Mark Ryan Trachtenberg
David Leonard Trachtenberg
Barry Herman Trachtenberg
Leslie Mania Strongwater
Candice Joelle Strongwater

In their great-great-grandchildren...
Taylor Lynn Trachtenberg
Megan Hope Trachtenberg
Brandon Sidon Trachtenberg
Jacob Matthew Trachtenberg
Ava Kate Trachtenberg

Tattered Letters, Shattered Dreams

Table of Contents

Foreword 4

Acknowledgements 5

Introduction 7

Family Tree 10

Biographies 12

Warsaw Ghetto Map 16

Warsaw, 1938 17

Warsaw, 1939 83

Warsaw, 1940 131

Warsaw, 1941 161

Warsaw, 1942 187

Warsaw, 1943 – 1945 193

After the War 199

Photo Album 205

Personal Stories, Leona Trachtenberg 216

Personal Stories, Anna Meroz 228

Personal Stories, Victor Hochberg 261

FOREWORD

Six million Jews and an untold number of other innocent victims died in the Holocaust. It is a part of our universal history that millions of adults and scores of children worldwide have read about or studied.

Far fewer, most likely, have ever contemplated the impact on the millions of other lives destroyed by the separation of families, the hearts of mothers broken, never to heal from the loss of their children or the anguish from a gaping wound felt deep inside that comes from knowing you survived, while others just as deserving – even in your own family – did not.

Tattered Letters, Shattered Dreams provides a rare glimpse into the lives of one family – that of Leona Zagraniczna Trachtenberg – and how she coped with just such devastation in a time of worldwide upheaval.

From 1938 through 1941, the personal letters to Leona from her mother and her sisters, tell more than the story of a family broken apart, but also of a family struggling to live, to reunite, to support each other and to keep hope and courage alive inside the Warsaw Ghetto.

While the world around them fell apart, they shared motherly advice. They talked of the concerns of the day, of friends, of fashion, of parties and ordinary activities. Sometimes in words – but sometimes in between the lines of their text – they give us a peak into that universal relationship that exists between mothers, sisters and daughters, particularly in times of crisis.

Their message of love, hope, support and encouragement at a time of mankind's ultimate act of inhumanity to his fellow man, only affirms one of the essential lessons of the Holocaust – that every life is precious and has meaning.

The world will never know what it lost when these lives ended, when these families were separated and lost to each other forever.

The letters of Leona Trachtenberg and her family show ordinary people can make an extraordinary difference in the lives of those they touch and in the world in which we live.

We are grateful to Ellen and Dan Trachtenberg for sharing these personal letters from their family, and giving a human face to those who suffered such indignities and whom we will never know. Through this book, their stories will never be forgotten.

Susan Llanes-Myers
Executive Director
Holocaust Museum Houston

ACKNOWLEDGMENTS

The creation of this book was several years in the making and it became a labor of love for me. I found the letters in a cardboard box when we were cleaning out some cabinets at the house in Seminole, Oklahoma after Morris died. They were all folded up, out of sequence, in bits and pieces. I deeply appreciated Leona's entrusting me to care and preserve the papers and the family history contained in them.

We are greatly indebted to Leona, who had the courage to leave her family and her homeland, to create a new life and a new family for herself in the United States. We are so grateful that she had the foresight to save these pages from the past.

Although most of the letters were in Polish, some were in the other languages that Mania spoke — Hebrew, Yiddish, English, and German. It took some time to find the proper translators. I want to thank Thomas Brenstein who not only translated the Polish letters, but was particularly moved by the beauty of the language and the content, that he was compelled to meet Leona in person. Heartfelt appreciation goes to Alicia Kelly and her daughter, Eva, whose translations of additional material shed new light on the family's history.

I especially want to thank Lisa Moellering, Director of Collections at Holocaust Museum Houston, for her interest in the collection and for her encouragement in this project. Additionally, at Lisa's initiative, and with her help and that of curator Valorie Olsen, I created an exhibit of some of Leona's letters and photographs for public display in the museum library in 2003. This exhibit illustrated the story of one family's efforts to emigrate from Poland and their subsequent fate in the Warsaw Ghetto. It has been my great pleasure to work directly with Lisa in many areas at the museum and to learn from this very special lady.

I would like to thank Janice Ly, the graphic designer at HMH, for her talent and assistance in helping to design the exhibit. Christina Vasquez, Director of Education at HMH, was extremely supportive of the exhibit and its power to teach, offering me great encouragement for the book. I promised her she could use this book as a tool for the teachers she trains. She would honor the memory of all the teachers in Leona's family.

I am also indebted to Susan Llanes-Myers for her support and friendship over the years. She is an extraordinary teacher, an extremely competent administrator and a beloved director with a passion for the museum and its survivors. She has taken Holocaust Museum Houston to new heights and has made our name known all over the world.

I have known Jodi Braham, the graphic designer, since she was born, and take great pleasure in watching her mature and her talent blossom.

Special thanks to my sisters-in-law, Marcia Strongwater and Sylvia Trachtenberg, for their love, friendship, and encouragement over the years.

I remember with love, two very special family members. Dan's brother, Lenny, left us too soon, but his memory will live on and comfort us forever. And I remember Morris, Leona's beloved and my father-in-law, who cherished his family and his Judaism, and whose intellect lit the way for all of us.

Thanks would not be complete without my remembering my own parents, Moise and Lillian Aronson Fishman, whose presence I miss dearly. Whoever I am today was made possible by the love, values, traditions, and lessons they imparted to me. I still have their family story to tell.

A very personal thanks to Dan, my partner in life and my link to the past, and our three sons, Mark, David and Barry, and our daughter-in-law, Stefanie, who are our links to the future. Their fine characters and outstanding accomplishments give me hope for the future. This book is also for our grandchildren, Jacob and Ava, so they and their future siblings and cousins, can know their family and bear their name with pride. May Jacob and Ava pass to future generations the love of family, love of Judaism, love of country, and love of life that emanate from these letters.

Ellen Fishman Trachtenberg
September 5, 2005

INTRODUCTION

This collection contains letters and other documents belonging to Leona Zagraniczna (Singer) Trachtenberg, who was born in Warsaw, Poland, November 23, 1917 and died in Englewood, New Jersey on August 12, 2002, having also lived in Seminole, Oklahoma and Houston, Texas.

Leona was the oldest of three daughters of Mania Hochberg and Jacob Zagraniczny. Jacob, born in Rowno, Russia in 1888, the son of a well-known cantor, was also a cantor, musician, and teacher, well-versed in Jewish studies. Mania was born in 1897 into a large family of eleven children. Her mother was a midwife and her father, who died when she was eleven years old, had studied medicine in Switzerland.

After Mania and Jacob were married, they purchased a seminary for Hebrew kindergarten teachers and added a Hebrew kindergarten. However, in 1928, Jacob left Poland in order to improve the economic situation for his family. Since he was not able to procure a visa for entry into the United States, he landed in Canada, then crossed the border into the U.S. with a false passport. The fact that he was not a U.S. citizen greatly limited his job opportunities and ended his dream of being reunited with his family.

After Jacob left, Mania began musical studies at the Warsaw Conservatory of Music which allowed her to obtain a position with the government and gave her the means to support herself and her daughters.

Once Jacob realized that war was inevitable, he asked his cousin, Morris Singer of Tulsa, Oklahoma, who had emigrated years earlier, for help. Morris managed to provide one affidavit for immigration so Leona, being the eldest, was chosen to emigrate. Leona arrived in New York City on June 7, 1938, aboard the boat, *The Batory*, with the expectation that her mother and sisters, Sarenka and Tamara (Marcia), would be permitted to leave soon and the family would be reunited.

These letters, kept by Leona in a cardboard box, are the correspondence from her mother, sisters, friends, and family from 1938 until the letters stopped in November, 1941. As Mania was proficient in several languages, the letters were written not only in Polish, but also in Hebrew, Yiddish, English and German.

In these letters, Mania tried to advise her daughter living so far away in America. She also tried to protect her from the hardships they were experiencing and from the tragedies that occurred after the Warsaw Ghetto was established in November, 1940. The sisters' letters were livelier, typical of teenage girls, filled with accounts of parties, friends, school, fashion styles, and heartbreakingly, their hopes for their future in the United States and the reunion with the father they barely knew. Almost until the very end, they were hopeful that they would be allowed to emigrate – even though it might take several years for their visas.

The personalities and unique qualities of Mania, Sarenka and Tamara, shone through in the many letters from 1938 and 1939, allowing today's family members to "get to know" these relatives they were deprived of ever meeting. As the conditions worsened and the ghetto was established, paper became more scarce and the letters reduced to brief messages on postcards. Some letters were sent to a cousin in Italy for forwarding to Leona in the U.S. or mailed through Lisbon, a neutral city. Most of these postcards from 1940 and 1941 asked for help and acknowledged the receipt of packages and money orders, their only means of survival, sent to the family from the United States. Unique to this collection are the receipts for these money orders and food packages sent to Warsaw and later into the ghetto, which had been saved by Jacob.

Leona, meanwhile, was torn. On one hand she was trying to live her life as a beautiful young woman of twenty and plan for her own future, while still taking care of her father. On the other hand, she felt guilty that she was free and not suffering the fate of her loved ones. She felt it was her responsibility to save her family, to get them out of Poland, an impossible feat. When she arrived in New York, her father, unable to provide a warm home environment for her, encouraged her to move to Duncan, Oklahoma where she was lovingly welcomed into the family of Fannie and Sam Raizen. She attended high school in order to improve her English skills. She was vacationing with the Raizens in California when Germany invaded Poland on September 1, 1939.

Leona did not learn the details of her family's deaths until the late 1960's when she visited relatives and friends in Israel. She received some comfort from being able to reminisce with these survivors about her mother and the sisters she had cherished. She lived the rest of her life feeling guilty that she had not been able to save them even though there was nothing she could have done.

Tamara was born August 18, 1922, described by Leona as an extrovert, full of life, fun-loving, sensitive, with a great sense of humor. She was also an accomplished pianist who studied at the Warsaw Conservatory of Music. As conditions worsened in the ghetto, Tamara was distraught, constantly in tears at the sight of corpses lying on the street, covered with newspapers. She organized concerts to raise money for the orphans in the ghetto. She also took bread from home (where it was already scarce) to give to the emaciated children she saw begging for food. Tamara, once so vivacious, stopped talking. She died of typhus contracted in the deplorable conditions of the ghetto on June 12, 1941, in the arms of her beloved uncle Victor, and was buried in the Gesia Cemetery. In her futile attempt to protect Leona, Mania never told her of Tamara's death. Instead Mania told Leona that Tamara had run away with a youth group and she feared that she would never see her again

Sarenka, born June 24, 1921, was only seven years old when her father left. She was described by Leona as a sweet, shy, reserved girl with a beautiful soprano voice. She graduated from the Comercium in 1939 and delayed further education in anticipation of emigration. Several months after Tamara's death, Sarenka married her sister's fiancee, David Lazar, who later perished. When she became pregnant, her Aunt Ida arranged for a doctor to abort her pregnancy due to the horrendous conditions in the ghetto. Too weak to get out of bed, she and Mania clung to each other when Nazi soldiers screamed for all Jews to report for deportation to the camps. Mania refused to leave Sarenka and vowed that they would die together or survive together. The soldier, upon reaching their room, pulled Mania off of her daughter and then shot Sarenka in the heart.

After Sarenka was killed, Mania was dragged by her hair, down the stairs, to the Umschlagplatz (deportation point). She was herded into the "death wagons" by the butt of a Nazi's rifle. Suddenly, this weakened, grieving woman, jumped up and with the same extraordinary strength and courage with which she had lived her life, slapped the German soldier standing over her. He looked dumbstruck for a moment and then reacted by shooting her in the head. She died in the street in 1942 at the age of forty-five. Mania's death was witnessed by a friend of hers who had escaped to safety in the sewers.

Meanwhile, Mania's mother had been placed in the ghetto hospital by her daughter, Ida, a pediatrician, in the hopes of saving her life. But the Germans emptied the hospital and killed or deported the sick and elderly.

Through family connections, Leona met Morris Trachtenberg who had emigrated from a small shtetl in Russia in 1921. They were married in Oklahoma on December 24, 1939 with Jacob chanting the prayers under the chuppah. Mania and the girls were so elated that Leona had found such happiness and were looking forward to meeting Leona's husband.

Leona and Morris moved to Seminole, Oklahoma where they reared three children (the oldest son, Lenny, died of cancer in 1975). Jacob lived long enough to see all three grandchildren, before he collapsed and died on a street in New York at age fifty-nine. Leona had six grandchildren and four great-grandchildren when she died in 2002.

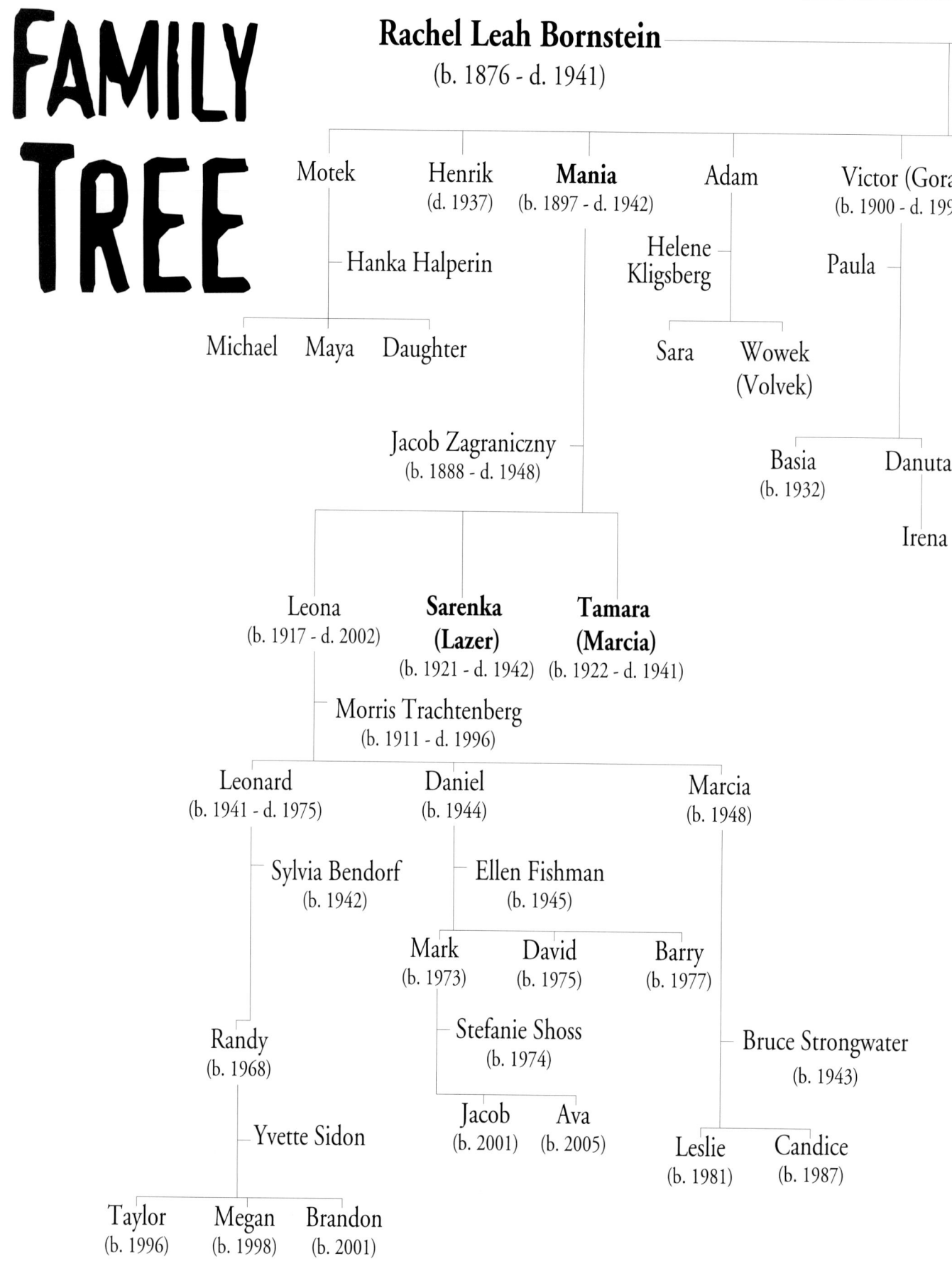

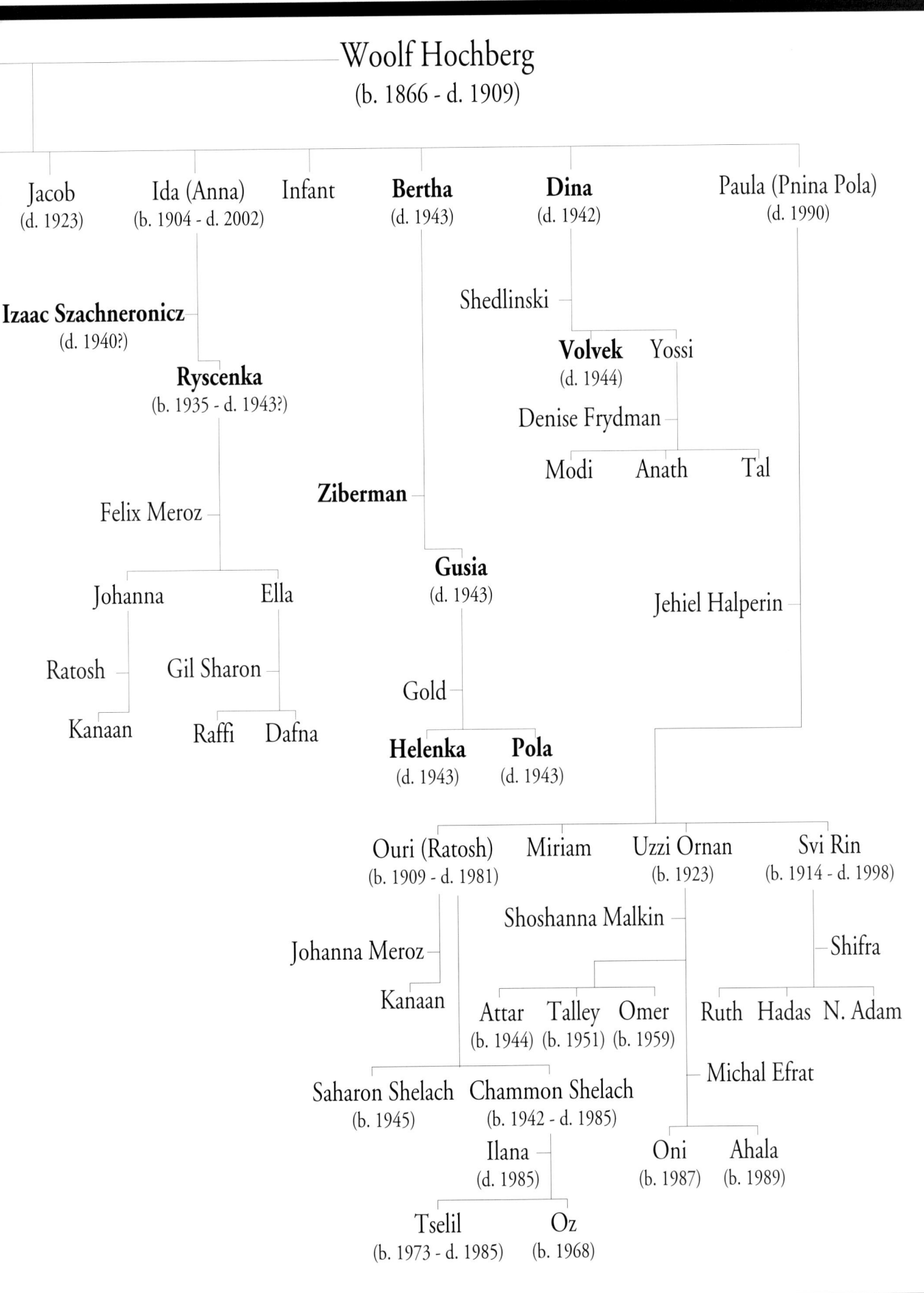

BIOGRAPHIES

Rachel Leah Borenstein Hochberg *(b. 1876 - d. 1941)*
Ruchla was a midwife who reared ten children by herself after her husband, Woolf, died at age 43. She was killed, along with other ill and elderly patients, after being taken from the hospital in the Warsaw Ghetto.

Woolf Hochberg *(b. 1866 - d. 1909)*
Woolf received a diploma of medicine in Geneva, Switzerland, after passing the examinations without having gone through medical school. He saw some patients but he mainly worked at the shoe factory he had inherited. He died from pneumonia contracted when he was imprisoned in Pawjak jail, where he was being held on political grounds, resulting from a case of mistaken identity. Their children:

Motek (Marek) Hochberg
Motek was forced to run away to Russia as he was a journalist with communistic ideas. His children still live in the Former Soviet Union. He was killed in a Russian camp.

Heniek Hochberg
Heniek also ran away to Russia and died as a political prisoner there in 1937. He was the editor of a Russian newspaper, "The Red Flag". His son, Felix, is a Russian literature specialist in central Russia.

Jacob Hochberg
Jacob was the "black sheep" of the family. He volunteered for the militia in WWI, escaped at age 16, and went to Vienna. In 1918, he became a Polish policeman and married a non-Jewish woman. He later went to Russia where he died in 1923 in a prison camp in the Gulag.

Adam Hochberg
Adam earned an electrical engineering degree in Geneva, Switzerland. He was eccentric and wrote poetry which was published in Polish newspapers. He had two children:

Sara Hochberg
Sara was a communist who ran away to Russia.

Wowek Hochberg (now known as Vladislav Gora)
Wowek (Volvek) teaches political science at Warsaw University. He was well known in his field and won prizes.

Wiktov (Witold, Victor) – Hochberg (Gora) *(b. 1900 - d. 1994)*
Victor was an electrical engineer. (See his Remembrances for details of his story). He had two daughters who still live in Warsaw.

Basia (Barbara) Gora (b. 1934)
Basia is a professor of agriculture and a translator. She never married after her Russian boyfriend died. She survived the war because her father hid her with Christian families. She was active in the Hidden Children's Group in Warsaw.

Danuta Gora
Danuta is a retired professor of pharmacy at Warsaw University. She is married to a Greek man and has one daughter, Irena. She was also hidden by her father with Christian families.

Pola (Paula, Pnina) Hochberg Halperin (b. 1890's - d. 1990)
Pola was a Zionist who emigrated to Palestine in the 1920's. She and her husband, Jehiel Halperin, had owned a seminary for Hebrew kindergarten teachers which they sold to Mania and Jacob before they emigrated. Her children:

Miriam

Uzzi Ornan (b. 1923)
Uzzi was a Professor of Hebrew Linguistics at Hebrew University in Jerusalem and is a distinguished visiting professor of Computer Science at the Technion in Haifa, Israel. He has published dozens of articles and several books.

Svi Rin (b. 1914 - d. 1998)
Svi was a Professor and Department Head of Oriental Studies at the University of Pennsylvania.

Uriel Halpern Shelach (Jonaton Ratosh – pen name) (b. 1909 - d. 1981)
Uriel was a famous Israeli poet and a leader of the Canaanite Movement, a radical Israeli political group. He had two children by his first wife and a daughter, Kanaan, by his second wife, Johanna Meroz, his first cousin, daughter of Anna. His children:

Chammon Shelach (d. 1985)
Chammon was a magistrate in Jerusalem who was killed with his wife, his daughter, and four other Israeli tourists by an Egyptian soldier in the Sinai in 1985. He is survived by a son, Oz.

Saharon Shelach (b. 1945)
Saharon is a noted Israeli mathematician and a Professor at both Hebrew University and Rutgers University. As one of the most prolific contemporary mathematicians, he has published more than 750 papers. He was honored by the Hungarian Academy of Sciences in 2000.

Anna (Ida) Hochberg Szachnerowicz Meroz (b. 1904 - d. 2002)
Anna was a pediatrician in Warsaw with whom Mania lived in her last years in the Ghetto, whose first husband and daughter were murdered in the Ghetto. Her brother, Victor, got her false papers and saved her life as well as many others. She married Felix Meroz, emigrated to Israel and continued to practice medicine. Her children:

Ella Sharon
Ella is a violinist, and with her husband, Gil, performs with the Amsterdam Symphony. Gil is an internationally known musician who was honored in 1997 by HM Queen Beatrix of the Netherlands for his outstanding merits in the domain of chamber music. They have two children.

Johanna
Johanna married her cousin, Jonaton Ratosh, and has a daughter, Kanaan.

Bertha Hochberg Ziberman Gold (d. 1943)
Bertha was a teacher. Her first husband died of TB and left her with one daughter, Gusia. She married a widower with grown daughters, had two more daughters, and the second husband died. She died of typhus in the Ghetto and her three daughters were murdered in the ghetto. Two of her daughters were in Januz Korshak's orphanage in the Ghetto.

Dyna Hochberg Shedlinski (d. 1942)
Dyna was a nurse whose husband ran away to South America, leaving her with two sons. She was killed in Treblinka in 1942. Her children:

Yossi Siedlecki
Yossi lives in Israel, is married to Denise Frydman and has three children – Moti, Anath and Tal.

Volvek (d. 1944)
Volvek was killed in the war.

Mania Hochberg Zagraniczna (b. 1897 – d. 1942)
Leona's mother. (See Leona's Remembrances.)

Jacob Zagraniczny (Zar)
Born in Rowno, Russia, in 1888, Jacob died in New York City, on August 29, 1948. Leona's father. (See Leona's Remembrances.) Their children:

Sarenka (b. 1921 – d. 1942)

Tamara (b. 1922 – d. 1941)

Leona (b. 1917 – d. 2002)

Morris Trachtenberg (b. 1911 – d. 1996)
Morris Trachtenberg was born in Korostyshev, Ukraine to Brucha and Labe Trachtenberg, one of 6 boys and one girl. After his father's death, ten year old Morris and his twelve year old brother, Jack, emigrated to the United States and lived with their aunt and uncle in Philadelphia until their mother's arrival. Morris graduated from pharmacy school in Chicago and then moved to Oklahoma during the depression to work for relatives as a bookkeeper in Seminole, Oklahoma. He eventually went into the pipe and supply business with Jack and their older brother, Bill. Morris was also related to Morris Singer who brought Leona to the U. S. After seeing a photograph of her, he told his cousin that if he brought her over that he would marry her.

Leonard Wolf Trachtenberg (b. 1941 – d. 1975)
Lenny was the oldest child of Leona and Morris, a graduate of the University of Oklahoma with a BBA in business administration. He worked in the family oil well supply business. Lenny died of Hodgkins disease at the age of thirty-three. He is remembered for his courage, charisma, and his love of family. Lenny was named for his grandfather, Woolf Hochberg.

Daniel Stephen Trachtenberg *(b. 1944)*

Dan is the middle child of Leona and Morris, a graduate of Tulane University and University of Texas Law School. He is an attorney in Houston, Texas and a very active member of the Houston Jewish community. Dan was named for his aunt, Sarenka.

Marcia Trachtenberg Strongwater *(b. 1947)*

Marcia is the youngest child of Leona and Morris, a graduate of the University of Oklahoma with a masters degree in psychology. She has been a psychology teacher at a private high school in New Jersey for many years. She was named for her aunt, Tamara.

Leona's Friends…

Marie Melamed Parreau

Marie was a childhood friend of Leona's who was studying medicine in Belgium at the outbreak of the war. She survived in France and settled there after the war, having lost her entire family.

Danka Zdunska

Danka was a childhood friend of Leona's, known for her mathematical prowess, who emigrated to Israel in the late 1950's from Poland with her husband and two daughters. The Trachtenberg family retains close ties with Danka and her family and Danka and Uncle Victor were very close after the death of his wife. Her brother, Natek (Nathan) was Leona's boyfriend for several years.

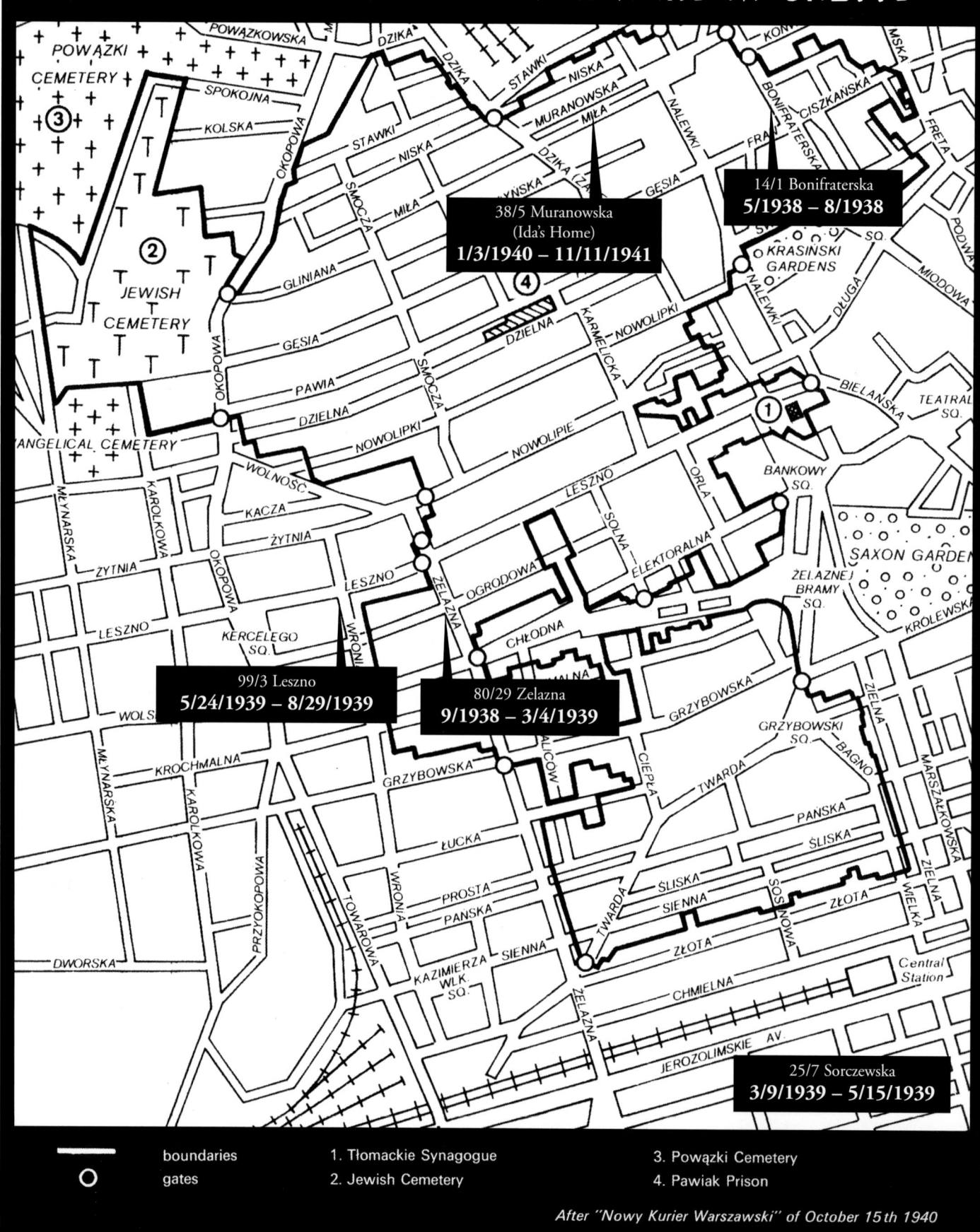

WARSAW 1938

The earliest presence of Jews dates from the 15th century.

The 1792 census shows 6,750 Jews, 1/10 of the city's population.

Nineteenth century Warsaw was the capital of Polish Jewry and an important world Jewish center.

The Jewish population of Warsaw was approximately 375,000 (29.1% of the total population).

It was a vibrant, diversified community.

There were 53 Jewish schools, 27 Jewish newspapers, and over 300 synagogues.

August 23, 1938. *Postcard from Mania to Leona saying that she could never tolerate living in a provincial city in Oklahoma after living in Warsaw. The lines that are not readable were crossed out by Marcia.*

October 16, 1938. *Letter from Aunt Anna written on her medical stationery*

July 31, 1938. *Top part of the letter is written in Yiddish to Jakob by Mania, followed by messages to Leona from her friend, Hanka Singer and her sister, Sarenka.*

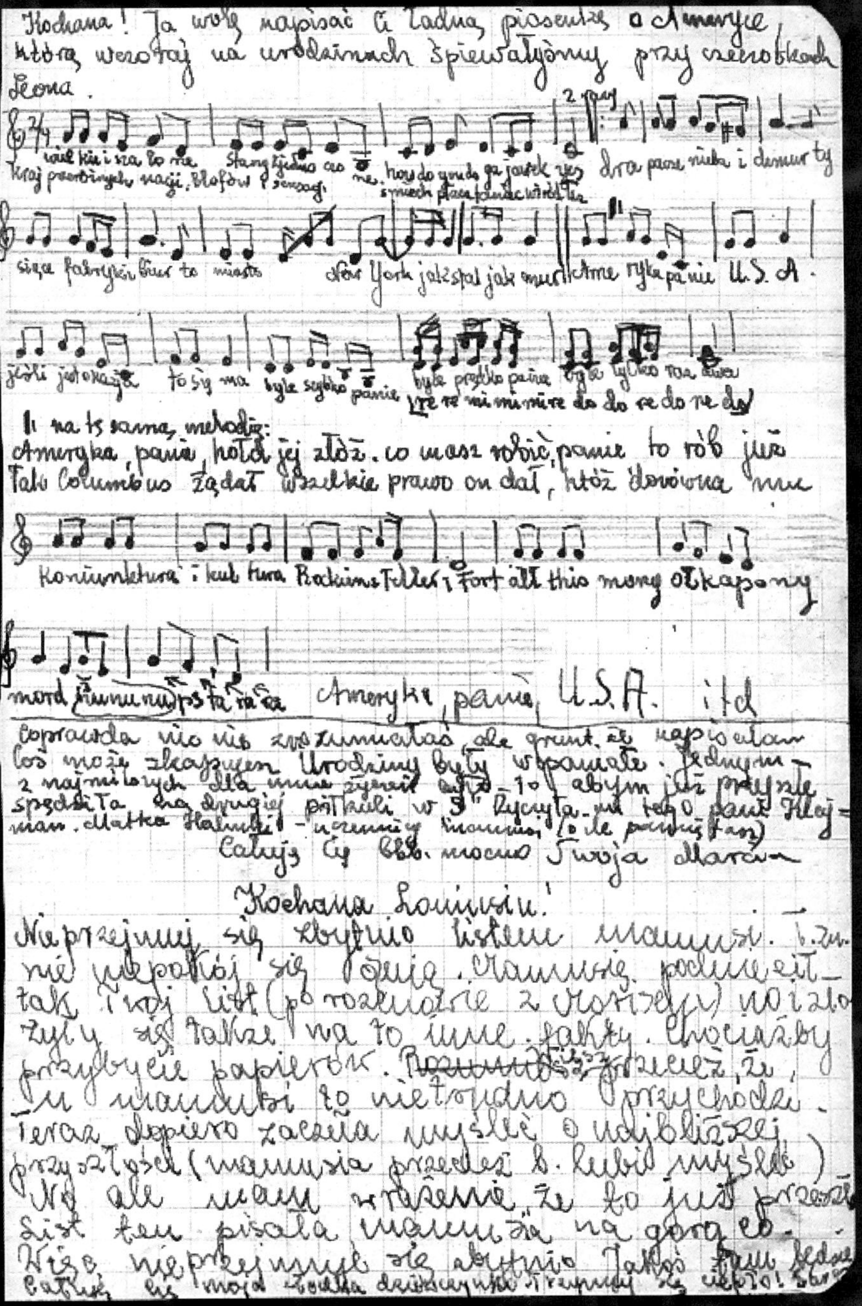

August 22, 1938. Words and music of a song about America, composed by Tamara and sung at her birthday party.

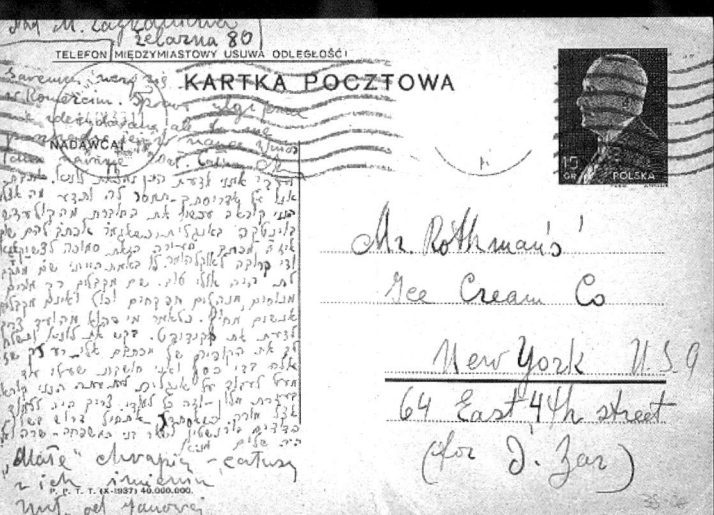

September 14, 1938. Postcard written to Jacob and Leona in care of Jacob's sister and brother-in-law's ice cream shop in New York City. The first half of the letter was written in Polish to Leona, the rest in Hebrew to Jacob.

Translator's note: Letters of May 1938 are addressed to Leona Zagraniczna in care of an emigration camp set up in Gdynia, Poland, while awaiting to be boarded on the ship "Batory".

May 25, 1938

Dear!

Your departure was so delightful and fabulous that no one present at the train station will ever forget it. You are sweet and brave, all that truly matters in life. I remind you that you must have a receipt for your travel basket. If you did not get it, you need to immediately. The only thing that you left behind was your diary from Plock. If someone decides to go over there, she will take it to you. I took a taxi-cab straight from the train station to the house; Ignas paid for it. Our entire group returned back to our house – would you believe that even Ester and Tolek came over, even though they had been fighting, and finally made peace by shaking hands (according to Mietek and Ignas solely for the appearances sake). Ignas provided us with all the vodka. I drank brudershaft with Mietek and Ignas. The entire group partied till midnight. Of course, Marcia and I, went to bed at 10:30 pm. I feel fabulous – just wish to hear from you that you have lost nothing and stay healthy. Do not expect me to come but who knows; I still may come over. Mietek and I are supposed make a decision tomorrow. Mina came over to the house. She was late. Passed her secondary school examination. Kisses.

    Mania

Dear Loniu!

Your departure was truly joyful. Our entire company had a fabulous time, including me (though I did not drink any vodka). It was awesome. Well, I kiss you heartily and even stronger than that.

    Sarenka

P.S. Loniu! Did Natek ride with you? Best regards for him.

Dearest angel!

You have no idea how happy we are about your departure. I was just a little sad at the train station. Afterwards, Ignas and I returned home by car and the rest of our group met us here. We all wanted to drink to your health but mommy said that you will be better off than any one of us and we ended up drinking to our own health. Mommy is incredibly happy and she feels fantastic. I kiss your sunny face and you my eyes, don't you? Keep warm! Dearest, gorgeous puppy. Ciao!

    Marcia

May 25, 1938

Lonius!

Just a moment ago, Polcia Lazer came over and here we are writing you again. We are all most interested in the chocolate issue resolution. How much will they allow you to take? Probably, you will have to eat some. Possibly, we could accept some which you sent with Natek or through the postal service, if he doesn't plan to return to Warszawa. Just tell him not to eat any of it as he had more than enough in Rowne. We are concerned about his stomach as he showed some signs of coming down with a serious sickness in Michalin (and Dr. Lejbowicz isn't around). We ate four boxes of chocolates together with the rest of the troops. And we want more.

    Mania

Dear Lonius!

It turns out for the best that I am over here, as I can remind you that you are not permitted to transport any opened articles. Therefore, you should open them all. Dear, I was unable to say my good-byes properly. Thus, I am doing it now and wish you that all your dreams come true. I ask that your first letter be equally beautiful like Marysia's letter. I believe that, even if you do become homesick, it will be only at first.

    Pola (sweet), right?

Dear Loniusiu!

How are you holding up? Did any quarantines start already? Remember to write us letters and to get a nice tan while on the ship. That album you left behind will be sent over to you through someone going to Gdynia. They might even be: mommy, Mietek, Mina, Wiktor, etc.

    Marcik

Dear Loniuchno!

We are just so full of admiration for you. Polcia L. and I talked so much about you that mommy decided to write this card. The chocolates were so good that gorged on them to the point of feeling sick in my mouth. We swiped a total of 5 chocolate boxes. Of course, not a crumb is left by now. Well, I say good-bye.

    Sarenka

P.S. We got from Rowne a photograph of our dad in his youth. It is beautiful. We kiss you with all our hearts!!

May 26, 1938

My sweetest L.!

I expected to get some mail from you today but forgot that today is a holiday — I will wait patiently till tomorrow. Mostly, I am concerned about your receipt for the basket and that the tags on it weren't glued on properly. maybe it needs to be corrected! I want to believe that you are holding on as strongly as on your departure day at the station — healthy, happy and, of course, so sweet. In the morning, I went to see Izak and showed him the bump. He told me that it is nothing to worry about and that it will slowly go away. He fixed my leg and bandaged it which made my walking quite comfortable now. I was ready to take a trip to Gdynia but this "horrible" Izak told me that something else may strain in such a "long" journey and another blood vessel may burst. In this light, I am forced to forego this dreamed about trip to Gdynia, or more precisely, to see you. But to brighten up the moment, let me inform you that yesterday evening Wawus brought over a sweet letter from Rowne, from Jacob, with the news already known to us (the offer) and an expression of a great delight because of that. Aunt Sara is aware that your ship will depart on the 28th so there is no need to telegram her. You will be met by Sara Rothman your aunt, or possibly your uncle, David Rothman. The big Wawek had 38.6 degrees temperature on the day of your departure (strep throat) and that is why he couldn't be there. Remember about things and your health. I anxiously await any news from you and kiss your sweet face.

    Mania

Dearest Loniusiu!

My exams are tomorrow but I am not nervous. As you know, we (with meat ball) are planning to meet with all your schoolmates. Today, I met Bronka Klamar who asked for your address. She wants to send you something through someone. Sarencik is at school. Anka is here and wants to add a few words.

(not signed but in Marcia's handwriting)

Best wishes and a pleasant journey sends,

    Anka

May 27, 1938

Dear Loniusiu!

Just a moment ago I received 2 cards from you which greatly improved my spirits. I was waiting for over an hour for the postman and was starting to worry since, according to my calculations, today should have been a regular day for mail – and what do you know, our postman delivered the cards proudly to the school. Sweetest! I kept on wondering if Natek did manage to join you in the 2nd class (on the train to Gdynia). It was marvelous that he did it in my place. If you were to travel all by yourself, I am certain that I would have gone along with you. I will listen to Izak's, and now also your, advice to forego the trip. Grandmother ordered me to spend the money on oranges instead of Gdynia. Saruz bought yesterday a half kilogram yesterday without any further questions but it turned out to be unnecessary as I felt great (due to bromide, of course). Apparently, the distance put from last Tuesday takes its effect as I start to sleep 2 hours longer every night — first night only 2 hours, second night 4 hours, which makes me to believe that tonight I should be able to sleep at least 6 hours, etc. Needless to say, I will try not to oversleep on Sunday as the school starts for me. I forgot to write you in the last 3 cards (which I don't know if you received) that along with the troops from the station came the Malewiaks – and what went along with it – official apologies. Dearest! Count it out for yourself but we will be at Michalin starting approximately around July 1st and that is where you should mail all your letters. The first letter from New York will most likely arrive to Warszawa around June 25th — such a long time away. Write, write as much as you can along your journey. Send us a photograph from the ship and, especially, describe to us your travel friends and companions. Sarenka is at school. Marcia is taking her exams. After dinner we will write you another postcard. If you still can, give Natek my personal thanks for taking care of my little "puppy". Your fabulous departure continues to be the topic of the day by everyone around. Mrs. Mankowa even said at the house that it was worth paying 5 zloty for the tickets to see you depart.

    Mania

P.S. Janowa sends her greetings to both you and Natek.

My Sweet!

I have just returned home. I passed it with 4* (average)!! So long.

    Marcia

> **Translator's note:** Polish grading system ranges from 2 (equivalent to "F") to 5 (equivalent to "A"). Marcia's grade here would approximate "B-".

May 31, 1938

Dearest daughter!

Today arrived your sweetest letter from the ship dated May 29th. I am just speechless from joy with respect to your health and good humor. Maybe you will not get sick after all; that is, you have not been getting sick but I still would like to know all the details of your journey and how you feel throughout it. I was quite concerned with you getting off the ship in different ports (eg. Copenhagen), as I mistrust casually met acquaintances, but Natek just dropped by and assured me that the husband is a truly nice guy. May God let you feel always and anywhere as good as at the moment you wrote this letter. I await anxiously a joint letter from New York. Write about all of it — from "a" to "z". Kisses for all those who deserve them. Take care of your health and good humor. Everyone here is healthy. It is already my third day back to school. Kiss warmly your aunt and uncle. Do rest very well immediately after the journey and all these sensations.

    Mania

Sweet Loniu!

What letters?! It appears that you were born with the writing skills matching those of both mommy and daddy. You are just so lucky. Many say that you were born under a lucky star. Regards for my Kasprowicz and from this end to you from Lu Hanne, Lazers, Lubliner and all the others. We do not miss you at all since: (1) you are having such a great time and (2) recently we have spent so little time with each other (you were so busy) that we just got used to this. Have a great time and describe what the ocean looks like and your entire trip. Warm kisses. Did you write Pola Boren?

    Marcia

Dear Loniusiu!

We are truly fascinated with your delightful letters. Was it really that wonderful on Batory? We are certain that you will write us all about it in detail. We are all healthy. Regards from everyone.

    Sarenka

Dearest Loniusiu!

I am taking this advantage to send you warmest regards and kisses. I will write more separately (a letter) to New York. Stay healthy. Kisses.

    (name not readable)

> **Translator's note:** The front of this postcard starts with a note in Yiddish followed by another note translated below.

Heartful regards for the uncle and aunt and the rest of the family. Chana Zagranicia
Dear, sweet, beautiful, sunny girl!

I kiss you, kiss you, kiss you mightily, mightily, mightily. My dearest Loniek! When will I see you? Your letters read like fairy-tales. You are a delightful, girl, as always. Regards from the boys. Pass on our regards to aunt and uncle. Best wishes.

    Your Dzidziula

June 3, 1938

Letter written to Jacob in Yiddish.

Dear Jacob,

While you are reading my letter you must have been happy for several days. I am waiting for the thank you. Maybe you will mail something worth for her (?). Sarenka is a head taller than any of us. Marcia looks everyday more like Lonia. I am waiting impatiently for the news, how she came and who picked her up. How she feels after such a trip. She remembers you a little. I can't imagine how you look. I agree to travel to Israel. The story like Lonia writes, you have to ride second class and for three people it will cost a lot, unless I'll be able to sell my part(?). Maybe you will be able to send -----(?) because you can't take money out, than I'll go to Tel Aviv. If not I'll travel like Lonia. We are talking about travel like it is actually here. I would like to know how long Lonia will stay in New York. I am fine. My leg is bandaged. I fell in the bathtub, I slipped three weeks ago, a vein busted. I laid five days with ice on it. But now I have to see that my veins will heal. Yesterday I bought medicine for five and one-half zlotys and I'll need a rubber hose all the way up. That's the reason I didn't go to Newfeld(?) after school. I rest. I can't strain the leg. As you know with Lonia I said good-by in a happy way, without a tear. Now everything is upside down. I hope we will see each other soon. It left me with a hard sign on my weak nerves. I hope everything will quiet down. I hope we will all be happy. I hope to make money this summer and here I am spending.

     Mania

June 3rd

My dear!

Probably you have been in the big New York for the past few days. We impatiently await your description of this "marvelous trip". How is your health? You should rest well after such a journey. How did you find Jakub? He can be such an excitable person; just like Marcia. You also are not exactly like me. I am not asking you anything now. I believe that you will write me in detail all the experiences encountered by that "green person". Enclosed please find the address of that Spigel. Essigmowala wrote him about you plus encloses here with an address: Ms. Mara Spiegel, 601 West 142nd Street, Apartment 9D, New York. Would you believe that his mother had the audacity, upon receipt of that letter, to write her back requesting to send her some "lajka". Find him in the telephone book or send him a card — most likely it would be proper to visit him and chat "like humans" — it maybe worth something later. His father owns a travel agency which may come in handy (ticket to Oklahoma, etc., maybe some trips). An excellent excuse anyway and it may make you feel better. What happened to your travel companion? Did you meet anyone else? Maybe Captain Burzynski who, you may not even be aware of that, you traveled with? Write to Michalin. I will notify the post office to forward anything that comes to address in Warszawa.

     Mania

Translator's note: This card is addressed to J. Zar and includes a note to him in Hebrew. The remainder thereof is in Polish to Leona.

June 18, 1938

Peace unto you, Jacob!

Your letter caused me a great deal of aggravation. For two hours, I have been under its influences. Do not think that I will not travel if the opportunity to do so will be available. I wish Morris will be able to take me as he wrote like a teacher. First maybe I will really earn a little and second, this will be the closest way to come. This is anyhow the way it seems to me. I am expecting a longer letter and I will know what is going on with Lonia, where she will be and what she will be doing. I think she has to travel to Oklahoma even though I will not be able to express my opinion, because I do not know your plan. Over the summer days it seems to me she will need to rest a little; then, if she will have the opportunity both to learn and at the same time to earn a little money it will be good. I would like her to find the environment she deserves and that she will not regret all we have done on her behalf. She traveled at a very good age. She just needs the right surroundings to make her happy. The main thing is that she shouldn't always be longing and should live life to the fullest. Many, many kisses to you and to her. This too will pass. We will definitely meet soon. These days I will be with Neufeld. My leg continues to get better. Most mornings I go by foot to school. I only have to buy stockings made of rubber. The little ones are not at home. Good-by. Good-by.

    Mania

Lonius!

I waited peacefully until yesterday. Last night I started to worry. Today I am happy. I can feel Jacob's happiness, and yours, of course. It is so nice to regain something so far away that almost elusive. I try to imagine what the two of you go through emotionally. Until recently, I constantly thought about my leg. Finally, I allowed myself to be talked into seeing a private doctor, Borkowski. He operated on Mrs. Natanowicz. That visit put me completely at ease. Imagine that, in his professional opinion, my varicose vein did not burst open. Instead, he claims, there was a strong hit to my leg which burst a blood vessel. He prescribed a nightly compress of Goulard water with an addition of boric acid. I can walk to school with no worries. However, I must wear special elastic hoses which I have already ordered (10 zloty advance deposit). He said my leg will hurt for another 10 days; afterwards the pains should slowly diminish. He also forbade me to attempt the cure with shots – strictly the use of elastic hoses. Until visiting him, I usually took rides to school. Now I walk over there freely. Next time write to Michalin. We will leave for Michalin around the 1st. I am quite bewildered after today's letter. I am quite wordless. I await more news from you. Szrignerowa requests that you visit Marym as she is very worried about him. There has been no letters from him for weeks due to a "broken pen". My other monsters aren't home. We will write you all together after receipt of your next letter. I kiss you, my love.

    Mania

Dear Loniusiu!

Yesterday arrived your letter from Batory informing us of healthy body and healthy spirit and supported with your sweet photographs. I impatiently await your letter from a permanent or, at least, more permanent place though I do realize that all that "permanence" in reality is very inconsistent. I suspect that you will settle down somewhere more permanent around August or September. Only then you will be able to write about it. In the meantime, I read with a great worry a story in the local newspaper about a railroad accident in the USA and I dread the thought that you could be among those more or less fortunate people. After all, you are traveling, though I do not know exactly when, to Oklahoma. If you had some heart, you would send me a telegram and spare me my health. I already had one scare like that before, Lonius, after you departed on Batory. A few days later I read in the paper about a ship that sunk near New York within only 25 minutes (no human victims involved). And today, just when I imagine that you are en route to Oklahoma, the devil pushes me to go to Lomdowa to "read the papers" and to read this "happy" news. (About 36 people counted dead). What do you say, Lonius? How would you feel to have your little one somewhere beyond the ocean? At least write me immediately after receipt of this letter. I will try not to think about it, if I only manage, for a few more weeks. My thigh is still giving me some problems; that is, I can not walk to much on it — I tire easily. My doctor indicated that the healing process will take a while. I expect that to go away soon as, a day after tomorrow, I will take a leave of absence from my job at school. Write, my love, as soon as you can. Also, give Jakub plus uncle and aunt Bornsztajn hugs and kisses from us.

    Mania

Warmest greetings for the sweet Lonius sends...

    M. Najemanowna

Warszawa, June 20th

Sweet, dear Loniusia.

Your sweet letters and photographs make me very happy but do not forget to write your grandmother. Your mom runs over to my place to show me everything from you. She is so overwhelmed with joy and happiness that she doesn't know what to do with herself: dance, jump up, or just be happy. We are all happy including your uncle Izak. I give you my warmest kiss.

    Your Grandmother

 Translator's note: The next part of this letter is in Yiddish. It is followed by a note from Izak.

I also include my warmest regards and wish you a happy settling down.

    Izak

Dear, sweet, wonderful girl!

Your sweet angel-like face still shows before my eyes a few times a day. But I do not know how much longer it will happen. I can only hope for forever. I kiss you many times over! When will we see each other again? How I envy your mother and sisters that they will see you quite soon! Kisses and hugs for that dear uncle J. and also uncle and aunt B. Best regards to you from my sons. Always loving you,

    Dzidziula

P.S. Bad girl! Why didn't you send your mother a photograph from Batory as well?

Warmest regards sends…

    Edek

Dear Loniusiu!

A wretched thing happened. I wrote you a splendid letter and they lost it. Now, I have to start it over. I have so much to tell you about.

I am doing quite well at school. The math test I took all by myself and got a "3". Polish language also "3".** In other words, I passed my tests and on the way to enter a secondary school. But which one?

That was a very tough issue to resolve and we thought and deliberated over it for a long time. In the end, I decided on – would you believe it – a Natural Science major.** I chose it based on the fact that the jobs in this field require less work than in other fields. A day after tomorrow, I have a written exam in Polish language (3 hours) – draft and final – splendid, isn't it? Then oral exams from Physics and biology (easy). Harmony is already behind me which frees me up (the exam itself was a blow off). What's new with you? Did you write to that "German" woman? Everyone asks about you and I, quite proudly, tell them your stories. Regards from the Warsaw Zyngiers, Moskiewicz family, Lubliner, Hannelon, Ippa, teachers, Dorka Bats and who knows who else.

Why don't you write about your own impressions about this "dream land", about those skyscrapers, walking upside down, eating with feet on the table, etc. Do you manage to communicate with people, and if so, in what language? You write absolutely nothing about those things. I also wanted to calm down your worries; we do not, and I mean, absolutely do not miss you. We plainly forgot that you are gone that's how quickly we got used to it. Only when I walk by Rys, I always have to stop in front of a photo of some beautiful American girl in a Hawaian shirt and in my thoughts I send her a kiss. But I have to congratulate you, my heroine, for your successes on the ship. Most of all, for your "staying near by" and then (which I found out from your letter to Natek) bewitching Burzynski. I am truly proud of you. I kiss your nose with that line across it, your teeth and your chin.

    Your Marcia

Translator's note: Polish school grade "3" is roughly equivalent to US grade "C". Polish secondary schools require students to choose a field of specialization. (e.g. Foreign Languages, Natural Science, Chemistry, etc.)**

June 22nd

Dear Loniusiu!

Based on your letters, the journey was great, healthy and gay (Captain Burzynski, as the word goes, even invited you to dance with him). And everything continuous to be great for you. Indeed, you are the lucky one. If we envy you anything, it is only the fact that with you are with daddy. Nothing is getting better here. Poland continues to be Poland and "our" old Warszawa has not changed at all in any respect (unless you are talking about the weather which changes constantly). You ask if we got used to your absence. We are starting to get used to it slowly. But to tell you the truth, to this day I have a hard time absorbing the fact that you are gone. I don't know what it is but I just do not feel it at all. To this day I imagine that you have never left. Only after we received a letter from daddy with your note included there that I started to realize that you really were in America.

And that is the reason why I think about you so little (do not hold it against me especially since that is what we promised one another). You must know that if it was completely up to me I wouldn't think about you at all but different people keep on reminding me about you. Just a few days ago, while taking a walk on Leszno Street, I was stopped by Dincesowa (I believe that's how you spell her name) and asked about you, what news you write us about and, of course, asked to pass on to you her regards. All our friends and acquaintances keep on asking about you. You know it how proud I am telling them how happy you are, enchanted, etc. Mommy does not get upset at all and, actually, feels quite well. The school year is over which will allow her to get some rest. Her leg is also well.

I have passed my elementary school examinations. Tomorrow, I will be taking my entrance examinations to a secondary school. The only subjects tested are math and art. (As a matter of fact, I must practice in a moment some math problems). I will take the examinations but haven't decided yet which school I will attend. Choosing is the most difficult part of this process. I truly don't know what to do. I get such a wide variety of advice from friends that I am truly lost. I got mostly "3"s on my exit exams from the last school (on Pryluska Street); I am not very pleased. The truth is that this exam doesn't mean much but you still have to write on some topic in Polish plus orally answer in Latin or German. Thus, I am not sure what I will do. In the meantime, at least I passed to the next grade which allows me to take an entrance examination. What Warszawa news can I write you about? Since just about the entire our family added a note in this letter, you know they are alive and well. I can also tell you that the Laser family is in Michalin since about 3 weeks ago. (Kuba failed his written exam). Ms. Raszab, who we saw with Marcia, send you her greetings. But if I wanted to list everyone that asks to pass on their regards to you, I would need at least two pages and write in a very tiny and compressed handwriting. And since I prefer to write you about something else, I am skipping that list all together. Instead, I prefer to send you warm kisses from me and it doesn't bother me at all that they are only on this paper. But you have to share them with out aunt, uncle and J. Don't forget! Your sister who becomes 17 years old in 2 days.

Sarenka

Dearest! I am taking an advantage of your mom's hospitality to steal a few lines here and include my warmest regards and kisses. In your next letter write so much about yourself to last us reading until the next letter (maximum 10 days). Don't let us wait too long on your sweet letters as we are homesick for your hieroglyphs. Well, so much my letter.

    Marek

June 26, 1938

Dear sweetest daughter!

I am not sure if this letter finds you in Tulsa. I am guessing blindly but write you anyway so you can find something from us upon your arrival there. Yesterday we celebrated Sarenka's birthday. Would you believe that I bought from Feldblum 2 beautiful rackets for 55 zloty — I gave him an "IOU" payable in December as September, October and November my school wages will be shorted 50 zloty each as it is. I am crazy, am I not? What do you think? Oh well, but I do believe that both of them earned it. Both of them brought home passing school grades; it is Sarenka's birthday; Marcia also passed exams to enter an intermediary course and her birthday is in only 2 more months. Also, what counts, I relied on this stupid photography school thinking that I would save some money with it. In the meantime, it came out that we were Jewish and that it wasn't so easy for a Jew to pass exams even to a f____ photography school — if you do not draw a few geometric shapes for a perfect "5" you can forget about it. She passed the math but was failed in drawing. I am very pleased. Let her go now to Prylucka. Maybe she will be spared the dubious "pleasure" of attending non-Jewish schools. Maybe she won't even have to finish her high school here. During this summer, both of them will be taking English and Yiddish lessons. I look forward to hearing from you. I am curious if you are as happy in Tulsa as in you were in New York. I think that you will be happy no matter where you are due to your sweet nature. I see that my advice is useful to you everywhere (smile and good humor). Natek's dreams somehow do not produce the hope for results. He is taken advantage of from all directions. The truth is that he does earn something but the sums we are talking about won't get him anywhere. Write, darling, often. I would like to know how your summer goes by and what next. For some reason there were no more letters from Jacob besides the one from both of you. He also wrote that he will send some money which just cannot reach us – and I am "sinking" deeper each day. I borrowed already 100 zloty from Wiktor against that money that's supposed to come as I had to buy a graduation diploma for Sarenka, etc. (But later about that). Also, I bought on credit at the Rotenberg's some material for mine and Sarenka's dresses. I have about a half year to struggle through but, as I suspect, I will struggle through it successfully. You stay the way you are – healthy in body and mind as that is most important, as you say yourself…and it's true. Enjoy yourself to the fullest and forget everything else as it is the most important ability to have. Happy are those who are able to forget. The separation period will fly by as a fleeting moment. I truly believe that this beautiful, also somewhat long, summer will fly us by quickly. Let it be as quickly as possible! I kiss you very, very, very much. You have probably written already to Michalin but we won't leave for there until the 1st. Read my letter to the Morrises.

    Mania

P.S. Regards from Janowa, Landowa, Bradowna and others.

The day after tomorrow I will have my oral examinations. I am studying a little. I think I passed the exam in Polish quite well. I wrote 5 full pages about Zeromski. And I have a racket! And you don't.

Why don't you write? We are learning about your successes from the tenth hand. Write us, dear Loniusiu, lovely puppy. Kisses.

    Your Marcik

Dear Loniusiu!

I will be taking my Polish exam in a moment. I hope it will go well. No matter what I have to pass as it is "our" school. Well, hearty kisses. Regards for the Singers.

    Sarenka

Dear Loniusiu!

You guys invent such cool parties there. Most of all, I like this pretense of being "gentlemen" by women. At such a party you should be called "gentlewomen". But the party must have turned out great. I just cannot even imagine something like that taking place here. The girls would be too ashamed to ask the boys out. Maybe in a very tight circle of friends. Talking about the summer, I must tell you that after the school is over I expect to get an internship for one month. It is settled in stone yet but continues to be a good possibility. I expect that we will have a good time at Michalin; just like in all the previous years. Hearty kisses.

    Sarenka

(…) Now, talking about your most wonderful in the world summer — enjoy yourself as only you can do it. Sometimes, even such a fun summer can bring most unexpected results. I do kiss you again and with lots of warmth.

    Mania

P.S. Pass on immediately the enclosed letter in Yiddish to Jack. I wrote him not to treat you too lightly – you are a human being who must stand at some point on her own two legs. Talking about education, you both must choose a school there that will give you some future. If the pedagogies turns out to be good – great, if not, there is dentistry, etc. But for now do not even think about it.

    Mania

Dear Loniu!

I know what's new with you from your mother. I am so sorry for not meeting you at the train station to say good-bye but I was very sick at the time. I also apologize for Natek and Abram as I forgot to inform them about your planned departure. I wish you lots of luck on that foreign soil. Warmest regards from my friends, mother, father and myself.

Your Wawek

(...) So far I have 3 children: Karola and Reniusia for 9 zloty per day and my 8 years old student for 4 zloty... They gave me 50 zloty earnest money for that which money I will utilize to buy groceries. Thus, I will depart with that trio and someone else may join me there later. I am taking the grandmother with me. Also, Ida might still give me Rysienka and pay for her, of course. For helping with the kids, I hired my past student Fidelzajd without pay but I will do my best to see that she gets something from the parents. I left for us 2 rooms and the kitchen. Mrs. Perkal refused for her children to sleep by themselves in a separate room and insisted that they sleep together with Marcia. That cut down 2 rooms to only one plus our lovely attic which, if worse come to worse, I will finish somehow (I have 5 windows looking out to Bonifraterska Street). A small possibility still exists that Marcia will go to Lublinerowa and Ester in Rabka – I would like that very much and they do not oppose that idea – we may work it out after all – maybe some kind of an exchange. Her husband had a terrible case of paralysis connected with a very high blood pressure. They barely saved his life – he is very sick and requires the country environment but it is too early to move him here. I am not too envious to deal with it but Rabka would be a blessing for Marcia and I really cannot refuse Lublinerowa. We shall see. Maybe you can write her a few kind words (in a letter to me). She is very depressed nowadays. Went through a terrible ordeal: a few weeks ago she had a terrible cold, her mother ended up with pneumonia, and now her husband is so sick. She cries all day. Essigmanowa retired (some lump/gynecological matter).

As you can see – fortune is fickle. A year ago I myself felt horrible – now I am healthy like a horse and feel great. I even forgot completely about my leg. The girls are healthy and full of vigor. The only thing – we wish for a continuance of our peace of mind. Jack writes that his sources in America indicate that we will not have to wait 3 years. Things will move along at a much quicker pace – we shall see. Talking about our case that is one of the reasons why I wish you met Washburne. Possibly he is acquainted with the consul personally, even though I am clearly stating here that it will not help much. I am still considering to go to the one on 14 Dzielna Street referred to us by Mrs. Malonad. Last week I had a buyer for Michalin but the transaction fell apart as we needed Jack's authorization and the buyer didn't want to wait. Now is a good market for sales as everyone wants to buy but what would I do with all that cash with our departure being so far away? I gave Natek your letter. Also, I was aware that Abe passed away. I wrote Sam a letter asking him to advise you like his own child what to do next. I trust him. I await his response. I kiss your sweet nose.

Mania

> **Translator's note:** The letter is followed by another note in Yiddish

Dear Jacob!

I have written Lonia such a long letter that I don't have much to write to you. Read her letter and you'll know what's new by us. Write Michalin with news and if you started with the business? I believe Lonia will find her way. Don't worry too much. You can believe her, she is understanding and wants to be independent. It does hurt me, the story with her young man. I don't know if she thinks about him, but he does not have an opportunity to travel. His father lost his position. He makes, but has to give at home.

July 2, 1938

Sweetest!

Your new pictures are no less wonderful than all the previous ones. The one with you by yourself with a beach hat – you are absolutely gorgeous – a painting. What else to say – princess. While with that little "puppy" I hope that were thinking of your own sweet "puppies" from behind the ocean and it made you feel good. I have no idea who this little anthropoid creature is but the face is nice and reminds me a little of Elza or my sister-in-law from Russia. Dear, I am concerned that you are "annoyed" with American humor. After all, the joy of life is the only mundane happiness. Let's learn from them! And because we have to wait a little longer for our happiness, it will only make it so much sweeter and more enjoyable. But, let us not forget that this separation time will also count for something in life and, especially at your age and with your natural beauty, you can not allow yourself to think in such terms as: "they" enjoy themselves too much. You also enjoy yourself to the fullest, as long as summer and sun prevail, then study and also enjoy yourself as much as your time will allow you. Talking about your "freedom" – you will not change and stay the way you were and are – I am certain of that. Freedom is a feeling dreamed about by all the humanity. One only has to differentiate it from lawlessness and profligacy most likely noticed by you in the others around you. Do not identify these with the holy word like "freedom". This word should remain in our minds as an ideal. Do learn that a true freedom has a tendency of hampering you; thus, simultaneously, protecting you from lawlessness which only can lead you to no good.

Your opinion about M. agrees completely with my own, as well as, I believe, Jack's. I can only assume that I should not worry about his high appetite for women. Maybe I shouldn't enlighten you in these matters but men in his age and position are not very choosy. You write that he behaves decently at home. I assume that you are trying to put my mind at ease. Dear, I do not fear for you. You are a sweet, dear and smart girl and such girls are not threatened.

Yesterday I went to Warszawa. I met with Natek who insisted that I have a dinner with him. I did forego visiting Dzidziula as I had to distribute the teachers' salaries which took me over 3 hours to accomplish and I didn't want to leave the "puppies" all by themselves for the night. We all very healthy and full of happiness in expectation of the near future. I just have a hard time believing in its realization. I am in process of looking for a buyer for the villa. Nenfeld told Ida over the phone that it can be arranged and to look for a buyer. I have already notified some real estate brokers. As long as we live here, I want to take advantage of it to the fullest. I will notify the inspector only after I have a visa in my hand. I assume that the documents are already on the way here. Give our regards to Morris and his entire sweet family. I think that they even like me a little. Of course, the first one to get our regards should be Jack who sent me a beautiful letter written in Polish (for the first time). When he speaks or writes in this language he feels closer to his Loniusia who he communicates with in Polish. Those are his own words. Let him kiss you and hug you as much as he needs to.

    Mania

Dear precious angel!

Your photographs are so beautiful that it is impossible to put them down. Your letters are no less...actually even more so... The truth is that it's a great pleasure to read your intelligent event summaries, stories and everything else. Your words reflect (and those are not complements) maturity, wisdom and intelligence.

Why don't you write anything to Mietek Biedor, Pola Lazer and the German woman. (I believe that Polcia L. does have your address). We had a lot of guests from Warszawa this past Sunday. Everyone from last year was here except for you, Ksantypa and Guta (Mietek came alone). But in reality, you were the only one truly missing. The meat ball went to the beach and myself, Natek, Mietek, Zyga and others to the tennis courts. Some girls even took a few pictures of us with her own photo camera. We are having a ball. I came here weighing 49.7 kilograms and as of yesterday I weigh 50.7 kilograms. I will try to do even better than that but there is so much running around. Would you believe there is no piano around? Also, we hardly ever study English. But, instead, we enjoy ourselves. Regards from Abram, Bursztyn, Karola Perkal, the Lazers and many other who admire your photos and miss you. I kiss you my little meat ball (you became a little one).

    Your loving Marcik

Sweet, beautiful and dear Leoniusiu!

Oh, how I admire this carefree lifestyle! But maybe it is though only due to me being separated from it by the Atlantic Ocean. None-the-less, I am enchanted. And you know how much I dislike to worry about things. And, I do not worry. I do not care about anything. I do not even care about the future. This way I have no worries whatsoever. But I am not sure how much longer I will manage to stay that way. In the meantime, when I am asked, "What are thinking about?" I respond, "I'm not thinking about anything." And that's the way it is. This time I am enclosing 2 photographs which are both nice and memorable. Regards from Natek. He visits us every Sunday and is making plans to spend 2 weeks of his vacation here. Polcia L. sends her regards. Write her something. Kisses.

    Sarenka

Grandmother sends you her warmest kisses and requests that you attach to Jack's letter a note for aunt and uncle Borynsztajn requesting them to write her as soon as possible – she is worried and writing is difficult for her.

    Mania

July 4, 1938

Dear, sweet little kitty!

Your letters are astounding. It is almost inconceivable to believe that your sense of humor managed to stay this long at such a high level. Of course, I want badly to believe that it is all true and you are not faking it for our benefit. I am truly proud of you. I especially admire your strong will not to prolong your stay in New York. Fabulous. To hell with all the sentiments or, maybe you are living thanks to them. I believe wholeheartedly that you will perform the miracle of getting us quickly out of this rotten lifestyle (I am thinking of me and Jack) and your sweet sisters will shine there - their incredible talents are suffocated here. Tamarus, like a fire - passed her entry examinations to a Biological Secondary School with "B" in Polish and physics plus "C" in biology. Sarenka was supposed to go to "Comercium" (previously called Bonna) with a 50% discount in fees (approximately 250-300 zloty per year) but Marcik opposed it by pointing out that "idiots go to a secondary school and the meat ball has to go to Comercium" – she is too talented to waste her like that. But, would you believe, I have found something (I think) that would be an excellent option for her. I found out that there exists in Warszawa the only industrial school in the country which was converted into a Chemical Secondary School; a 3-year program. It trains chemistry lab technicians in different specializations, such as electrochemistry, cosmetology, food products analysis, tinctorial process, etc. The first two years everyone learns the same basics – specialization comes in the final year. I did see the school's principal who presents himself as a liberal with respect to the known issue (two Jewish women graduated this year out of a total of 30). I asked him for a discount. He promised right there a 30% discount and I am supposed to go to Warszawa on the 15th and file application for an even greater discount. It is a private school supported by a Creative Workmanship Association and costs 50 zloty per month the first year and 75 zloty per month thereafter. I believe that there is not much else I can do – need to pay and educate her at this school as it gives her a specialized skill and, simultaneously, it opens up the door to a politechnical college (chemistry?). I did inform the principal that she may even not finish the schooling and he responded that, regardless, even after a half year she will get a certificate allowing her to continue her education at a similar school in the USA. United States and other countries have similar schools. Do find out about such schools there and write me about it, my dear grown up daughter, and if my choice was a good one plus will I manage with it all. After all, I just cannot let her go to Prylucka to deepen needlessly her knowledge of the liberal arts which she has neither interest nor talent for. If not for her old grudge towards Landanowa, she could probably go there and avoid loosing out on her biology background. Prylucka would also, most likely, increase her tuition at least 250 zloty. If I obtain a 50% discount, that is about 300 zloty, I will let her go there. Exams only in math, physics and chemistry. Polcia Lazer would help her any laboratory work.

I got $60 from Jack. I may also get another little boy for 3.50 zloty (Czarnobrocka's brother). Early this morning I was looking over all my debts – about 500 zloty. I have someone who may potentially loan me money to pay off all other debts but it will not be enough for Sarenka's tuition. I hope that Jack will commit to provide for her otherwise I won't be able to afford her tuition and that, by itself, would be a sin. She is such a sweet and talented girl. I do feel sorry for him but what can I do. My leg healed very nicely. I bought a long stocking for it for 21.50 zloty. I kiss you very, very, very much and even more, more, more than that.

    Your Mania

July 5, 1938

My dear, sweet girl!

I you cannot even imagine what joy your card addressed to me alone has brought me. My sweet one! I just got off my shift and returned home both exhausted and somewhat upset. And there I found such a wonderful surprise. Whenever I went over to your house in a sad mood, all you had to do was to look at me and say just a few words to make me feel light hearted again. This card from you had an exactly same calming effect. "I will let you haaave it." Many, many kisses. Will we ever see each other again? . "I will let you haaave it." Did you run out of your photos from the ship for "Dzidziula"? Best regards from my boys. Yours, always loving

    Dzidziula

Dear Loniu!

You do not know what a pleasure you bestowed on us with your card written on the ship. We all thank you so much for remembering us. I overheard that you are doing extremely well and that you plan to study medicine. I am quite surprised by your decision; I do not recall you ever having any interest in that field. Please explain this to me in your next letter. I do not believe, Loniu, that you even realize how sweet are your letters and how much joy they bring to your family. I have just finished reading your most recent one and I am bewitched. Now, some pieces of news from me. In October I will be going to Brussels. I have not decided on any specifics yet. Szyfra is quite healthy already and wants to go to Palestine. Kuba did very poorly on his last exam and now he starts getting ready for his secondary school certificate exams. That is all. I do beg you not to forget about me and to write to me. Hearty kisses. Best regards to everyone.

    Pola

Dearest Puppy! (Your own term).

I read a few of your letters. I was speechless. I am enormously envious of you. Simultaneously, I am so happy for you and your happiness. I decided to write you a separate letter later hoping for one from you in return. Currently, I am taking advantage of your Mom's hospitality here at Michalin. My warmest regards to you. Guess who!

    Wisia

Warmest regards for you and Jack from your Grandmother who cannot write this herself due to a poor eyesight.

Dearest, beautiful sister!

Regardless of your assimilation there, I bet it is quite pleasant for you to get regards from your old friends. Would you believe that we will have access to riding horses at no charge? It is due to some friends of ours living there (at Flantz's place). We all thank you so much for your wonderful letters which deserve to be collected in a special album. It is only now that I am starting (that's the way it always is) to get to know your inner self. You are a loving, courageous girl, woman, daughter, sister and a doll. You are a sunshine on the other side of this Earth whose rays spread strong, bright light.

Dearest, is our case truly so close to being resolved? You asked about Natek. While in Warszawa, he used to come over quite often. We expect his arrival here to Michalin any day now. He is so sweet. He "appears" to be holding well but, every time your letter arrives, he is loosing his head. Thanks for you help in taking care of Kasprowicz. By the way, do you know what token of remembrance you left behind for us? A spot on the wall next to your old bed. You know which one. The one from linseed oil (after you got burnt in Warszawa). All one had to do to remember you was to look at that spot; here, we have your letters to look at and constantly talk about. You know what, I do not believe this letter will ever get mailed. We are all writing and writing in it for the past five days and we cannot finish it. You truly deserve to hear more from us but, you must understand, it is so much easier for one person to sit down and write until the heart is content. If given a chance to be alone, each on of us would do exactly what you do.

Yesterday we went to the tennis courts. It was great. By the way, we do not have any problems with that small boy. He plays the whole day with Moniuta and other boys. You have regards from Moniuty, Kuby, and Karoli Perkal, who were all supposed to add a few lines each but we can not wait for them any longer.

    Marcik

Michalin, July 5, 1938

Dear Loniusiu!

We are all truly marveling over your letters. We are full of enchantment. Speaking for myself, I can tell you that I have already "been" to this New York and I met with everyone there. No need (so sorry, those are two separate words) to wonder why. Your letters are so vivid. I can see right in front of my eyes those enormous skyscrapers which leave no impression on the people living in the city, numerous neon-signs, elegant cinemas and theaters, variety of aquariums, monuments of art, and wealthy inhabitants. And in the midst of all that is our Loniusia who was known for her beauty in Warszawa and now plans to become a Miss New York. But this Lonius is not only beautiful but also a smart, sensible, and a good girl, who manages to unite her family after 10 years of separation.

Michalin is not as bad as we thought it would be. I got acquainted in the right circles and we will manage somehow. We even got a chance to play tennis; a wonderful game. We will be playing volleyball; the net is being readied, similar to one from last year, as I speak. We are here only for a few days now so not everything is ready yet. Grandmother is with us with Rysienka. She changed a lot and became a sweet girl. She walks by herself around the villa and plays with a baby-shovel and a ball. She is an awfully cute child. Well, I give you as many kisses as you will let me. Warmest regards and kisses for Jack and all those uncles.

    Sarenka

Translator's note: The front page of this postcard contains a note in Yiddish (most likely to Morris Singer, an addressee thereon).

Dear Cousin Morris,

I believe that my Lonia is at your house for several weeks and feels good. I am waiting for a little letter from you. How did you find her? I received many letters from her about the trip from New York, but not from Tulsa. The last letter was from St. Louis. I send regards and waiting impatiently for a letter.

    Your Mania.

July 7, 1938

Our dearest!

Today arrived your letter from St. Louis and a postcard from the ZOO. We felt suddenly as things start to move forward again. The faster the better. I am enclosing immediately my words of thanks at the degree level deserved by you (in accordance to your own plan). I await important news from Tulsa from both you and cousin Singer. How are things in regards to my application? He didn't respond to my letter dated May 21st. I would like to believe that it was due to a serious position taken in respect to our matter. If things cannot be taken care of as quickly as the five of us hoped for – let's not despair. Let's not rush things, etc. What's crucial that all five of us are committed – persistent but constant efforts by the two of you will bring results. I wish that Jack's case also moved forward. Is it truly possible that nothing will ever fall in the right place? I would like from him an authorization to sell or transfer of title ownership into my name which is very important. No matter what he says, I prefer not to keep it. I would like to sell it; the quicker the better. For now, I just wait...and wait. Do write me, my dear, how things go for you now? You are the most loved child in this world. I do not want to miss you – I just want to see you soon. I try to make myself busy to avoid having time to think about you and missing you. I have no slightest doubts about your success there. I don't stop kissing you.

    Mania

P.S. Regards from grandmother and Janowa.
    Warmest regards and kisses from the Lasers.
    Sarenka kisses you too.
    And Marcik kisses even more.

Dear Loniusiu!

I am so happy with your successes. Here you were considered a princess and you continue to be one; you were a goddess and you continue to be one. In general, you have not changed at all except for a new talent discovered by others. You are a fisherman? Well, well, who would expect. Is fishing that popular in America? Is it fun to fish in a pond?

Dear Loniusiu, we are having a ball here. We play volleyball, tennis (a very pleasant sport), ping-pong, take walks on the beach, have friends, and everything is a-okay. I kiss you my sweet girl.

Sarenka

Just look at her! How dares she kiss you on my behalf and leave only ¹/₁₀th of this page free. Dearest! We do have a great time here. There are so many people in Michalin. You may meet just about anyone you would like to or not. Aside from last year's company and other friends, there are at least a half of last year's guests. (Hersz and Abram B. asked to pass on to you their regards – we talked briefly with them, Lazerow and Karol P.). Thanks for your sweet letters. We are overwhelmed by America... We just cannot understand why you continue to talk about mommy's leg while this topic stopped being actual years ago.

Marcik

Dear Loniu! I have been in Michalin for over a week now. I am taking a two-weeks vacation. Wawek took a two-day trip to Gdynia. He is well. Kisses.

Elen

Dear Ms. Lonko! I take this opportunity to enclose a few words. We are boarding with your Mother – arrived on Friday and managed to settle in. What is new with you? How are you doing and feeling in the foreign lands? You probably don't need any more glue. This memory will probably bring a smile on your face. Our best regards.

Rigen and wife

July 12, 1938

Sweetest and dearest girl under the sun!

I am not able to satisfy your enormous appetite for our scribbles. You are setting up a record. Today we read with a tremendous intensity 4 of your letters in a row (I guess they arrived on the same ship). In accordance to my calculations, I expected to get something from you yesterday, that is at least 3 days after your letter and postcard from St. Louis – I was restless for an entire day – maybe another railroad collision. I am a worrier – you know that quite well by now. And here are 4 letters – all of them charming, sweet, full of humor and hope. This hope is kind of amazing. I just have a very hard time believing that things will move at such a high speed. Let it be. I got a very sweet letter from Morris (along with your annotation). It appears that I was absolutely correct in my description of his personality – well, I am a "wonder child" even in the field of psychology and Jack was wrong. I am very pleased with your personality, or more correctly your disposition, which plays a major role in people loving you and that's the reason why you have it so good now and always will. I am flattered with a fact that a part of you is "me".

Jack wrote me already that without my teaching credentials nothing can be done. Singer wrote me the same thing. He also expressed enormous happiness about my "Hebrew" offer which he read with a great pleasure but he will not be able to utilize it. Jack ordered me to write to the Rajcyns. But I am not writing, knowing and feeling deep down, that I have a sweet and capable representation there; I am also afraid to get ahead of you with things. Besides that, your 4 letters clearly indicate that something is being done. If the consul agrees to issue visas – remains to be seen. Do find out and let me know (if the documents are sent) what answers should I prepare for potential queries by consul and what are my plans for the USA – after all I can not say that I want to study there (which can be said about Marcia and Sarenka). Possibly I will listen to you regarding "ORT". If I only could be sure that it will happen very quickly, I wouldn't even enroll her at the Chemical Secondary School which I dream about for her. I believe that her preference would be children's clothing but I do not think it is worth anything – if "ORTt" it has to be a seamstress for women's apparel and, of course, Raffinowna. Advise, my dear. A few days from now, I will be going to Warszawa to apply for a discount at the Chemical Secondary School which I wrote you about earlier. If I managed to get a 50% discount it would cost 30 zloty per month without a streetcar, 37.50 zloty with it, but I doubt that they will give me such a large discount. They did promise me a 30% discount; that would be 40 zloty per month. It is another great financial undertaking which I could do without if things would really move on this quickly. Do write me. Actually, it is a very silly request. You are absolutely lovely and you write me more often that I could ever expect from you. Let Jack write me more often. I am sure that he works a lot. Since your departure from New York, he hasn't written me once. Kisses.

Mania

Dear, loveliest Loniusiu!

It is so sweet of you to shower us with all those wonderful letters. I flew over like an arrow from the neighbor's villa at the news of 4 letters from you simultaneously. Things are truly groovy, great and wonderful. All of us are so happy that we don't know what to do with all that happiness. The stories you tell us are most interesting. Those "mature 13-year olds"! But I hope that America will not influence me in that way. In Michalin, against everyone's expectations, the relationships shaped quite nicely. Good camaraderie, parties, fun and, in general, everything is great. But, as you write yourself, this is the very last summer spent here by us. Utinam!! Utinam!! Let it be soon that we see each other in that sunny palace in Oklahoma. It is really so near? I am not sure how I will manage to order it all in my head. So many sensations each day. A truly American pace. You know, we finally got a volleyball net. We pieced it together after a lot of effort and collection of any string available all over Michalin. Are you having as great a time there? Did you get adjusted to the environment and social integration in this small, yet beautiful, town-garden? Write us...tell us all about it. (Though, we don't have to remind you about it. You are truly, as you have written many times in your own letters, a sweet and dear girl. A wonderful puppy). Ouch, Rysia is screaming now. She is such a ham. She is truly very smart and sweet. You cannot even imagine how much she has changed. And our grandmother started to worry that we will leave her behind soon the moment she heard letters from you and Morris! But it's all rubbish, silliness, least of all important – you know...

They are calling me for dinner. I will be back shortly...

Dear Leono! Do you have any idea what I am doing right now? You can only guess from the change in hand writing. Well, as is proper for a proper girl, I am resting after the dinner. I plan to become very fat. I am in the forest. There is a lot of fun on the clearing. Others are playing ball but I am true to my own goals and here I am finishing your letter. Give my regards to Kasprowicz. Kiss your family. I say to you good-bye now and (accompanied by the noise of the ball game) I will try to catch a nap. Bye.

    Your Marciuchna

Dear and sweet Loniusiu!

Is the end truly so near? I have a hard time believing it. I just cannot comprehend it. For over 10 years nothing happened at all and, suddenly, such a little girl who until recently was called a sweet child (or an angel) manages to perform a miracle. Everything will be completed before this year is over. Is that what you call a "miracle"? Talking about "ORT", I haven't made up my mind yet. The level of education there is very low. Marcia already wrote you anything that is newsworthy. Heart kisses (I am finishing writing this in the dark).

    Sarenka

Letter written in Yiddish.

Dear Yakov,

I am writing to Lonia, but I don't know if she will be in Tulsa, therefore send her the letter and the few photos. Don't be mad at Morris. I think he did a lot. Seeing the copy from the letter from Winnetka College and my letter to Lonia. Go to Maladowski and you will get personal regards and you will be in touch. Her husband has recently traveled to her. You better write to Pincer (?) address. Yesterday I rented a room with kitchen privileges; a very nice room on the first floor, from a young widow who lives by herself with all the furniture. She didn't have any place to dispose of it. I'll slowly be able to sell my things. In the meantime, I will take everything to Michalin. The piano and the cadenza, I'll take with me. It cost me 77.50 per month with using the radio 79 zlotys. She will pay one-third of the electricity and the gas. Also the oven is a partnership. It is not too expensive. For my other apartment, I paid 60 zlotys, but coal cost 25 zlotys. It should be a warm apartment. Be healthy, watch your stomach. When I come, I'll help you with this.

July 15, 1938

My dear!

At this very moment I am on the way back from Warszawa. I received 3 letters from Jack. Here I am so concerned about him and he chooses to write to Dyncia's address. I feel so sorry for him. He is still under the spell of a sweet dream – Loniusia. Is it really true that it all will be over very soon? Sweetest one! Will we truly see each other shortly? Jack sent a letter to Sztojmek in care of me in which he confirms that affidavits are on their way. I have a hard time putting faith in all this. Hearty kisses.

    Mania

Dear Leone!

What's new? Everything is well here; I would even say, too well. Again I do not have, and I mean it this time, my piano. I don't know what to do. I kiss you, my dear, with all my might.

    Your Marcik

Dearest Leoniusiu!

I miss you very very much. Everything here is truly quite well. Best regards from numerous people.

    Your Sarenka

(...) quickly as long as the consul likes it. Let me know what your average day looks like? Are you learning anything yet? (Of course, I mean English). Did you decide to study medicine? I would like you to, so much, if only possible. Jack writes that the cost would be around $200 per school year; of course, not including the boarding. It would be good if you stayed with some relatives if there is no university in Tulsa. It would be a waste of money to spend it on boarding. But I am not an expert in that area. I am sure that Jack and others will take care of this in the best way possible. As long as it works for your best. The time will fly by making it feel like just a moment. May your vacation be happy and pleasant. Work makes us forget about anything else. Study and do not dwell too much on us. Just as we do at your own, sweetest in the world, demand. You look like a gorgeous prima donna. And Jack! But I suspect that this effect was "fabricated over the years by the photographer" (Maniusia). Well, even my own photograph shows some truth, doesn't it? I kiss you heartily my love.

    Mania

P.S. Warmest regards for Morris. I asked Szlojmek to kiss all the relatives working so hard towards our freedom. Did you get our photographs?

Dear Loniusiu!

Again, we received 2 letters and 1 postcard from you. The pictures are wonderful. I am truly speechless. I could not take my eyes away from them for quite a long time. They are absolutely fascinating. Fabulous! Your facial characteristics are just identical. That photograph will end up on top of the piano as soon as we arrive back to Warszawa. We will use the frame of that meat ball. (Annotation on the side of the letter: That will not happen, will it? We will get a completely new one. Mania)

Is it very hot there? You know, that dress you have on in one of the pictures, is very pretty. In general, you like "Princess". There is a possibility that I will go to Druskiennik with one of mom's friends (vacation boarding house).

We are having a great time. Lots of laughter. When will we see you? We still did not start learning English but the intentions are there. Can't say the same about the piano. Must say good-bye.

    Marcia

Best regards from the L. family.

    Pola

July 18, 1938

Dear Loniulko!

I am enclosing a letter for Sztojmek. I outdid myself to be polite and warm – per your request. I do like him but I was not very keen on, and do not consider it to be proper, writing him a letter in care of your address. I do no know his address. If you can sneak it in the local mail system – great. Dearest! Those pictures! Since yesterday, I am still under their impression. I have received my set today but I saw copies of them at Natek's. He received his copies a day before and stopped by yesterday to visit with us for a few hours. He earns some money but is not able to put any of it away. According to him, he still owes about 300 zloty.

Who knows, perhaps things will work out as we planned them. Slowly but I am becoming a believer in seeing you soon. Anyway, I should not regret anything that I've done so far. Maybe that's why you felt so good lately. Of course, our departure will be somewhat different from yours. We await your further instructions. Is the Oklahoma climate really so unbearable? That's something to consider. Your writing style is so descriptive that I feel like I'm right there with you, my daughter. The prices are truly cheap, if earnings level is that comparative to ours here. Jack writes me that, as a teacher, I can potentially earn as much as $60 per week – if so, thing are really cheap, very cheap. Well, no need to worry ahead of time. There will be plenty of time for that after arrival. Again, and as always, kisses.

    Mania

Dear Loniusiu!

As usual, I was left with a tiny space at the bottom of this page. Also, they through their meanness they have written already about everything that I planned to write you about. But that's okay. I will think of something new to write you about. But, first of all, I must tell you how lovely you look in that picture. You even look somewhat "Americanized". You appear on it to be a fully grown woman and, after all, you are only a full grown teenager (I heard that even 13-year old girls are treated as fully grown ladies in America). We are having a great time here. As a matter of fact, I am just about ready to play volleyball; they have already started without me. Later today we will go to mail this letter. Kisses.

    Sarenka

July 21, 1938

Dearest Loninku!

We write you again without even waiting for your response to our last letter. It was written in a very lighthearted tone due to mailed affidavits. But come to think of it, the affidavit wasn't supposed to be mailed until today. I guess, we will see soon for ourselves what it will accomplish. We are thrilled with your and Jack's happiness. From the "five" of us, I'd venture to say that we are here most happy as we are all together. But in our minds we live with you in that part of the world. I believe that Jack is worst off as his experience with happiness called "Loniusia" was so brief. But the hope of near union keeps him on his toes too. He writes me that most likely I will get into a university, a Pedagogic Department, which will allow me to earn about $60 per week. I read Dr. Carlton Wasburne's book on pedagogic, an inspector for Winnetka schools, titled "Winnetka System". It is a new teaching method where the key idea is to conform the school itself to each child's needs. The last chapter deals with additional education required of the teachers and mentions the Graduate Teachers College of Winnetka. Write there and request the school's brochure. Also ask if they would consider accepting a foreign teacher and, if so, on what conditions. I am also considering to write directly, in English, to the school's director with an acceptance request. I am more than certain that they would accept me since I am a full time teacher. Furthermore, in my letter, I will express to them my great interest in pedagogic and how much teaching methods overlap with those of theirs. It would be wonderful if they considered both of us and accepted as students. What do you think, Lonius? My fantasy carries me far, all the way to your beautiful Oklahoma. Dr. Carlton Washurne's address is at Winnetka, Illinois. He is a superintendent of the public school system. Do find out where exactly is this Winnetka. I believe that Illinois is another state all together. His address comes directly from his book. It maybe a long shot but be sure to write him anyway.

    Mania

My Dearest!

What's new with you? What do you do? How are you managing with your English? We do absolutely nothing. We spend so much time having fun that there isn't even time to read a book. We are having a blast. Live it up! Stay warm!

    Your Marcia

My Sweet and brave Loniusiu!

I am so very happy for you, your happiness, and new experiences. The goal you were trying to reach for so long is almost here. I kiss you from so far away wishing you all the best in life.

    Aunt Beata with children

This time they didn't even bother to leave me as much as ¼ of a page. I kiss you with all my heart.

    (not signed; Sarenka's handwriting)

July 25, 1938

Dearest daughter!

Your letters dated July 8th and 11th arrived today. Most of the time we receive a few letters at once; I guess the ships don't travel back and forth too often. I summary, it appears that your letters for the entire week arrive on the same day, Mondays. You are a brave and sweet soul. You fish, have good time as only you can and, best of all, you don't worry too much. And what is there to worry about? You are a lovely princess – there isn't a soul who would disagree with this statement. And a fact that you have a very loving family (me!!!). You do not know discord or bad relationships. What next? Be merry! Time flies by quickly in hope to overcome soon this separation and realization of our dreams. Most likely you are already studying some, playing some (or more than some) and we won't even have a chance to turn around before we will be together again. Yesterday, I read a monthly magazine borrowed from Lejbowicz (I gave him one of your photographs and, by the way, you should write him in person). Among others, there was an aphorism of Einstein. Someone asked him how his theory could be explained in simple terms to an average person. The great professor replied: "If you spend two hours in the company of a young and beautiful lady, time flies so fast that it seems to you to be no more than five minutes. On the other hand, if you keep your finger over a burning candle, five seconds could be for you an eternity. The reason for it must be looked for in the Relative Theory." As you can see, my kitty, Einstein's theory can be applied to us as well. If we live happily and worry-free, the time will fly by like those five minutes by a side of a beautiful girl.

Enclosed, please find a letter for Mr. and Mrs. Zinger. Actually, I wrote it on Morris' advice who indicated in his letter from Texas that I should do it. Apparently, you moved in with them for good. I guess we don't know who's at fault in their marital problems. But do not judge everyone based on their poor example. A much better example to look at are the Bornsteins who managed to stay together about 40 years. Learn to take advantage of every situation. Be at your best toward both of them. They just may learn something from you which will score you a "brownie point." Try to influence their daughter to improve her relationship with her mother. After all it would not be proper for her to act mean towards her mother in front of you. In other words, Lonius, spread around you the warm rays of our own family's harmony and love. I believe that you will be very successful at it. I am also enclosing for you a copy of my laughable attempt at a letter in English to the director of that institute that I mentioned to you in an earlier letter. If you wish, you may show it to Morris or even have it typed and sent, on my behalf, to another college. Or, you can correct it and return back to me for signature. You may even just mail it to Winnetka's address taken by me directly from that book. I have no earthly idea when that college is located. I may be wrong but I think that Illinois is a name of a state. I mailed the original to Winnetka yesterday and the enclosed copy is just for you to have something to laugh at. But I do expect to get hold of the prospectus for the Graduate Teachers College and pass it on to me, as I requested of you earlier. Something may turn out of this. You know how much I love to plant seeds. Something just may grow from them. Also, send a copy of my letter in English to Jack. But rewrite it first. It may be useful to him

The entire week, my dear, I am at peace. I start to worry some on Sundays. But it doesn't last past Mondays or Tuesdays past 11 am; mail delivery time. Stay healthy, my dear.

    Mania

Warmest kisses for my sweet Loniusia from grandmother. I would like to write you much more but my eyes are in a very poor shape. Grandmother is worried about her brother and sister. Pass it on to Jack.

Mr. Frances L. Murray
Dean of the Graduate Teachers College of Winnetka

Dear Sir:
Excuse me, that I write not so quick but I desired first of all to read your prints, and I was very tired, than I changed my dwelling and the beginning at the school year occupied me also very much. I obtain this year the first class than after seven years, my class is out. I am also the Secretary of the Pedagogic Council and had very much to write. After read the description of the College, my interest for you beautiful work is greater and my large desire is to make application to the Graduate Teacher's College, but I think it can be able to the following school year. First of all it is possible that my resources shall be larger. Secondly, I have rich relatives in the U.S.A. and it seems to be near to Winnetka. I have cousins in Tulsa, Oklahoma City, Duncan, Chicago, and Wichita. I believe they shall help me in the living that is so expensive in Winnetka.

One of my cousins took my daughter the past year to U.S.A. for study and paid for her school fee. If you are interested more for my life and work, my daughter can go to you and by word of mouth tell you all that is interesting for you. All my training are work in schools, self-study and examinations. The one at the systematic school that I attend was the Frobel Cours in 1914 when I was 17 years old and the Conservatory for Music, when I was a mother of three children and a teacher in public school. I am a little more than forty years old (1897) but I study all my life and I think that the man who love study and work as I is not old, if this age is even hundred years.

My new class has again 60 children — a very sweet class. I stopped in the first class and shall go the second year (8 years old) 5 are 5 years old and 47 7year olds. I can meanwhile the children not very good, than I work three weeks (without tests) but day by day I learn them and their different. I divided my work to all the year in crumbs of interests and I begin from home and afterwards school.

We go out from the home and go to the school. The children tell me what name is their parents and relatives, what they did to house, how they amused, how they go to school, whom they meet on the street, etc.

We amused that they and I are a new family, and I tell they a story by a little girl (Anderson). The name of the girl was "Ala". They designed the girl and write her name. The Polish language is phonetic. The reading is a easy thing. I attend the analitac synthetic method…After a month or two, I shall see who from the great class had difficulty for reading and then I shall divide the class into groups and so in the systematic. In every group I place one or two of better children and they shall help me in my work all the year. I divided also the classroom, to distribute the class accessories etc.

So I think to work with much love to the little ones. If you please send me much as matter to the work for the first class and I shall be very glad to send you all the relations that interested you.

    (scratched out) Yours very sincerely,

P.S. Forgive me please, my English. My work seemed me to be progressive, but I seek always new methods and ways to put the principle in practice and I feel a need for improvement. The best references of me and my work can give my client, the leader of the public school…in which I work nine years. I have much money and also a own country house and can receive a loan if it is need.

I greet you
Yours very sincerely,

    M

P.S. Forgive me, please, my English

July 28, 1938

Sweet dear L.!

Today 2 letters arrived from you plus another one from Jack with a copy of your letter to him. I am responding to them all together on this postcard. I don't want to waste money on postage (which is scarce to begin with). If I understand correctly, our case is reaching its culmination point. Jack already insists that I obtain employment referrals. Of course, I will leave here without them, but that request by itself makes me laugh. I mailed the letter to Winnetka. I am curious what will come out of it. We all are healthy (even grandmother who thanks you for your memory and sends you many kisses). Ida comes over every week to read your letters. She feels quite hurt that you seem not to remember her and Izaak. Lonius! When I told her to add a few words to my letter, she had tears in her eyes. My little kitty, you cannot fight anger with more anger. Instead, use warmth to resolve the situation. And be sure to know that she, nothing ever changes, is certain of being right. At least she thinks so (again, Einstein's theory). Loniusiu, try to be like I wish for you to be and how, in reality, you truly are. (It's my only wish in this matter!!!) Your letters bring me tremendous joy. Same for Jack's letters which appear to be more level headed. Let's all have a little more patience and things will work out themselves. Hearty kisses to both of you.

    Mania

P.S. After all you send Jack copies of all my letters so I am just taking an advantage of this (thriftiness is the first step towards wealth).

Oh, so thank you for your sweet letters which arrive interchangeably: from Lonia, from Jack, from Jack, from Lonia. I kiss both of you heartily.

    Your sweet Marcia

Dear Loniusiu!

I am so very impressed by all your social ethics there. I kiss you so very very much.

    Sarenka

Translator's note: Mania starts this letter by transposing a return letter from Winnetka college.

July 31, 1938

Dear Miss Zagr:

Mr. Washburne has handed me your letter of July 22, in which you say you would like to enter the Graduate Teachers College of Winnetka for study. We are very much interested in what you have to say of your training and present work. We do not accept people in the Graduate Teachers College without some kind of direct contact between them and either ourselves or people with whom we have worked before. So after you have received this letter if you are still interested in making application to us, we will try to put in touch with Mr. Gillianus, President of the New Education Fellowship, who is either in Finland or England traveling and whom Mr. Washburne knows well.

A year of study in Winnetka is expensive. You couldn't possibly pay your fare back and forth from Warsaw and attend the Graduate Teachers College of Winnetka for a year without it costing you $1,500. That seems like a very large sum of money to me and I presume it will to you. But living in Winnetka is expensive and although the fee for the college itself is only $250 a year and that is reduced to $150 for a foreign student, still it can't be done for less. I am sending you under separate cover a copy of the catalogue of the college and a description of the work in our early years and after you have read them, if you are still interested in making application to us, we shall be glad, as I told you above, to put you in touch with Mr. Gillianus.

Thank you very much for your interest in our school and for your feeling of confidence in what we are doing.

Sincerely yours,
Frances L. Murray
Dean

My sweetest!

What do say about such a "love" letter from the dean of school and, on top of that, with such a speedy response!? The Educational Directors of this college are: Flora J. Cook, Perry Dunlap Smith, Carlton Washburne (also Chairman). The Dean is the above-referenced Frances L. Murray. Now, I am awaiting their catalog and job description, both promised in writing but not received to date. Thus, I am composing them another sugary sweet letter in English. I plan to maintain this contact and if it turns out that the Consul rejects my visa application, I will whisper a few more sweet words to Mr. Murray through Mr. Lilliac. Read Morris the copy of their letter, then pass on a copy to Jack. Maybe one of them will decide to get in touch with either gentlemen but I do not believe that it's even necessary. If there is a necessity for a contact in the future, I will just do it myself. In summary — a barrel of laughter. Yesterday, I stayed overnight at the Zynglers. Best regards from everyone. They informed me that Lew is already in America. I'm enclosing his wife's address.

K. Molodowsky-Lew
c/o Buff

144 East 22nd Street
New York City

Do not ignore such contacts as Jack did in the past. When you are in New York next time, immediately visit them. Remember how important it is. She brought her husband over after everything fell into place for her. She is very brave and has tremendous connections as a poet – an acquaintance with her can be nothing but beneficial to you in every aspect. And you do know her husband (he is the one that once said that he looks at you the entire surroundings light up). So make sure that, at least for a moment, his and her surroundings light up in your presence and both of them become willing to do something for both you and your wonderful family. Do ask her how did she accomplish her success (I overheard that her husband's fame had a lot to do with it). In other words, attach yourself to them – they are both very intellectual people. He completed university studies in France. Her education was in a Russian school, then a training with Jedlick to study Hebrew (she mastered it in only three months). After that she studied Yiddish which she speaks beautifully. Pola was helping her with translations from Yiddish to Hebrew. She was very tight with Pola. Tell her or write her that you are a daughter of Mania Zagraniczna, who is a sister to Pola from Tel Aviv. Just wait and see how they will treat you after that. Mietek's address is: M. Biderman, Panska 3 m 8. Hearty kisses.

    Mania

Dear Jakubku and sweet Loniusiu!

Three more days and…the end of my vacation! Too bad but it's time to go back to work. The summer passed by with lots of fun. Who knows, the next one could be a 100% even more fun. Then it won't be just fun but outright fantastic. I'm waiting patiently.

    Marcia

 Translator's note: The next page contains a letter in Yiddish followed by the following notes in Polish.

Letter written in Yiddish.

Dear Yakov,

I am writing to Lonia, but I don't know if she will be in Tulsa, therefore send her the letter and the few photos. Don't be mad at Morris. I think he did a lot. Seeing the copy from the letter from Winnetka College and my letter to Lonia. Go to Maladowski and you will get personal regards and you will be in touch. Her husband has recently traveled to her. You better write to Pincer (?) address. Yesterday I rented a room with kitchen privileges; a very nice room on the first floor, from a young widow who lives by herself with all the furniture. She didn't have any place to dispose of it. I'll slowly be able to sell my things. In the meantime, I will take everything to Michalin. The piano and the cadenza, I'll take with me. It cost me 77.50 per month with using the radio 79 zlotys. She will pay one-third of the electricity and the gas. Also the oven is a partnership. It is not too expensive. For my other apartment, I paid 60 zlotys, but coal cost 25 zlotys. It should be a warm apartment. Be healthy, watch your stomach. When I come, I'll help you with this.

Dear Loniu!

I am with your Mom in Michalin. From time to time I read your letters which appear to indicate that you are having a marvelous time.

    Hanka Singer

Loniusiu!

Just look at this Hanka, little crud. I let her have a small piece of this page and utilized all the remaining space here. I'm forced to pass on to you just my regards and kisses. I will do better in my next letter.

    Sarenka

August 8, 1938

Jaremcze

Dear Loniu!

Please accept my apologies for not responding to your sweet letter until now. It may be quite hard for you to comprehend how excited I was to receive it. I am very grateful to anyone who writes me or visits me. I may remember how hard I work which causes me not to have time to socialize with anyone. That hard work had a serious impact on my health. As you can see, I am in Jaremcze. I forced myself to treat myself. Even I have a hard time believing in it myself. I was forced to leave Warszawa with no delay. Recently I felt just awful and I lost a lot of weight. I left behind over eight kilograms of live body. But the happiness of that fact had also some serious consequences. I weakened my heart and I am at a risk to have some heart murmurs. Aside from that I am prognosed with Basedow's decease. Those disease require a lot of time to heal properly and one is not permitted to work. And am used working with no breaks for rest. During the summer there were house remodeling, shipments, etc. Plenty of worries. One can get used to just about anything. But what's important that I'm getting my rest now while I admire the natural surroundings of Jaremcze. Wasn't it just yesterday? Lonka Zagraniczna causes havoc in Jaremcze! And today she admires the United States. It the past she could only dream about this wonderful country. Nothing but dreams. The dreams that became a reality.

As for me, I don't believe that I will ever break away from my unlucky streak. I have a lot of problems with Sewek and Edka. I have to be smart to stir this in the right direction. The is the deciding moment. He wishes to continue with his education. You know well his skills and interest in the medical field of surgery. Oh, well. He planned to join the army for a mandatory few weeks of training and then enroll to study medicine for a year. So far neither did materialize. The army doesn't accept Jews so far. Yes, they will accept, but not before a third period and by then it's time to take the entrance exams. What can he do? He must complete his army training before anything else. And try to make any decisions under such conditions. With all the doors being shut in our faces. Edzia decided to attend a commerce school. Since we will be forced to do bookkeeping very soon, her education will be very handy. Aside from that she is already studying some foreign languages. I don't think it will come hard to her. Could I direct her future anywhere else?

Would anything else be any better? Hard to say. The difficult task and responsibility of shaping their future became all mine. And I am not so sure that I am doing a good job at it. But I will do what I can. And even more. Julek still serves and manages to get by. Franka is the same. No significant changes.

My dear! Enough of these boring outpouring of my feelings. I would like you to write me fairly often. If you only knew what happiness it brings me, you'd be writing me constantly. But you should be touring, playing and having fun. You need to take advantage of this rare opportunity.

I see Natek quite often. The poor soul misses you so much and tries to collect enough money to follow you there. I forewarned him that I will be the first one to tell you about all his infidelities. We had a good laugh on the account of this joke. Marcia and Sarna were laughing their heads of numerous times while I visited your Mom (with all that free time I have).

Enclosed please find some pictures. They are not the best ones, if you still recollect what's on them. Please, do keep your promise and send me a picture of yourself. Write me at the address in Warszawa. My next letter will be longer and more interesting. Kisses.

    Lonia

August 9, 1938

Yesterday both your letters arrived, I mean 4 from L. and 1 from J. Yours, as usual, in a heavenly spirit caused by apparently that "salt water bath and massage" plus a hope for the near future. J. indicates some wonderful news that upon my arrival he will become "kosher". L., if you don't understand what I'm referring to, ask J. directly and he will explain it to you. It would truly be wonderful development even my skeptical frame of mind. But, somehow, I'm having a hard time coming to terms with it. I have a hard time comprehending how this enormous machinery can be dismantled, just because of some clouds in the far west, in such a short span of time. It may be worthwhile to speed up our case. Is anyone else in the family mailing the documents? So far, the buyer for Michalin didn't show up and Nenfeld told me to look for another buyer. He told me where to look for one via a telephone and it all can be easily arranged (fictitious auction, etc.). Enough said that if we have a buyer, the rest will be taken care of. If I can't find one here, maybe I will advertise in Warszawa. Of course, all will change when the documents arrive. Also, I have a serious situation with Sarenka. If the case will take less than a year, why should she burden herself with passing entry exams to the secondary school and possibly not be accepted anyway. After all, she will lose a year there too to learn English very well. Therefore, I am leaning towards entering her only to "Commercium" and let her apply herself seriously to study English. Tomorrow we will mail a family letter which should bring you some happiness. Grandmother thanks you for a picture and sends you warm, warm, warm kisses. Ida rented from me a second room (the one for Siecinski family) and Rysia, grandmother and Rutka sleep there. Also, I took in Basia Czarnowska from my class in lieu of paying off a debt I owed.

    Mania

Sweet Loniusiu!

We all thank you for your lovely letters overflowing with humor and happiness. Slowly but surely it starts affecting us as well. I'm just not sure what to do with that birthday party. Your letter came this time but the next one, if it comes at all...Mom isn't that stupid and may not go for it at all. Thank you so much for your taking care of Kasprowicz. I kiss you (and you kiss him to lessen his nostalgia). Bye, bye, bye.

    Marcik

Dear girl from beyond the ocean!

You just cannot imagine how much happiness your sweet letters bring us. Only Mommy's letter can come even remotely close to yours. Kisses.

    Sarenka from abroad

August 10, 1938

Sweet Loniusiu!

My warmest greetings to you. Write, my sweet one, to your aunt Berta at least once with all the detail of your activities there and future plans. No changes with me. At the present I am in Aleksandrowo which is about 2 kilometers from Falenica. Thus, we see each other quite often. Give my best regards to Jack, as well as all the other members of your family. I await your response.

    Aunt Berta

Dear Miss Loniu!

It is so much more pleasant to write this note to you since, just like your dear Mother, I have nothing to do this year with our school's summer camp which allows me to rest completely in Michalin. I understand that you live like in a fairy tale. I must believe that it's a result of doing by all those people wishing you well. Unfortunately, I do not have a photograph of you in Warszawa. Thus, grant me this wish to have a photograph of you from that country of eternal happiness. Your family basks in your happiness. I assure you. And me too.

    Greber

Dear Loniu!

I never even considered that this note to the "girl from beyond the ocean" will bring me so much joy. I thank you so much for your remembrance of me. My trip to Belgium moves on like anything else dependent on others. Manka is afraid somewhat. I do understand that and do not hold it against her. I am waiting for a final decision. In the meantime, I am residing in Michalin and, taking an advantage of the short distance to your trio, I read all your letters. Your letters...I must tell you (read it as "I must write you") that I become a fan of your letters and their contents. I had no idea of your writing talents! But most of all – that cheerful tone of the letters. You must be truly happy. It turns out that one can know a person for a long time just to find out that one doesn't know that person at all. Let's take you as an example. When you claimed last year to bring everyone else to America shortly after you, I had my doubts. As it turns out, you have accomplished so much in such a short time. You deserve many praises.

Talking about any news about us – you must be aware that there are no excitements whatsoever. Everything is same as always. The only difference that if my plans will misfire, everything will become just so much more dreadful. And I am not equipped with endless reserves of optimism. Szyfra is healthy by now. She planned to write you a letter but it didn't materialize. She had to leave earlier today for Szczawnica. I beg you to add shorts notes addressed to me more often, or even better, make them longer letters.

    Pola

P.S. Best regards from everyone. Lonius! In every letter and to the end of time I send my best wishes to Morris and his wife and, even more warmly, I thank them for their attitude towards you. Don't forget to pass it on to them!

August 11, 1938

Dearest!

I cannot stop admiring you. At this very moment 3 letters and 2 postcards arrived from you; the last one dated August 1st. Of course, such delights can be experienced only during vacation time. The news about mailed documents I received, as I wrote you earlier, from Jack. I'm starting to believe though not without some reservations. After all, I still have some important tasks to complete here. I would like so very much to sell the villa to unburden Jack financially upon our arrival. I try not to even think about how we will manage there but, after all, such thoughts follow my old habit of bouncing around my head by themselves. It would be wonderful if I find gainful employment. Jack has no doubt in that respect. The recent news from Jack that my arrival will lift some burdens off his shoulders made me very happy. I am waiting and waiting. I live (all three of us actually) with the constant thought of a speedy departure. All those warnings about our clothing, undergarments, etc. are quite funny to us. Is it really the right time to start worrying about all those little things? What with the documents from various cousins? I received a letter from Morris about you but I had hard time translating it. I mailed it to Jack for translation. Apparently, Morris took a liking to you from the first time he saw you and promises for himself and all others to make you feel like at home. About your qualities, which I wrote him about in detail in one of my previous letters, he agrees with me in full claiming that I didn't exaggerate about them at all. Szlojmek wrote to Jack (I have a copy of his letter) praising your beauty (as well as your sisters') and telling Jack to be proud of you (…)

 Translator's note: The rest of Mania's letter is missing.

Dear Loniusiu!

Yesterday was my birthday. I wrote you a postcard but I don't know if it reached you since Mommy forgot to write "Hazel". Anyway, for the second time I thank you both for your memory and your letter filled with paper-made kisses. The official birthday party will take place this Sunday when more people are able to attend it.

I could write you a lot more but I don't want to repeat all that's in the card in case it does reach you. You know, Polcia L. definitely departs this October. Szyfra is in Szczawnica. You asked about that acquaintance and Druskiennik family. Well, I planned on going to see them but, in the end, I didn't go as everyone had such a great time in Michalin.

What do you do with yourself? Natek became an uncle. The end of vacation is just behind the corner in two weeks. Too bad…then again not really. Vacation should last forever. Today I started my seventeenth year. It makes me very proud of myself. Well, I better finish these incomprehensible rubbish. Kisses.

    Your Marcia

Sweet Lonius!

It was a stupid mistake with that "Hazel" – was it a name of a boulevard? I was going to step inside the house, look it up and correct that part of the address. But I became so busy that I completely forgot and dropped the card in the mail box with everything thereon except that word "Hazel". Nothing new took place since yesterday. You probably had a great laugh at my expense because of that letter of mine in English. Unfortunately, I did not follow your, albeit late, advice. Well, maybe it will reach you anyway. Write me, now that you have "sobered" somewhat, your true impressions of America. Before I take that final serious step, I would like to hear from you one more time if you are really happy there. There is all the same old crap with us here. Not a single change. Kisses from Sarenka and grandmother. I left them no room to write on – too bad for them. Read a lot in English.

    Mania

August 22, 1938

I received your 2 letters today and a card from August 10th. After reading your last letter written during a state of depression, needless-to-say, I became quite depressed myself. But in the end, at your own request, I smiled though not without a drop of bitterness. I have been on the crossroads for the past few days – that was caused by my trip to "HIAS" where Samplowa, in the first row, informed me that the documents appear to be in order but it is not so easy to take the entire family. Especially everyone at the same time. She told me: "Lady, you have a job here. Send your children first and let them settle down for themselves. Only then you should go. But if want it this way, it's just fine with me. I would advise, however, to take a year of sabbatical, etc. Go over there during vacation time. After 3 months request a return to Poland. That will make your visa valid for 2 years." In summary, it's a fairly stupid situation. Also, Samplowa advised against selling our villa - only after obtaining a visa. I filed an application for 3 references, requested that the Consul registers our case, and I wait. I wait somewhat sad and stupefied as I am not sure what I will get in the end. If I only knew that at least you are happy. But truth to be told, I don't even believe in that. I do not want, my dear, any sacrifices on your part. I enrolled Sarenka into "Commercium"; she will be used to some office clerical work. I am not sure if I shouldn't just send Sarenka by herself to you; both of you could live in New York until a better settlement at some point. At that point it would be easier for me to leave my job and join you both with Marcia who, after all, has her school and conservatories here completely free. It is my opinion that we shouldn't rush anything at this point (what an irony!!!). Who knows, maybe after getting my visa and a few good incidents from the enemy's camp, I will "tune" myself into this immigration business. Right now I am not coping too well with it, my dear. This immigration does not appear to provide me with any wonderful prospects for support there. Tough, we said "a" and it's time to say "b" but not a time yet to say "c" (in my opinion). From your letter, I am guessing that your position in Tulsa is not only not fully guaranteed but also not so great to begin with. Therefore, it is my opinion, that not only Should you agree on New York but also quite happily embrace that thought. First, I just cannot imagine how you could even live in that Tulsa – boonies – I wouldn't agree to it for any treasures in this world. Second, a case of Natek – in New York one can quicker consider such a matter (Jack). Third, Jack will certainly not find anything for himself in Tulsa or entire Oklahoma. Fourth, even though I deserve a good rest, I refuse to do it in such inhuman conditions (like a kitchen) and I will accept employment opportunities only in New York.

Samplowa warned me that your contact with Jack must be very well "thought out" and that until I receive my visa you must stay with Morris. I asked her what if you'd study in a different city. She responded that for verification checks you should always list his address. I wouldn't hesitate for a second to send Jack even now to Canada to take care of all his matters (but it's his own business). Then send you to New York per Morris' advice. I really would like to see you settled there for good. I give you my consent to get a job. maybe you can live at aunt Bornstein's. And, as you say, take more time to learn the language better. Your personal well being lays close to my heart. If your engagement with Natek it really that serious, I am not sure, if you won't have to return to Poland. In my opinion, his departure can be a very problematic one. Does it make any sense to suffer like Jack? I don't know...But, we shall see. Anyway, you must sacrifice my dear at least two years and, in the meantime, our situation may (...)

 Translator's note: The rest of Mania's letter is missing.

(...) it didn't feel right to me from the very day I saw Natek's ring on your finger. I feel sick after reading your letters to him. We drank bruderszaft*, I got used to him and I did understand that you departure was late by at least one year. You would never let me utter a word every time I touched this subject and that, my dear – was wrong! What happened to our intimate communication when the whole world knows about the topic discussed? I want you to write me directly and seriously how do you visualize to resolve this matter. If you cannot immigrate Natek to you, are you resolved to return back to Poland? If though, I don't think that I will go to America at all. Let it be. Jack should go to Canada and find out if he really lost his Polish citizenship. If not, then return together with him. One may rightfully say that it's craziness and I shouldn't deprive Sarenka and Marcia from their future opportunities in America, but I don't want to be in America without you and with so uncertain means of support. Forgive me, my love, a lack of logic in my letter but I am very upset. Read from within it all that causes me tremendous heartache and depression. Then, do sit down and write me seriously, and I do mean very seriously, what should I do in regards to all the matters affecting both of us.

    Mania

P.S. Write Jack and inform him that his money for me did reach Wiktor in Warszawa. Probably that was an exchange for $50 (second time since your departure). Hearty kisses.

    Mania

* Customary practice of drinking with a person as a pledge of friendship after which the parties address each other by their first names

Dear!

I prefer to write you a pretty song about America which we sang yesterday at my birthday party with Leon's help.

"Enormous and crazy United States, how do you do, go Jasiek, yes
country of many nations, bluffs and sensations, with laughter intermixed with tears
with buildings reaching sky and clouds, with thousand factories and offices
that's the city of New York, like steel, like a wall, that's America, mister, USA
if you have an occasion, do it quickly, man, hurry up, one, two..
re re mi mi mi re do do re do re do"

Then to the same melody:
"America, Mister, bow to her, what else can you do, mister, just do it
Columbus demanded new laws and got them, who will be equal to him
markets and culture, Rockefeller and Fort, all these money, well, capons
morality hu hu hu psta ra ra, America, mister, USA"   etc.

I am sure that you didn't understand any of the above, but what counts, that I did write it down for you. maybe you will get some parts of it. The birthday party itself was wonderful. One of the nicest wishes I got was that my next birthday be spend on the other side of this Earth in The United States. Mrs. Klajman wished me this. She is Halinka's mother (mom's student if you recall). Hearty kisses.

    Marcia

Dear Loniusiu!

Do not take mom's letter to your heart. I mean, do not worry about her. Mommy got very excited after your letter (after your heart-to-heart with Morris) plus some other factors played a major part here. Just to mention one – an arrival of documents. You know very well that mom does it all the time. She has just started to think about the future (and you know how much she loves on ponder on things). But, I believe this all is history now. Mom wrote her letter when she was still very excited. Thus, do not worry too much about it. Things will be okay. I kiss you with all my heart, my sweet girl. Take care and stay warm.

    Sarenka

August 23, 1938

Dearest and sweetest!

Forgive me for my outburst yesterday. Today, in a much calmer state of mind, I digested it all over again. It's very hard for me and the word "immigration" by itself interrelates to many technical difficulties. And before one can transplant a tree to a new location, such tree will go through an assimilation period; a mental adjustment in my case. It appears that you are just about reaching that moment of "coming down to earth". I am just entering the stage that you are leaving which overwhelms me. I live with a hope that my mind will adjust to the required changed and allow me to move forward without any scruples. The issue of your move to New York and our potential meeting you there simply overwhelms me. But it also makes me pleased as the thought of Oklahoma simply irritated me. It may be good for the summer only. How would it be even possible for us to adjust ourselves mentally to live in such a little provincial city after living in Warszawa? No way in this world! Your unhappening (so far) medical studies do not worry me. Your reasoning is very logical. Some evening courses with a daytime job will introduce you back to a social schedule you are accustomed to. Hold on with all your might to your plans. Most importantly – J.! I would prefer that you live with aunt B. Samplowa's concerns, in my opinion, have no grounds. Anything can be done – just very carefully. After all, any matters related to you will be directed to Morris who will always know how to reach you. The fact remains that he promised to educate you and, therefore, you went to study in New York at his expense. In summary, I am very happy with this New York resolution.

> **Translator's note:** The following 12 lines in the letter are marked over with a pen and not readable.

(...) as you seem to be already doing with the might of a twenty year old, study a lot, work (if work is available), and the time will pass by like a brief moment in time. I do not believe that a decision to return to Poland would be very wise – but I am leaving that decision for you to make. I am going to go back to work as if nothing will happen; also I will work on my English. In the meantime, the time will show if we get visas. I will await your letter from New York quite impatiently. You just must move there. Did you remember to pass Essigman's letter to his acquaintance there? When you settle in New York, I will take care of sending you numerous introductory letters to friends and acquaintances. They will allow you to mingle with many people and, possibly, provide you with an employment opportunity. Also write to Lonia Goldfela. She has there some very close family. All will be well. Chin up! Crossed out sentences are Marcia's doing.

Mania

August 25, 1938

Dear daughter!

Again, 2 more letters arrived from you today along with 2 postcards. Our responses are much cheaper; what I mean is that we respond mostly on postcards. By, what counts, that every piece of mail from you gets responded to. Our guests – old acquaintances of ours. Ms. Estusia lives on top (pays me 40 zloty for room plus patio and kitchen privileges). Ida rented a room (after Siecinski) for 100 zloty which includes dining with us (dinners for grandmother and Rysia). Our room is constantly occupied by either one or two strangers. That's all. Leaving for Michalin, I barely scraped to pay for the train tickets. Thus, as explained above, we managed to survive this summer. As you can see – that's all there is here. The means of survival there – I leave that to my adult smart daughter. I conclude that you have already learned the lesson for yourself that one cannot count too much on Jack. He always counts on miracles. I am not upset with Morris at all. To the contrary, I like his way of thinking. Let's just hope that his plans do materialize. In truth, I wish you were already in New York and write me from there if there is anything for me to come for. The moment I return to Warszawa (September 1st), I will start my efforts to collect those introductory letters for you. I believe in Morris to help you find a job. After all, I would expect him to have some contacts. You need to join some organization and socialize with people which, in turn, develops relationships resulting in employment opportunities.

    Mania

Dear Loniusiu!

Please do your best to constantly write to us. They are so nice to read. After that "blow up" letter, the life wasn't too pleasant for a while. I am so very happy that I got some genes after our Dad – even if it's only childishness. The pictures were mailed to you quite some time ago. From among your girlfriends, we saw here such as Polcia, Irka Ergin (Hirsz) and Tusia Zonand. Also, Anka Brand, Gewikoman and others. Everyone asks about you. We don't have to await a mail delivery on Mondays or Tuesdays as we get it more often now. It appears that we get at least 5 letters every day (we shall see if this trend will continue). Natek will be here shortly. We all took some pictures for you but they haven't been developed yet. I kiss your lips, nose and feet.

    Marcik

Dearest!

The letters we got recently - completely changed the mood around here. Your outburst was matched by Mom's. Best regards from everyone. Kisses.

    Sarenka

> **Translator's note:** This letter contains two notes: it starts with one from Sarenka and ends with another one from Mania. Neither note is complete.

Dear Loniusiu!

Summer vacation is over and it is time end the summer pleasures as well. It is time to do some "work". (I wrote it in quotation marks as I will be going to school one more year. I assume you will too.) My vacation turned out to be great. I continue to be playful and I have no idea how and when I will manage to put a stop to it. I am quite comfortable that way. You must know, my dear, that I am enrolled at a high school specializing in administration and commerce (they accept all students as long as the examinations are passed). It should be noted here that the school, aside from such achievements as a high level of education (subject are taught well and in an interesting format), lasts only 1 year, is coed and is attended by many good looking boys. It is a great virtue, isn't it? But jokes aside, I really like my new school. I am especially pleased with the fact that I won't be too bored with commerce side of it. Along with such classes as bookkeeping, business correspondence in polish and German, commerce, etc. we also study general law, present economical issues, government administration and other interesting topics. (...)

(...) certainly we will manage it. It's okay – as long as we get visas. Don't forget to write me the family relationship with Szlojmek and other detailed information the consul may be asking me about. I am actually somewhat surprised at the lack of any contact from him. We did receive all your mail written to Bonifta. St. address since I notified the Post Office about the change of our address. Have fun and do not worry about anything as you advice me yourself. Concentrate on working on yourself and having fun – the two smartest things to do in this world – give lots of pleasure and advantages both spiritually and materialistically. Your annotation helped me make my decision to leave everything behind us without looking back. I do believe that Szlojmek will help us settle down. He doesn't write to me. Pass on my warmest regards for him. Also don't forget to give regards to Singer (did my letter reach him?). Also, say hello to Rachele whom I remember well. Also pass around my New Year greetings (including yourself and Jack). Immediately before your letter was delivered, I was struggling with my letter to Winnetka. If it isn't too far from you, you may want to visit there and talk to Dean Murrey. I am truly interested in this institution and it may provide me with an employment opportunity. Officially, they do not accept any candidates past age 40! (...)

September 14, 1938

My happy Lonius!

Today, after a week's break, we finally received your postcard "from the sky". Truly you were born under a lucky star. You outdid us in just about everything…That's great. You dumped some heavy lead at my feet recently in a letter but…I got over it. When I receive from you a letter full of sweet lightheartedness – and stay calm and patient awaiting what the time brings along. Some of our documents were ready but I refused to accept them as they were completed 10 days too early. I waited a few days then paid 39 zloty and picked them up just to immediately return them back. The documents were in the name "Maria" instead of "Maniusia". In other words, I have to wait another 5-6 days and their date ca not be changed since the filing stamps were executed already. Any day now, Samplowa leaves for the USA herself. She is sending her daughter and her husband ahead of time. I am curious where you are and what you are doing. On one hand, waiting for our arrival does make sense – you won't have to enter the hard life in New York by yourself, so feared by Jack, and you have an opportunity to study English. On the other hand, we should consider a quicker settlement for you as my own arrival heavily depends on it. If only Duncan had a dental school and if you were allowed to help Szlojmek in his business in exchange for him paying your school costs – it would be a dream come true. To wait idly – which I am not accusing you of – would be a waste of so precious time. maybe there exists another school that would fit you better. What's the story with Reinhard? Did you consider it? We feel wonderfully at home in our new apartment. The shortages at Walerianska, etc. are not felt here!!! The work started without any incidents. Marcia behaves as her usual self. Sarenka studies well. The matter of her school discount continues unresolved and, so far, I had to pay 20 zloty. Kisses.

    Mania

P.S. The girls are asleep. Janina sends her regards.

 Translator's note: Following Mania's letter to Leona the postcard includes a note written in Hebrew.

Jacob!

I do not know where Lonia is. I am writing on your address – transmit to her and she will know what is with me. I am reading now the brochure from the college in Winnetka in English, when I finish I will write them another letter. This small town is close to Chicago and quite close to Oklahoma. If I would really be accepted there it would probably be good. Over there they accept only experienced teachers, principals, supervisors, etc. and they do not accept people from the outside. That is to say someone from the board has to know the candidate. Ask Lonia and she will send you the copy of their letter to me – the only bad thing is that this will cost sufficient amount of money and I think that I still have to work a little more on my English. As of now I read with the help of a dictionary, and this is my entire studies. One has to learn from a teacher. When I will settle – I will start requiring the condition of the Bornstein uncles and the other members of the family – Sarah and more. Good-bye.

    Mania

September 21, 1938

Dearest Loniusiu and, no less dear, Jack!

Again, I write a common note to both of you as Lonia hasn't provided me with an alternative address. Also, I have no idea of her whereabouts. Today, after more than 10 days of silence, your postcard arrived in which, Loniu, you write about your new idea – something comparable to Sarenka's "Comercium". In my humble opinion, this may be the best resolution to your situation. First of all, you will avoid New York, so feared for you by Jack. Also, while at that comercium, you will have an entire year to improve your English and to prepare yourself for a clerical job. It will come in very handy for all of us or you in your future studies. Thus, I salute your energy, smarts, bravery (an airplane!) my good and dear girl. I salute dispairing and so calm down Jack!?! (Wiktor butted in and wants to tell you – my advice to you is do what YOU want),

    Mania

My dear child, I order you to write more often as your Mother is starting to show some "dangerous signs" during such long breaks between your letters.

    Marcia

Dearest Loniuszku!

Looks like you will be attending a similar school to mine. That makes me quite pleased. Kisses.

    Sarenka

My love!

maybe this method will work and I will write a few words in response. I heard that you are having a great time and even managed to fly on an airplane. Who knows, maybe on that occasion a few details escaped your head. But I will find out for myself in about a month or so unless I hear from you prior to that time. In the meantime, enjoy yourself and good luck with that commerce school. Write more often to Danka.

 Natek

September 21, 1938

My dearest sweetest daughter!

I received an hour ago your letter dated August 31st (and earlier your postcard dated September 2nd). Its tone stirred me beyond words – firm, serious and sensible. I am very proud of you though helpless regarding any advice. I know that you do not seek any advice and I will not give you any. Maybe it is egotistical on my part. But I am afraid to voice my opinion. As you indicated yourself – I am not a disinterested party. The future is blind to us; contrary to the past and the present. And only the past and present give us some guidance towards the future. Our personal observations serve us as a beacon and treasure to safeguard from potential catastrophes. I see a lot of you in myself and I cannot help but be impressed. I strongly believe that, being in your shoes, I would do exactly the same thing. That is all I can tell you. I wish you were here to hug you. Know that you are loved; most loved in the whole world.

 Mania

Loniu!

I am with your family at their new apartment on Zelazna Street. It's been a long time since I have seen them last. I did hear about it too. I am extremely busy. There isn't much time left for friends, even the closest one (as in this case). But it is not an excuse why I do not write to you. The reason for that is, it is my opinion at least, that you still owe me your first letter, which I am still waiting patiently. My regards and warm hugs for you at least to an extent allowed me by both my shyness and my Anglo-Saxon Puritanism. I wish you all the best in your life.

 Mietek

My warmest regards while we await your letter.

 Guta

September 24, 1938

Dear Loniulko!

I have just received your letter written already from Duncan. I am so relieved to know the whereabouts of my little angel and that you are safe with Szlojmek. I am truly ecstatic – know that I am smiling with delight. All that you do is smart and sound. May we receive our visas as soon as possible. I am again in the mood to move to America. Yesterday I received three personal reference letters which I will pass on tomorrow to HIAS. (Scurplowa advised me to obtain them and attach with all the other documents for the consul). They were very expensive – 40 zloty – but if they help to speed up our case, I am happy. All efforts aside, I do not believe that we will leave before this calendar year is over – may I get the visa! In the meantime, I am sure you will manage to adjust to the American lifestyle and hopefully find a job. We all will manage one way or the other. University studies – after all we do not live for them but instead utilize them to live better. Talking about Marcia, she is still so very young and...(remainder of the letter missing)

Loniusiu!

Why did you stop "showering" us with your frequent, sweet letters? We had so many changes here. We are now living on Zelazna Street (between Lesznem and Ogrodowa Streets) in a beautifully finished second level apartment facing the street. It also has a balcony extending over the street which we use for watching people as well as sun tanning. We also acquired quite a few new friends who often stand in the way of our school homework but we manage to forgive them. Ain't that the truth, Loniusiu? Recently, we all went to the cinema to see "The Boarder". (Absolutely fantastic!!!!!!) Just yesterday, we went to Miejskie cinema to see "The Charlatan". Truly magnificent! I happen to be a very important person. At my secondary school, I wear a red emblem. I do not have too much extra work related to it. Most of my old school mates moved away. We have a lot of new students. There are only 5 students taking a German language course and next year, when biology and humanities get separated for that course, one class will have 3 students taking German and the second will have only one (if I don't attend); you know her: Lila. (By the way, you have warm regards and kisses from everyone in the family). The school itself constructed new levels (from prior three levels to seven now). There are wonderful new classrooms but...I would rather leave for America. You know why? Because now, our Secondary School No. 2 will stress math over German!

I have already taken one lesson with Lefeld (the second was canceled due to some meeting he had to attend). He is so nice. He is so much better than Dabrowska. She is absolutely furious with me since, some time ago before vacation, she requested that I see her before my first lesson. (I do not believe that it was her splendid generosity; more like she wanted to make sure that I am ready to play and avoid any humiliation as her pupil). I did not go as I did not even know any piece to play until the last second. I was afraid that she would yell at me. The lesson went quite well (at least I think so). I was the only one among all the students that wasn't asked to practice exercises! He told me to keep on playing! Afterwards, I went to see Dabrowska. She was furious and when I tried to tell her something she interrupted me and demanded to know why didn't I come to see her before the lesson. Stupid goose!

I saw Marysia Gasior. She confirmed receipt of your card but it didn't say anything beside your regards, etc. so she is quite upset. She said that if you can sit down in America to write something you may as well write a longer note. (Apparently there was enough empty space left for at least 3 more sentences). And on top of that, you forgot to write your address. You callow, callow! You have regards from M. Raszab and Sara Weber who I also saw recently. Yesterday, I was stopped on the street by Hermann. I told (...)

(remainder of the letter missing except for the very ending added on top of the page)

Janowcik sends you her warmest kisses. She is so attached to us. Changed a lot though.

(letter not signed but in Marcia's handwriting)

  Translator's Note: This postcard is written in Hebrew to Jack Zar in care of Rothman family. Mania adds a note thereto for her daughter.

October 4, 1938

My darling!

Today I received a letter from the consul in which he "is commanding" to send him different details – that is to say – registration, the one I was waiting for until now. Meanwhile I tried to prepare different papers and now I have to wait four more days to get the matriculation and additional like these. And then I will go to the board and I will give everything needed in order for them to add it to the affidavit and all together I will send it to the consul. This is the way they showed me at the board. In brief – the case is getting closer. Yesterday I got your letter together with Lonia's letter. Do not be angry at me, for I am a little afraid to travel. Despite this I will not delay my travel even in one day. "to our birth place" I will not long. If I do have pity, then it is only for my relatives, mother, and also for the job in the school. To your opinion, I will also be able to work there. I wish it will be good. Maybe Shlomke will really help us to get settled. In brief, like you say – everyone is alive – we will live, too. Our treasure has a lot of energy. I hope she will really get a position there and then if both of you work – already we will not die. And if you will succeed to open any kind of shop – how good – because then all of us will work. Write for goodness' sake immediately in which way Shlomke is your relative. It seems to me that his mother was the sister of your brother. Send a small amount of money. I was hoping that you will send by yourself when you heard that I had to change the apartment. I had to pay rental money for two months, to transport the movable property and additional like these – good thing I had your money for debts – but now we remain without a penny and the owners of the debts do not wait. I still have to pay promissory notes until the month of February – in each month. It seems to me that on January, I will get an increase – I wish to travel before and not to get it. I am leaving everything for them for their dealings with our brothers.

I have already seen beating with my own eyes – so far I did not believe – now I have depression from the street. Write immediately. Do you really need all the documents that you asked for in one of the letters. Everything cost money. I am reading daily some English pages – the girls are not learning yet. Marcia does not have any free time. Sarenka will start soon with a private tutor, like I did with Lonia. She studied for eight months well with a private tutor, and therefore it is easier for her now. I also had to study, but at least I am reading. Also this gives me a lot. Light literature I am already able to read. I have excellent book of her "Flowers of Poetry".

Lonius!

By means of this note I want to save 30 groszy. I received today your sweet postcard. In four days, upon receipt of our birth certificates and six housing references, our documents will be sent to the consul along with previously prepared personal reference letters. The reference letters were suggested by Scurplowa some time ago. Based on our second correspondence with the consul, personal reference letters, birth certificates and housing references will speed things up. The documents did cost so far about 80 zloty. But, it appears, we are quite near our goal. And our financial position is not suffering due to these costs. Kisses for all of you.

    Mania

 Translator's Note: The following postcard starts on the reverse side with a note in English written by Mania. It continues in Polish by sister Sarenka.

October 8, 1938

My pretty Polish maiden-

I read the article in the newspaper and was very glad to see that my little daughter is so interesting for the county agent of Jefferson. It is harm that you did not send me the article with the photo. I am very curious to see my Warsaw Beauty in the American newspaper. I received already a letter from the consul in which he bid me to register. Do not fear. I am willing to sail to you in the land that "one is more sure of living". The conclusion of my pretty 20 year old Duncan girl is alas! A very great truth. Greet our very dear cousins and the beloved children.

    Mania

Dear Loniusiu!

It appears that you have become a very important person. The newspapers had articles about you and your lectures on Poland. They made a "somebody" of you. At this rate you will soon stop writing to us. I hope you know that I am only joking. I am very happy for you and your successes. You are so lucky. Here, everything is normal. We settled into our new lodgings. Janowa's sleeping quarters are in the kitchen where she also cooks for us since the woman, who rented us part of her house, dines outside all the time. Also, she is almost never home anyway. She only returns to sleep here. Overall we have already adjusted to these new living conditions. Our room is very nice, large and fashionably decorated. We received a letter from consul informing us to file our registration application with some additional documents. Besides that there is nothing new. I attend "concercium". I truly like this school. They teach us to use typewriters. I kiss you my beautiful Polish girl. Marcia is presently at the theater but she sends her greetings.

    Sarenka

October 16, 1938

Sweet Loniunko, Angel,

Recently I received from you 2 postcards, yesterday 1 letter, and finally today Naten came over and showed me another sad letter from you to him. What strange suspicions about me! Simply, some time ago Michalim Naten came over and talked us into taking photo pictures. I was not in the mood for any pictures at the moment which you can clearly see on my face. Afterwards he sent you directly this "beautiful" picture of Maniusia. What can we do – he is quite worthless as a photographic artist!! I am just not photogenic. Aside from this distress, everything else is in order. My humor, strictly speaking, is directly related to your letters: talkative after your happy letters; poor when I feel that you are homesick. And that how it is, my sweet daughter! But time will clear up everything as you know very well yourself. Thus, do not be homesick, either for real or make believe for our benefit – I consider it unnecessary. I look forward to receiving the clipping with your picture in that Oklahoma newspaper. I have no idea why but Naten was extremely keen on taking those pictures. I guess he believed that they would stir you. That was unnecessary. I do want you to have the greatest time of your life and study to the best of your abilities. All of us here are quite happy. All documents were sent already to the consul. Let us hope! Kisses.

    Mania

Loniulko!

Natek continues to ask for any letter for him from you. When Danka received your letter, he came over and said that it is one thing for you to break up with him but he cannot understand why you chose to stop writing him. Of course, I did not show him your letter addressed to me but I did feel obligated to show him your letter received by us today. The main thing is to get him prepared slowly – a little at a time – it cannot be done in a single shot. After this letter he calmed down a little and. continues to wait. You, naturally, cannot and should not base things on sentiments. Besides that, the European continent is becoming so cloudy that who knows if we will even a chance to run away from here. It is impossible to consider him in our own equation. Hold on tight and always be as lovely and sweet as you are now. Kisses.

    Mania

October 16, 1938

Dear Loninechno!

Thank you so much for remembering about me. I heard about your successes in every respect and I am very happy for you. At your age you went back to school! I imagine how nice it must be for you there. I also heard reports about your interviews with the Polish Star, etc. I am truly proud of such a niece! Our best regards for your daddy and, if you correspond with your aunt and uncle Borenstejn, also for them. Kisses and please send me a photo of you and your daddy or just you in an American dress. After all I have to "advertise" you among the family here. I have been back home only a week now. I was hospitalized for 10 days after a surgery to remove my appendix. The surgery was successful. Hearty kisses.

    Ida

Best regards and kisses.

    Isak

Recently there was a family gathering at the grandmother's place. It was very nice. We sang your songs. Look, how this sweet old woman, writes beautifully again.

    (not signed but in Mania's handwriting)

October 17, 1938

Lonius,

I am presently at Nenfeld's place. He says that everything is doable. Jack must provide me with a power-of-attorney document. It has to be notarized before a public notary who will testify that the document was signed by him personally (of course provided that he has documents proving that his name is J.Z.). I assume that public notaries do not inquire any further. Nenfeld had a similar case two weeks ago. What is this all about that even with a power-of-attorney document, unless it clearly specifies that he relinquishes his share to me, upon sale his share of money is "frozen" under the currency regulations. I will have no access to these monies and they will stay in a depository account until he claims them in person. Nenfeld will write me tomorrow the required power-of-attorney document in two copies: in Polish and in English. The document has to be signed by Jack in front of a public notary; then someone else (as listed in the document) has to witness the public notary's signature. Jack does not have to go there in person but, afterwards, the document has to be confirmed by the Polish Consul in New York. In summary, I am sending this document to Jack. If there is no way for him to sign it before a public notary (any city will do), we will have to take an alternative course of action which will take longer (e.g. fictitious auction). In other words, we will sell it regardless. Imagine that Ida and I are matchmaking Nenfeld to Jadzia! What do you think of our new profession? I start to wish to see you all soon. My sweet, dearest, most loved angel, Loniulko. Kisses.

    Mania

 Translator's note: Letter includes a short note from Mr. Nenfeld who appears to be an attorney.

October 17, 1938

Miss Loniu!

Your mom is at my office regarding the villa. I am very happy for your chance at a new life. My best wishes for you. Please give my best regards to your father and I kiss your hand (I hope it is permissible now).

    Henryk Nenfeld

Dear sweet Loniusia!

It has been a long time since I have written you or received anything from you due to the fact that your mother lives so far away from me and has no time for frequent visits. In the past, when you lived much closer, I used to walk over to your place. But it all may be for the best as it is probably time to disaccustom from one another to hanker less later on. After all, sooner or later, my loved ones will depart to be with you. I wish them it happening as soon as possible though, for me, it will be a very sad moment. But that's how it has to be since, after all, it is for the best of you all. May God grant you all this wish quickly. Now, my dear, what is new with you? How is your health? How is your daddy? Do write me about everything. I kiss you from deep within my heart and my best wishes to your daddy and your dear relatives.

Your longing grandmother

 Translator's note: This letter continues with a note from Ida in English.

My dear Louia!

I write to you English, but I please pardon, then I cannot so good to write, in these language. How do you do? When will to go to you your mother and sisters? I think to go to America to the exhibition, but I don't know. When I shall have the money I shall go with Dyniecika. Please write to me and send me your picture. I send your many, many kiss my suite girl.

Your Ida

Dearest daughter, my dear being!

Yesterday I visited the Zyngiers. I had a great time. Dentner was fascinated by your newspaper appearances. He is learning English. He knows it much better than I do. In a few weeks he will be in London. Benen left already a few days ago but left a postcard for you. Ida has been recovering for the last two weeks after surgery to remove her appendix. It turns out that all her health problems were related to her appendix. Now she feels great. Nothing new with the three of us – all is okay. Marcia works; Sarus less. At least she is working on her English. Scurplowa, in her time, told me to obtain personal reference letters. This blond guy with HIAS heard about it and told me to also obtain 6 housing references and birth certificates. However, after receipt of the registration document, the new clerk who replaced Scruplowa told us that all these documents are not necessary and they will not speed things up. However, taking into the consideration that they cost me about 80 zloty and are valid for only 2 months – one of which they sat idle at my place – I attached them all anyway. I do not know if the consul will be angry with me for trying to be "too smart". It can't be helped – no risks, no rewards. Since it all had to go to waste – I sent it. We will see what happens – after all Scurplowa was an excellent clerk and this new one – just that...new. Most likely it will speed things up and, if not, should not cause any damage. Anyway, the forms must be filed twice. I wrote just yesterday that, in my opinion, all the remaining affidavits should be filed as well. Especially, since we hear that cases are not processed as easily as during your days. Most likely they will be selecting emigrants with the strongest guarantees. These are only rumors, however Morris wrote me a long time ago from HIAS in America indicating that he had read that more than one person should file documents simultaneously – after all we are talking about three people. Aside from all that, write me more information about my cousins. Abe – how many children; where; family relationships. After all I may need all that information. My dear, do not waste any time thinking about us – I stopped worrying about you. Now we live only with a hope of seeing each other soon. Time flies when you work (and have a good time). But it is still hard to comprehend that it is already October and you have been gone from home for 5 months. The next 5 months will pass by even quicker – school. Finally the following 5 will be quite distant from the first ones. Do you remember this joke about a hanged man who at first kicked with his legs, then got used to hanging and stopped! I urge you to have a great time and do not miss anybody. I suspect that, besides your sweet cousins, you have some other friends. Only make sure that they are compatible so they don't waste your time. As for me, as always, I still read a lot but I can't say it improves my education.

    Mania

October 18, 1938

Lonius!

We meant to write you a letter for the past two days but, as you can see, we have not done it yet. In the meantime, we received another letter from sweet Sam and 10 photos!!! What wonders. We are truly impressed. Sam looks about 15 years from what I remember. His wife – the girl is incredible and it is hard to believe that she is a mother of three children. The children are lovely. But the one most lovely under the sun is my "angel". I kiss your sweet nose, my Loniu from P.T. Frolic around, my dear, on bicycles and horses. Maybe you can teach us how to do it too. At this point the only thought occupying my mind is to depart from here to see you. I am hopeful. After all my expectations from life are not unreasonable. Just enough to have some food on the table. All of you girls received an education – the only thing left is marriage. But jokes aside, the main thing is that we all finished our high school education. It is never too late for further higher education if there is a desire. One can be gainfully employed and be a student at the same time. I have finally made up my mind on this subject. Europe has fallen on some very hard times nowadays. New incidents take place on a daily basis. Especially "our brothers" are in some very peculiar situations. At the university – you should see this with your own eyes – and not only there.

Pass on the letter to Sam and express to him my endless gratitude for taking care of you. What luck that you ended up staying with them. Sam writes that both his wife and children got so accustomed to having you around that they will never let you leave them.

    Mania

Dear Loniusiu – Amazon!!

Those photographs are beautiful, quaint and you look wonderful in them. This horse is quite photogenic and, at least Wawek claims so, a thorough-bred. He knows those things. You can only imagine how excited he was looking at that photo. With regards to the table-cloth, I am not sure what it is all about. Never-the-less, I will buy a linen one of these days, I mean during a single day, and I will start going around to collect signatures. Just let me know what to use to preserve these signatures in order for both of us to finish the embroidery together in America of the ones I will not finish here. Also, should they sign with a pencil or a pen?

I have for you some most recent news. Imagine that Mietek, or more precisely Gutter, opened a store on Bielanska Street with halva and other sweets. Actually, they had it already a full month (…)

 Translator's note: The missing part to the above letter is followed below.

(…) How do you like Mietek as a merchant? In truth, he only takes care of business in town; I mean that he doesn't stand behind a counter with a white apron like Guta. Mietek told me that he is taking his job as an opportunity to earn some cash which will enable him to emigrate. Look what this world does to people. I too think of Mietek and store in one sentence. But it's okay. Maybe it is a way for him to make a new, better, more secure life for himself in this country of future potentials – America.

We spend time having lots of fun. Not like you on this farm and riding horses but not any worse either. We go to cinemas and for sightseeing walks (Warszawa grew a lot. You won't be able to even imagine how much. But it's not important to you, is it?) We like our little room. Now is about 10:40 pm. Mommy is asleep, of course, and Marcia practices some etude. And I sit by a round table and write this letter which you will have in your hand to read in about 2 weeks time. Our windows look out at Zelazna Street. Across from us live very nice people. Some young carpenters. Marcia and I watch them intently. Kisses.

Sarenka

Dear Marciu!!!

Well, just look at this, what a scatter-brain I am. That meat ball is laughing at me that I have no idea what I am writing. Thus, Loniu! Now, both my mommy and Sarenka are laughing at me together. I said that I would tell on her: The meatball does not do her homework! You know, I am completely ready for our departure to America. I have a very stylish coat (made out of Sarenka's old navy blue one) with black fur (flaps) – just like you always wanted. But I wear it only on special occasions. Besides that I got, again, another navy blue dress, a blue dress (old one), one pair of hose, and navy blue gloves. School is okay. Tests, tests, tests!!!! On Monday in German, on Thursday math (on the last one I got "C"), there was already one on physics, and there will be one in chemistry. Reports, reports, reports!!!! In every class. Repetitions, repetitions, repetitions!!!! Cheat sheets don't work – too few of us. Everyone has to fend for themselves. They announced 6-8 oncoming tests in physics and another 4 in chemistry. Did you hear that Marysia Melamed flunked her exams? Apparently, she was having such a great time partying in the "big world" that she forgot completely to study. We heard all that from Polcia L. who dropped by our place two days ago. She sends you her super warm regards. She is enrolled now at the French Institute. Very pleased with it. Plans to go to Tomaszowo to make herself more fit. What's new at your school? Do you also have tests? Write us more about yourself. I need to finish for now to complete my homework and practice piano (even though tomorrow is Sunday). You know, tomorrow I am going to Ateneum Theater with some fool to see "The Sanctimonious Hypocrite". I admit that I'd rather not go to the theater with this cretin. But it is too late (he already bought the tickets). Your photos on the horses are fabulous. Are you still riding? Pass my regards to your girlfriend, that sweet girl compared by everyone due to her looks to Sarenka, and to that little boy pretending to be a count from "Mr. Thadeus" (sorry for my sentiments towards my equal peers) and to Fenia and Sam and you.

Marcia

Sweet Lonius!

There is still some room left so I will add a few more words. Imagine that I was talked by a doctor, a colonel, a director of the Surgical Institute at Pilsudzki Hospital, into taking a shot containing 20% of regular cooking salt administered directly into my old lovely varicose vein in order to get rid of it and to avoid constant wear of the "elastics". It's been already 2 weeks since I have done this. The vericose vein truly did go away. There are still a few smaller one left. He, Ida and Izak are trying to talk me into 2 more identical "pleasures". The procedure is extremely painful but I think that I will go along with them. I would like to leave without my "calf problems". Hitting the leg doesn't cause any pain already for some time. My dear, avoid falling off the horse; it can be very dangerous.

Mania

October 18, 1938

Dear Loniusiu!

What fabulous pictures! They overwhelmed me. Are all Americans as care-free as this cousin of ours and her family? Do all of them look so youthful or become so youthful after arrival? On that photo with the chickens you truly look like Zosia from "Pan Tadeusz". Not only because you are feeding the chickens but also because you look like a 17 years old lass. I am beside myself and at a lack of the right words to express my enchantment. I am so happy that you are having such a great time. But, do not fear, we are not holding back either. There are a lot of new male and female friends at my new school. Also, I have to tell you about my new wide belt with a satin top. I am not sure that I will ever get used to it. It is on me right now and it is difficult to bend over. Kisses.

Sarenka

> **Translator's note:** "Pan Tadeusz" (Mr. Thaddeus) by Adam Mickiewicz, a poet, is among Poland's most renowned literary works.

My sweet American beauty,

Please grant this minor favor of writing me a small sweet letter. I do not mind to number three or four in a line for one. I sent you, with Michalim, photos of my children signed by each personally. We are all so proud of your successes and fame. I pray to God that your luck never leaves you. Again, I await your letter impatiently and envious of everyone else getting one.

Aunt Berta

Dear sister!

Do you remember us going to school together? You in your blue coat and me in my gray one; always at 8:05 am? We used to run like two little calves.

Do you remember your secondary school examination? We went to Frydman's store for some ice cream and promised each other to never tell anyone? Or when you rang the doorbell and I ran over completely naked to open the door for you?

Do you remember both of us in Michalin when we got older? How we both got sick with stomach problems? How Mrs. Estusia used to pass our food on to us through a cabinet and Kazimierz used come over asking if "corpses" are still alive? How Natek got sick at our place? How Oliver used to come over? How Ksantypcia learnt the nickname given her? Do you remember how later we went to Warszawa to Lejcowicz? How we finally got cured (castor oil and $1/2$ cracker)? How later I used to go to school and you attended English lessons? How you were learning to sing and I was accompanying you and later you tried to teach me?

Then, when you were going to Desu? How once we went together to Starorypinska (I came over to you at Rywfinowna)? How we were later accosted by that photographer and we ran away from him? How you didn't want to ride back and put me on a street-car while yourself walked back (in your green outfit!)?

And, then, you were leaving us. How we saw each other for the last time; you left and we all returned home with the whole mess (and chocolate candies underneath our coats) and later on that evening baked a cake in your remembrance.

But I did forget how you lectured me about positivism and neorealism; how you forced me to do my homework even on your last day here; how you checked my report. But I also do remember how you got to fly in an airplane; go and see some of our cousins; go to school and listen to teachers' lectures; how you were coming home, eating dinners and then reading books; then studied; ate supper; go to bed.

Pretty soon we will be reminescensing about our arrival, how we greeted one another, how we went together to tour the city; how...; how...I don't even know what else, you know.

After that we will be also saying: "Do you remember? Yes, I remember, I remember."

Warmest regards from Marysia Ranab, Pola Lazer and Franka Goldfeld who I saw recently. And something else from Gersztowa but her regards. She said: "When you write your sister, you can tell her that I asked about her." And she did want to know every detail. Write, write, write. I kiss you with all my heart.

    Your dearest Marciuchna

Dear Loniusiu!

Today is the first time I came over to your new flat and just had to write you. I am looking at your photographs and am fascinated by them. That is all I wanted to tell you. Warmest regards and kisses from your family.

    Moszkiewiczow

What splendid pictures! I am simply speechless. Wonderful, beautiful, angelic (after all you are an angel). Everything is fine here. There was a lot of work but most of it connected with the holidays. They came. They went. That's the way it is. Too bad. To end it we are going tonight for an evening party to Finkiel's house. We were invited by our boyfriends. We have a lot of fun but do not get a chance to ride horses. That can be done only by our "American sister". Just wait, pretty soon we will be equally important. From our old group of schoolmates almost half is gone. There are 31 of us left: 10 in humanities and 21 in natural sciences (it's mine). What a terrible pen to write with! But it is mine purchased for 1.75 zloty. It is very sweet because it is mine.

    Marcia

November 1, 1938

Sweet Lonius!

Write us how you are doing at school. I mean, obviously you are doing well, but how many hours daily do you spend in lectures, what you do the rest of each day and how is your on-going relationship with those sweet Raizins. Is anything said about us? How is your sweet stomach, your skin, etc. Please do write more clearly. Almost every postcard leaves some unreadable words after long suffering at deciphering your handwriting. Things are truly well with us here. After your care-free, at least in appearance, letters I trod on air. Of course hope, mother to the fools, aids my blessed condition and wait. But…we will see each other when we see each other.

    Mania

Since this "mommy" of yours left some space here and we never waste anything, we send you a few kisses.

    Your kittens (not the false ones) and puppies (the gorgeous ones)

(…) Unfortunately, that crazy man ended up at our house. We had some problems with him. Some time ago, Sarenka met him in the city and told him that had moved to a new place. Where? To Zoliborz. Subsequently, I met him and told him some tall stories. Finally, when I told him the truth, he did not believe me. Later, he somehow did find out where we live, showed up at our doorstep and documented where we live. And that is the commentary to this "bible".

Will I ever live to see those wonders you write us about? Yeeeees, but wheeeeen?? I feel like after April Fool's Day (it just happens to be Tuesday tomorrow but that is not material). How are you doing? Write me about your school. What do the exams there look like? Will you have to take some exit or entrance examinations between schools? Polcia B. claims that you must (since you are attending an elementary school there) and thinks it is a great idea. Well, ciao for now or that meat ball will yell at me.

    Marcik

Dear Loniusiu!

Your birthday is almost here so I wish you...I think you know very well what we want to wish one another. Regards from friends, schoolmates and family. Hearty kisses.

    Sarenka

I was dwelling for a long time how to address you in this letter and decided to leave it out all together. I will just get right into the meat of this letter. Well, I found out that you are doing great in Oklahoma. I assume that there are cowboys and Indians all around you. When I was younger, I read a story by May or Mayne – the story took place in Oklahoma where the cowboys were shooting simultaneously from two revolvers and were catching with their lassos anything they could manage. Please, write me if it is all true. There is nothing new at our house except for Mika getting married. That's about all.

    Mietek

P.S. Did you marry and divorce already?

We don't need any boys like "Mietek". Your sisters have plenty of much more intelligent (at least so they claim) boys. Sarenka dates constantly now.

    Mania

> **Translator's note:** The letter starts with a copy, in English, of the response letter to Mania from Winnetka institute signed by Professor Washburne. The translation picks up the actual letter to Leona written in Polish.

Graduate Teachers College of Winnetka
Mrs. Mania Zagranicia
Zelasna 80 n 29
Warsaw. Poland

My dear Mrs. Zagranicia:

Mrs. Murray has handed to me your letter of September 26th. I am writing to my friend Dr. Ziemnowicz in Cracow and also to Mr. Nielsci in Warsaw for information in regard to the likelihood of your fitting into our situation here and being able to make use of the training after you go back to Poland. I think it might be a good plan for you to go to Cracow to see Professor Ziemnowicz who has visited the Winnetka schools and whom I visited when I was in Poland. You should of course, write to him for an appointment. His address is Dr. Chrecrystew (sp) Ziemnowicz, University of Cracow, Poland.

I can assure you that your application will have careful consideration.

    Sincerely
    Carleton Washburne
    Education Director

Lonius!

I don't remember if you received a copy of my last letter to Winnetka. I did mail you a copy. I really thought that they will not respond to it. And here, look, how seriously the matter is approached by a director himself (the first letter was written by Dean Murrey). Now I can go there without any further worries. I am certain that they will accept me. Of course, it is a moot point for now, but if I obtain a visa, I am not sure if it wouldn't be a worth enrolling with them for a year. Needless-to-say, I will do my best to keep in touch with them. Such letters may even turned out to be helpful in dealings with the consul. And, if this place isn't too far away from you, maybe you should make an effort to visit it. You would be quite welcome there if you mention me as your referral. ("My dear!!!" is truly something even though I am aware that this is a formal way to address people there; but it could be without "My"!) Laughter aside, this contact may truly become quite useful at some point in the future. Possibly, in the meantime I will make a written contact with Professor Zimnowicz.

We are sending you ahead of time your early birthday wishes via Jack. I say via Jack as we directed him to do something which we cannot do ourselves due to that enormous distance between us. The entire family, just like us, is well. Many kisses.

    Mania

Dear beak!

You are becoming such a pig. You don't write any more. But that's okay. We also have no time and can stop writing. I showed your photographs at my school. Gerslowa asked to tell you not to stick your belly out so much. Then she compared you to a standing amphora with legs looking from the profile (you understand). Thanks to your pictures we wasted half of our German class. Kisses. Grow tall.

    Marcia

Dear Loniusiu!

I am just a stupid meat ball and that is the reason for not writing you a letter so far. But I will start right now. Well. This sister of yours, Tamara, lost a few marbles. Do you even realize what silliness she writes you? But, let her be. What's new with you? Write more concrete information about social relationships there. Kisses.

    Sarna

November 3, 1938

Dear Loniusiu!

Today your early birthday greetings arrived. I am happy that you are doing so well. It never truly crossed my mind that you would adjust so well and have such a great time in that other hemisphere in "H'america". I kiss you, my sweet, on both cheeks and wish you further successes.

Sarenka

Sweet Loniusiu!

Your lovely letters raise my spirits and add belief in the future. A few days ago Mr. Jusp Szczerba called the school asking Lublinerowa if I possess outstanding teaching abilities; have I published anything which, after my potential arrival to Winnetka, could be published there as a scientific treatise; and if I am fluent in English language. I have forewarned Lublinerowa that there might be some questions. She indicated that I am a very talented teacher but she is not familiar with my scientific work. She also informed him that to the best of her knowledge (I was not at school at that time) I plan to immigrate and have already sent my daughter. Also asked Jusp as "one of our own people" to provide a neutral response not to undermine my own efforts. I do not know if anything will come out of this but, as you already know, I have already written to Winnetka with a different approach in anticipation of the outcome of this call. Prof. Ziemnowicz made an inquiry in the Ministry, the school superintendent's office followed, then passed on to Jusp, etc. We will see what will come out of this. Hearty kiss.

Mania

Dearest, beautiful,

Kisses from all, both us and your old friends, Moszkowiec, Goldkorn (your old school friend), Micio Biderman and others. Winter camp again in Rabka in "No.1". Good bye.

Marcia

November 5, 1938

Dearest Loniulko!

We received the beautiful cowboy to our delight. Nothing new from the consulate. Your last letter full of compliments for me filled me with an incredible pride. You are spoiling me. There is no more need to improve myself any further. If recognition comes with little work or expense (postage stamp) – why bother working. On the other hand, I reread my letter to Winnetka again and I liked it even more myself. If nothing else, I hope to benefit some from this contact. Alas, you know well, that my deep down dream is to avoid retirement (especially kitchen duties!!!) and if by chance I was accepted to this institute for a year, as Prof. Washburne promises, I should get some work – at least that is what I think. Then, during a winter break, I could meet with Prof. Ziemnowicz, who already knows about me by letter introduction from Prof. Washburne. What do you think about it, my smart sweet loved very much daughter? Gracious God continues to provide me with stimulations to set my frame of mind towards ours, may it be as soon as possible – journey. Well, after all the tommy rot the landlord put us through – I left the lodgings at Bonifraterska Street a month early before the lease expiration (Walerianc, Matusik and Saskow families still live there) – decided that it is proper to inform me that she is planning to sell the flat. If I had known that, I would have never moved out from Bonifraterska Street. As I said before, this is just another good reason to leave all these pleasures behind. However, it is possible that I will get a loan and, if so, I will prepay Dyncia for the next, let's say, half year. This amount would help her buy the flat: a room with a kitchen. She would live in the kitchen (we in the room) and after our departure she would be left with both. Wiktor offered to loan her 200-300 zloty but she does not want to be in debt. I would like to help with setting her up in her own place before we leave. She eats dinners at Berta's place. It would cost me extra since I do not expect our wait to be longer than 2-3 months only. Continue writing to this address; if something happens I will notify the post office.

Mania

> **Translator's note:** The letter starts in English but switches to Polish in the middle of the first page. The translation picks up at the conversion point.

November 12, 1938

My beloved child!

I received the beautiful photos upon the horses. You are like a film actress. It is the opinion of everyone who sees your wonderful shape. My correspondence with the consul will be late upon the least for four weeks. I received back yesterday from whom the formulary, than I have not written the name of my husband and if I am married or free. I was yesterday in HIAS and have heard, the consul gives visas but not so quick as for a year. I hope to obtain a visa but when it will be able, this is a hard think to know. It would be very good to send to the consul a recommending letter from a senator or another important man (as it was done by your visa). Than now very much peoples waited for a visa and the consul chooses the best papers. Write to Morris, perhaps he will help us, as he took pains for you.

Well, admit my darling, I did "sweat" enough, didn't I? I am not sure what to do with Krakow. People are accepted at Winnetka only after a personal interview with the dean or someone from the Advisory Group which has its representatives all over the world or with someone well known to any one of the three Directors. In this case, Prof. Ziemnowicz (sociologist) is known to Prof. Washburne. I would like to talk to this Prof. Ziemnowicz; maybe I will hop over to Krakow during the winter break. In the meantime I will wait for any visa developments. Perhaps something will clarify by then. Nonetheless I need to start making more efforts on all the fronts. I overheard that someone obtained a visa due to a certified letter sent directly to the consul in response to which the consul promises no difficulties in obtaining one. The applicant showed this letter from the consul during his interview appointment (to obtain visa) and was granted his visa with no delays. (At this point I just wish to get an appointment invitation.) As I already explained to you in "my English" the correspondence with the consul will be delayed a few weeks due to a silly error on my part. While completing the application I missed the entries for my civil status and husband's name. Now I remember that, due to my "odd civil status", I was not sure how to complete it and Sarenka was to question this issue at HIAS upon submission of the document. Enough said as I feel stupid about it. I rushed with all the additional documents which no one requested so far but cost me an arm and a leg (quite possibly unnecessarily) but the truly important document – I did not complete correctly. I trust that my daughter, my sunshine, forgives me for that. But I am concerned about it myself even though I do not wish to leave before the school year is out due to a one-year sabbatical issue. But this worry may be moot since nothing may be resolved by then anyway.

Even if they do issue a visa with good application documents it usually is only for 11 months. Kiss yourself from me and give my best regards to Fenia and Moris.

 Mania

P.S. I question if would manage there with my "English". Apparently Winnetka is the suburbs of Chicago. They sent me a brochure about the institute – extremely interesting. I am in the process of translating it for our own Educational Board.

November 13, 1938

Lonius!

Before I close this letter let me write you about my newest and most ingenious idea. I am considering (as of today) to write a letter to Prof. Washburne explaining that in the meantime (as our correspondence crossed in mail) I received an affidavit from my cousin there. Thus, he would be "absolved" from any responsibility should the institute decline my acceptance. Also, explain to him my civil status and ask him kindly for a recommendation letter to the consul. What do you think? (I will mail you a copy.) Am I risking? I also want you to take a trip during your winter break to Winnetka (47 minutes by train from Chicago). Contact there Prof. Washburne after first writing him a letter that you wish to tour the institute. It truly is an interesting facility. Possibly it might make sense for you to transfer there after you complete this school year. They admit from two sources: teachers without any experience fresh from college and experienced teachers from amongst administrative staff and visiting faculty. The selections take place in January. They consider only a small group of potential candidates that could benefit the institute in their respective specialties, e.g. pedagogy. You could say that your mother insisted that you visit the institute for both yourself and on my behalf and, should the professor deem you a worthy addition, you would like to follow in your mother's footsteps, etc. I trust that you can chatter away about your "love" for pedagogy. My only goal for this visit is for them to see you. If the cost is not too great, may be you can talk one of your cousins into accompanying you. Discuss this matter with one of your teachers. Stay healthy.

 Mania

Loniusiu!

Close by, at the Traugutt Park, there was a ceremony to unveil a new monument – a large boulder dedicated to the teaching profession. It was beautiful. I attended with a delegation.

 Marcia

Like the mountain streams
flow down this green Earth
Let your young life flow alike
Sweet, pleasantly and happily

Besides that we wish you, ourselves and Jakub a prompt reunion in person and a long and happy life together (like in a fairy-tale), basking in happiness and good weather, in sweetness and beauty, in an enchanted house somewhere in America, for that is someone's wish…

    For our dear Loniusia on her birthday
    Mommy, Sarenka and Marcia

 Translator's note: This letter written in English and dated November 16, 1938 (copy), appears to be directed to Prof. Washburne at Winnetka (mentioned above). It was mailed to Leonia along with another letter.

November 16, 1938

Dear Sir:

I read your letter and have been very happy at its contents. I wrote to Dr. Ziemnociez for an appointment. I think it will be able for the Christmas recess. Now I must tell you a news, that can perhaps throw a light on my application to the College and can also throw down your great responsibility for so an expensive travel. I feel your comprehensibility scruples in this matter.

For my plan contributed a accident yet all our life constants from accidents. After my oldest daughter's gateway to U.S.A. I took much more interest for the American school life and so during the summer recess I have, I intend to make use in an intellectual, not paper sense, and it is characteristic for my family. My late father was a physician with a very great number of patients and has never seen neither university nor even any school. And when he was in my age as a father of ten children he has gone out to Swiss and took a course for medicine by a private professor. His keepsake for us is a diploma of a autodidact for medicine.

Excuse me, please, sir, my long, long letter. I think all this can be a little interesting for you as a pedagogue whose method depend upon adaptation of individual differences of children (peoples) and support for self-study. Please my unknown sir, if it is taken to report for our Teacher Bunch your plan at Winnetka (now I make a translation – report from the description at the College and shall read it on the next conference).

When I resolved make application to the College I have written to you and in the same time to my cousins. Now I received an affidavit from one of them for me and my two daughters. The one is 17 years old – study at a commerce school. The second 16 years – study at a "nature liceum" and also in the class for piano at Conservatory. I have therefore a possibility for immigration to the U.S.

And so I am bold, perhaps over bold, to request you for a very considerable thing. The Jewish immigration from Europe is now great and the Consul truly gives visas, but he raises difficulties and delay it on a very long term. My large desire and also possibility is to make my travel June recess and then summer times I should arrange my children at the relatives and should go out to Winnetka for an immediately personal interview.

If it is possible, write please to the consul in Warsaw (Gasna 11) a recommending letter in which you can assure him that my intention is for study and after to work either in U.S.A. or again in Poland, where I have a constant position. I am not depend on a certificate, I have "papers" enough. If after a year you will find me worth an evedence you will give me it. Only possibly don't refuse my hearty request and help me in the quick possibility to receive the visa.

Yours very sincerely,
M Zagranicia

Dear girl! (but spelled with "cz" the way Miecio pronounces it)

I noticed that you maniacally shower people with complements. Is it possible that as ugly photographs like mine can be so liked? After all my face on them looks very flat and all of them are "mommy-like". We are all so happy that you are having such a great time. We also have great time (but mostly having to do our homework). The meat ball hooked up with someone called Heniek ever since the last summer and I am into Bens and Ajzyks. There are so many row with that. Most of my notes end with a P.S. "Stop finally..." (you know what I'm talking about). Today I showed Ipcia your photos on the horse (she is so awfully sweet; I like her so much). She was enchanted and looking at each picture she kept repeating: "What a lucky girl". Nothing new at school. The girls keep on asking if you are still single.

We got 5 of your letters at once and it was already 11 pm. We read them, laughed so hard and enjoyed them so much that afterwards we couldn't sleep – mommy and me, the meat ball snored the night away – almost the entire night and the following day I skipped school. Would you believe that Rebeca threw me out of her classroom on Thursday? She asked what did Jews visualize God to be like during the biblical days. Some answers were: a bush a flame, a man, etc. The overall mood was quite gay; just like most of our religion classes. At some point, Lila (who sits behind me) said "like a stove" and I jumped in immediately saying "like a plate" and burst out laughing. Well, a moment later I went out through the door still shaking hard from my own laughter. In general, I have a hard time concentrating during religion classes this year. I just don't understand any of this. I would give myself at least 4 "F"s in religion class. Enjoy yourself, my dear, it is good for you. Do laugh a lot and you will end up looking like Sarenka (reference to her weight). Dance, dance my golden one – from Sunday to Saturday – and eat until your heart is content.

Your Marcik

November 19th

Dear Loniusiu!!!!

I have been trying to write you for the past few days but just couldn't get myself to do it.

The cow didn't want to write anything, therefore, we are mailing it as is.

 Translator's note: The last note above was started by Sarenka who never finished it. The last sentence was added by Marcia (her handwriting).

November 20, 1938

Lonius!

Enclosed please find a copy of my latest idea. He just may be willing to help me and I don't believe that he would want to cause me any harm. It just places on my shoulders a moral obligation to study a year in Winnetka – I do not know if financially I can afford it. Again, my worries may be moot as they accept only a select few with pedagogical accomplishments and my application can be denied. Besides that, we can always come up with some lame explanation to excuse my inability to study there. On the other hand, all graduates of this college leave to prearranged employment positions and if my finances permitted my studies there – it may be to my best interest to be accepted there. But we will see. Let him provide for now a recommendation letter. I question myself the intelligence of this concept but I must try and it costs me nothing. My dear, please do write much more about yourself. Do you plan to continue with the next semester in high school? I think that you should. But what qualifications will this give you or future possibilities? How far are you from Chicago? What kind of "order" rules at Sam's household? Do you dine all your dinners outside the house? What exactly does Sam do for a living? Is Fenia helping him in the business? What are the trades of some other Jewish families in Duncan? What are our potential future possibilities there? How I wish J. was legalized before our arrival. Would my arrival help him in that respect? Somplowa at some point indicated that you should remain in Oklahoma at least until we obtain our visas as there could be checks made if Zinger truly provides you with your livelihood. It does not mean that you have to reside at his house but he always must know of your whereabouts and he is responsible for providing you with the funds to cover the costs of living. She was under the impression that you plan to live with J. – that is why she said all that. All his letters, if I am correct, are officially addressed to Sam. You should address all your letters to him the same way. J. did write me that people at HIAS informed him that it was not necessary, but I do not know…It cannot hurt. Kisses.

    Mania

Warszawa, November 23, 1938

Sweet Loniulko!

I feel as if just gave birth 7 hours ago. On this occasion, even though this card will not reach you for another 2 weeks, I wish you again all that you wish for yourself. Our general wishes are the same, thus I wish for their speedy fulfillment. I suspect that as we write this card our primary birthday wishes are already in your hands. We tried to mail it appropriately so you would get them on time. So far there is nothing new to tell you about on this end. I hug your sweet hand and give you a hearty kiss.

    Mania

Dear Loniusiu!

What is (or rather was) the weather like on your birthday? We have an ugly Autumn. Mommy said that 21 years ago on November 23rd, your birthday, the weather was exactly the same. When she finally got up three weeks later everything was already white. So far we had beautiful weather: strong sun and temperatures around 608 degrees. The typical gray autumn skies were not here. What the weather will be like here next year I will not know – I will be already there. What did you do on your birthday? Did you have a good time? Did you get spanked 21 times or received 21 kisses or whatever else is the custom there? I kiss you.

    Your silly Marcia

Dear Loniusiu!

When you receive this card it will be about 2 weeks after your birthday. You will be able to tell us how you spent that day. And 4 weeks later we will have your return card from you telling us what a great time you had and how you spent your 21st birthday. Kisses to my older sister.

    A little bit younger, Sarenka

Translator's note: The postcard itself is not dated, however, the postal stamp thereon indicates the date of mailing to be December 10, 1938.

Lonia! Mazultow!!

The meatball bought herself a hat! Ha! Ha! Ha! Also, we have turtle-necks – the meatball has a blue one and mine is a navy color. Furthermore, the meat ball sign up for an English course with the Methodists on Sewerynow Street. Hearty kisses. Same Überraschungen.

    Sarenka (with a hat on)

Lonius!

I wasn't writing awaiting your next letter but Marcik doesn't allow me to wait any longer. They played us for a fool with that apartment. I lost a lot of money due to that. The physical move itself cost about 50 zloty. But, so be it. It was my own fault therefore I must take the consequences. I could have stayed longer on Bonifraterska Street. Walezianscy weren't scared with the notice to move out and continue to live there to this day. I grabbed that room for its beauty. Who would suspect that they tell me to move out after only two months. I took a loan for 700 zloty from the school superintendent's office. I gave it already to Wiktor who will find somewhere another 400 zloty and I will get a place of our own with Dyncia. If I get a visa, we will treat me as a sublease and she will pay me back as a rental money. Instead of paying these pigs, I prefer to help Dyncia get a flat of her own. If I don't get visa, God forsake this possibility, the ownership of the flat will be split in half with an allocation of half of rental money, if any. I am trying to send Marcia to Rabka, same as last year. From your debts I still owe Loni 23 zloty, Trzebuckiej 25 zloty, Fejgii 10 zloty, Kanfie 40 zloty. Aside from that some older debts reminded me lately of their existence. Jack sends me money but I would like something more systematic. I was thinking of a financial aid from him somewhere around $20 per month. When I pay off the debts and own a place, I won't need his help any longer. Reiterate this card to Jack. All of us are healthy. Kisses.

    Mania

December 25, 1938

Lonius!

Yesterday we, meaning myself, Sarenka, Hanka Zynger and Halinka, arrived to Krynica. We joined a winter camp called "Stars". I am sure that you must be absolutely shocked with my extravagance but I decided to, at least once in my lifetime, live like others do. I had some money for a new flat but after searching and searching to no avail or satisfaction, I decided to loan myself some money from that account. I hope to repay that debt at some point (maybe with J.'s help) before we finally find appropriate accommodations. In two days Marcia will leave for Rabka. As usual, she is quite tired at this time of the year and claims to have "subfebrile condition". Again, as usual, it will pass once she gets there. In reality she is just fine and after two weeks of rest and some mineral treatments she will be even better. I can only wish for time to go by quicker but I kind of doubt if it would bring something new. All consulates are buried in work. But it will happen. Continue to write at the old address as I am certain we will be here the entire January if not February as well. And even if we do move, the post office will be notified accordingly. Best regards to Sam and family. Kisses.

    Mania

Dear Loniu!

I am in Krynica with mommy, Hanka (Singer) and Hala. I did not notice that mom has already written you that but it's okay. It is so "cool" and merrily here, etc. I kiss you.

    Sarenka

Hugs and kisses from

    Hala

Also, hugs and kisses from

    Hania

POLAND
1939
JANUARY – AUGUST

March 22

Poland refuses German demands for Gdansk and the "Polish Corridor".

March 31

Britain and France guarantee Poland's sovereignty.

April 3

The German government issues a secret directive for the seizure
of Danzig, Poland, as a "free city".

April 6

Poland and Britain sign a mutual assistance pact.

April 28

Hitler renounces the non-aggression pact between Britain and Poland.

August 4

Poland rejects the USSR demand for permission for the Red Army to enter Poland.

August 23

The German-Soviet Non-Aggression Pact (Molotov-Ribbentrop) is signed containing a secret protocol
on the disposition of Poland, which will be divided between the two larger nations.

August 25

The Anglo-Polish Alliance is signed by which Great Britain will assist Poland should
Poland become the victim of aggression..

March, 1939. Letter from Marcia and Sarenka expressing their sisterly love.

April 22, 1939. Postcard from Mania with an additional note started by Marcia and then finished by Sarenka.

May 14, 1939. Letter from Mania discussing financial issues

March 9, 1939. Letter from Tamara with a diagram of their smaller apartment on 25/17 Sorczewaska Street.

April 29, 1939. Letter from Sara (Sarenka) to Leona in Polish, except for the last few lines when she practices her English.

June 3, 1939. Mania writes to Leona, complaining about Jacob and wishes her a good time on her trip to California.

Krynica, January 1, 1939

Dear Loniulko!

For some reason I have not received any letters from you lately and I miss them a little. I have no idea if the letters are in Warszawa without being forwarded or if you just don't write. I am taking advantage of all the therapeutic treatments available here. I have hydropathy, galvanic bathes (voltaic) and mineral bathes (carbonic acid). I will be here for a total of three weeks to complete all the phases of my treatments prescribed by the doctor. Today is the eleventh day. In two days Sarenka is leaving with Halinka and Hania for Warszawa; I will stay behind a little longer. This entire trip was not as successful as I wanted it to be due to a disappointment caused by Landanowa's grammar-school. Hofmanka got sick and I was informed that Marcia – I was so counting on her trip – is still in Warszawa. I sent an express mail to Wiktor asking him to send her over here but it does not look that he managed to accomplish it – she isn't here. I am furious with myself for not taking her with me to begin with. Rabka was somewhat cheaper but I also felt that it would be better for her. Also, Wiktor talked me into leaving before I could see Marcia go. What a terrible waste. Possibly she will go to Srodborow as suggested by Wiktor (Pola and Irusia are there). In other words, I do not know what is going on and it ruins my humor. I bought some used skis here and rented the ski boots. Sarenka is doing remarkably and is satisfied with herself. When we arrived here she had nasal congestion and a temperature; it disappeared here in no time. What's new with you? We still have no news. Maybe there is something waiting for us in Warszawa. I personally think that all delays are caused by the German refugees. Let it be. They deserve the priority. Give our best to the Raisins and Jack, of course. I wrote him twice from here and received myself 2 letters via Warszawa. Hearty kiss.

    Mania

P.S. Enclosed please find a picture of me. The one I took with Sarenka didn't turn out very well; I will send you one another time.

Dear Loniu!

I am here with your mommy, Sarenka and Hala on vacation. Between all of us we are causing quite a havoc but we are also having a ball. Your mom reminiscences a lot about you, and we all are sorry not to have you here with us. I am learning about the American lifestyle from your letters. Your pictures are truly fabulous. Take care. Kisses.

    Hanka

Dear Loniu!

It is the first time I am writing to you since you left for America. I trust that America suits you well. I would love to be there with you. But I am in Krynica and it is quite nice and lovely here. Hearty kisses.

    Hala

Oh, these girlfriends of mine, they wrote so much…that they didn't leave me hardly even a quarter page to write on. They were quite ecstatic, those buddies of mine, but I guess they have a good reason. Today I spent 5 hours skiing with some boy who claims to have known you for over 10 years now. He is Beli Blatt's brother (about 20 something). But this is not important. Hugs and kisses.

Your Sarenka

January 5, 1939

Sweet Lonius!

I just escorted Sarenka, Hala and Hanka. Sweet Marcik was very unlucky with her winter school break. Too bad. I spent a lot of money on behalf of all of us. I am staying here another week to complete my therapy. I was in a state of nervous prostration. The hydropath does wonders for me. I wrote Lublinerowa to extend my vacation by another 4 days. In the meantime, I will cut my therapy short by a few days and, this way, I will still get full 3 weeks. I went through so much over this past year that it all drained me emotionally. And, it is my strong belief, there is so much more to live for taking into consideration our "dream" journey. Thus, I was in a dire need of three weeks of rest and relaxation. (At least once in a lifetime!) I am enchanted with Morris' letters to you. I feel that he is honest. Overall, you truly lucked out, my dear. As I told you – the key is to win people over. I am quite surprised with the lack of response from the consul but, I guess, it will arrive some time. So far, I did not write to Winnetka. I will do it from Warszawa but I honestly doubt that anything will come out of it. Kisses. Best regards for Jack. He asks for more frequent letters yet each time I write you I also include greetings for him, the Raizens and Morris. He doesn't write to me but, most likely, there is nothing to write about. Maybe that is why I am not angry with him. Write him just that.

Mania

Dear Lonius!

Today we are leaving Krynica. We had a great time here. We had some jolly and pleasant times together. We will include a photo of us all in the next letter. Hearty kisses.

Sarenka, Hanka and Hala

Srodborow, January 13, 1939

Dear Loniusiu!

I write you from Srodborow since I never did go to the winter camp. Please, do not mention any of this in letters; you cannot even imagine what I went through here. Mommy, with our sibling, Hala and Hanka left for Krynica and I stayed in Wiktor's care until my own departure for winter camp a few days later. Now imagine that a day before my departure I got "sick". (I can tell you the truth; you are not like mom. In reality I am quite healthy, with ruddy cheeks and "fat"). I wrote mom to Krynica telling her some unbelievable fibs – that the camp never left town and this and that – and this fool believed every word I said. Thereafter she wanted me to come to her but I told her that I preferred to go to Srodborow and…here I am. During my "sickness" (just for a few days) I was pampered. I had a constant flow of visitors: Polcia Lazer, ours Ida and Izak (every day acting as doctors), of course Wiktor and – most important – a lot of my friends. Believe me when I tell you that since summer, early summer, we have our own close circle (I do not recall if I told you already about it). It includes Sarenka, Karola, myself and 4 boys: Heniek, Eljasz, Ajzyk and Leon. We often gather together and go eat, dancing, for walks, cinema or early evening parties. It is so nice. We have become a very close group. Recently I received a cute card from most of them how much fun they are having in Srodborow. So far there are 5 of us here but 4 more will arrive tomorrow. We do everything and go everywhere together. Currently, Aunt Pola and Irenka are also here in Srodborow. We all went to visit her.

I spend a lot of time outside in the fresh air. The weather is great. I am getting a nice tan and am renewing my strength for more hard work. Loniusiu, dear, did you know that Marysia Mel. visited Warszawa? I met with her. She turned out to be a beautiful elegant lady. Except she smokes. I could smell it when we kissed. Kisses, kisses and more kisses.

    Marcia

Warsaw, January 16, 1939

Jacob,

I have been in Warsaw for two days. During the time I have been in Krynicia, Marcia was sick again with influenza. Ida and Izak and Dintzik and Victor used to come here every day to see her. They deceived me that the colony of her school did not travel so that I will not come. And after her fever dropped they sent her to Shrodborove. As it is understood I visited her yesterday. I also spent the night. I took her temperature. It was 37.3. It goes without saying that she has to stay there for a few weeks. There is a high possibility that I will take an apartment over there next to the mill in Michalin until the summer, because here anyhow it is impossible to find an apartment for sale. As it seems to me it will be needed because we will not travel so soon. Today I received the papers of Shlomke and Zalmanke and I gave them to the consul. From there I received a letter yesterday that I am registered over the Poland quota, but it will be possible after more or less forty-three months. What are you going to say about this?

A year ago the matter used to be easier – now it is a totally different matter. It is needed to wait three and a half years and afterwards who knows? You must not get angry but seek for ways. First of all, the matter of your citizenship. Ask in your board if there is any way. They did not want to accept the new papers from me, but I asked to have them there because we are three people and finally he accepted the papers. But what out of it if Morris will be able to do something as he promised – he will try. As it seems to me, it is easier for a husband or brothers. But who knows. The most important thing is not to get angry, just do whatever possible. Who knows if it is not worthwhile even now to travel to Zalman's land. We also have to think about Lonia. Will she live there three or four years? It would be good if you could be together with her after this school year will be over, meaning in the fall. What shall I tell you – when there is nothing to say and nothing to talk about. Consult with the board and write what you will be told. My health has been improved tremendously. I am relaxed. Whatever will be – will be. I will wait patiently like I waited for ten years – just let us all be healthy – I cannot stand diseases. And this is unfortunately not in our hands. All the remaining concerns – vanity of vanities, all is vanity.

January 16, 1939

Lonius!

For the last two days I was back in Warszawa that is including the night I spent yesterday in Srodborow. It was quite a joke played on me. But she is fine now except for a slightly elevated temperature. I feel splendid. I rested well and my health visibly improved. Today I spent the entire day from 8 am to 1 pm at HIAS and the consulate. I delivered documents received in the meantime from Sam and Saul. Unfortunately, I received a letter which is not a denial but, I believe even worse, as follows: "Consul General informs that you have been placed on the list of people to be called upon in the future to file an official application for emigration visa subject to the assigned Polish quota. Your turn is expected to take place in approximately 43 months. In the meantime, you should neither write to the Consulate nor come in person. Vice Consul William H. Cordell." Well, here it is – three and half years. I doubt that anything can be accomplished now but…let Morris do what he can on his end – maybe something personal. I wrote a letter to Winnetka that I had elected to follow the quota as, there is no way, I would leave my children behind with acceptance from them or without. Do, my love, what you can. It is time to sit back and calmly consider all the options. Push Jack to get moving with his own case – even better, tell him to ask for advice from HIAS. But it looks like, aside from falling into the assigned quota, no one can do anything – except may be the consul himself. Write Morris about this development. After all, he predicted a denial. I am (after Krynica) much more peaceful, level-headed and I will just await my fate. I have done all there was in my power to do including expending monies for all the necessary documents. Now all I can do is wait. Kisses.

    Mania

Dearest Loniusiu!

We have returned from Krynica after a 2-week stay there. I had a ball there…and continue to have one here. I learned to ski. I like it. You asked in your card if Marcia and I are not trying to compete with one another. You must be kidding – it is quite impossible. Both of us have numerous and separate admirers. Hearty kisses.

    Sarenka

February 3, 1939

Dearest Lonisiu!

We are such horrible cows for not writing you in such a long time. Did you get my card from Srodborow? I wasn't sure that I remembered to write "USA" on it. I had such a wonderful time there. What's new with you? Please write to Marysia Gasior. I met with her in Srodborow. She is upset. I passed on your address through her brother. Kotlicka, Buirksman and Fejgin send you their best regards.

You would not believe what a row I had today with Urbanowa. I had no homework since I did not read a single composition it was supposed be based on (absence!). So I wrote it quickly at the school, was selected to read it out loud in front of the entire class and... I was okay. Charanka did exactly the same as me and we both were selected to read our homework. Ipcio is so sweet. Everything is hunky-dory. Ciao!

    Marcia

My sweet Leonko!

I let Marcia write you first and now, I must admit, that – following her vocabulary – she is just herself, a child, but I am the worst among those "cows". Your card sits unanswered after a few days now. Since it is the first, I trust that you will find forgiveness in your heart. I feel truly splendid. I am the first to admit that I have not felt that good in a very long time. Krynica did me good. I dream about another 3 weeks there this coming summer. It truly made me feel so much better. Recently I went to HIAS. They say that my case is looking extremely good since new immigration registrations get assigned numbers in the 25 thousand range (while mine is only in the 13 thousand range). Furthermore, the letters sent by the consulate do not indicate, like mine, that they were placed on a waiting list and will be notified of a scheduled interview within 43 months; instead they inform that their case will be reviewed in approximately 5 years. Something to be pleased about! They also told me that in my case the phrase "within 43 months", in reality, can turn out to be only 3 months – it strictly depends on their position at the time towards emigration. The same took place in your case. First they denied; then they relaxed somewhat (for I do not believe, not really, in the success of any our interventions, though I do not exclude completely the possibility thereof) and you left much sooner than we all expected you to. My dear, write Jack immediately that his 650 zloty did reach me. This last method works with no snags. Only Wiktor complained since he had to go to the bank. I hid the money in the basement and everything is "hunky-dory". If I don't find an appropriate apartment by March, I will move in with Michalim. Again, thank Jack for me for his sweet letter. Tell him not to worry; I saw the light and started following his directives. Kisses for Rajcyns and Zingers.

    Mania

Dear Lonius!

I wish you a great carnival season. I will try to send you a picture in a near future. Hearty kisses from me. Also best regards from everyone here.

    Sarenka

Dear Daddy!

You always insist that we be happy, playful and laughing a lot. But why are you so sad? Why worry so much? We accepted the following principles: "The most important thing is not to worry!", "What do I care?", "Do not worry ahead of time!" And we follow them all. Any time someone starts to worry about something, someone else immediately reminds her: "What? You are perturbed?" The other responds: Not at all!?" and start to laugh. In the end she even forgets the cause of her worry. "Laughter is healthy! You won't get fat while laughing!" Remember all this principles and put them into practice yourself.

It's not about – how you say it – bouncing around between clubs, cinemas, theaters or concerts. It's about being practical. Not spending any money and still having so much fun that it makes you want to c___ in your underwear. Being able to laugh at the worst joke. Organizing parties under the most primitive conditions. Those are the times when a person can feel the most comfortable, free, capable of enjoying life to its fullest. Maybe your present situation does not allow you to do all those things but when we arrive, we will bring with us a lot of joy, laughter and other things to change your present situation and to change your future forever. It is not too far away!

In the meantime, prepare yourself for this new lifestyle. Just like Lonia promises us a new, completely different life in America, so do we promise to change your life.

Laugh a lot!!!!
Do not worry about anything!!!
Kisses, kisses...
Do everything happily!!!!

    Your Marcia

 Translator's note: Marcia's letter is followed by a note in Yiddish to Jack from Mania.

Here you have a little happiness. We are all healthy. Two days ago, three of us went to the movies. The children really were happy. I have enrolled in an English course so I can be busy. Maybe I think, I progressed with questions and it also feels better than to sit home. I go twice a week. Be healthy.

February 13 but not an unlucky one (it's already evening)

Dear Loneczko!

I write this on a page from my biology notebook. Isn't it a sacrifice on my part? Sweet doll. Since you do not want to write in detail about yourself, I will do it about myself with a hope that it will serve as an example to you.

It is already a third week at school and I still have nothing completed. And do you know by what miracle? Well, listen. After my return from Srodborow, I jumped into everything in my own way – that is frantic way – work, completing unfinished stuff and I worked so hard (what a fool) that I ended up with a headache and feeling like a corpse. And that was when, as can always be predicted, mother threw a fit, wouldn't let me do anything, sent a letter to Hofmanka demanding that I be released from all the school responsibilities, demanding that she talks with Belfranci, demanding that I get extension on all my deadlines, that things can not continue the way they are, etc. etc. etc. etc. That's when it all really started. There was a conference at the principal's office that Zagraniczna is horribly exhausted, she is going through a depression stage (what a bunch of bull!!!) and that she must be released from having to take any oncoming tests. And I was in a paradise! The teachers (especially Polcia) started to come over to the house telling me not to worry about anything and that I will be given plenty of time to catch up. Have you ever heard of such an attitude towards a student? They talked themselves into me being very sick (all because of mom's letter) and on this account I do nothing except of going for walks and to the cinema. On Saturday, mommy and I went to see "Professor Wolf" (continuation of "The Charlatan"). There are a lot of beautiful new Polish films out. Today, I went for the first time to Conservatory but I had no lesson (what luck)! I was not prepared at all. Lefeldzik, that sweet man, had to go to the radio station for a rehearsal.

We are all having a great time. Especially yesterday topped it all. Four boys came over: Heniek, Eljasz, Leon (I wrote you about him from Srodborow) and Mietek Borensztajn. At the beginning they all sat in our room but were too noisy (mom and I were doing homework) and we threw them out to another room. They had such a great time there (with our meat ball) that the close proximity of them was too much to bare. We evicted them all the way to the kitchen. They turned it into a paradise for themselves. The kitchen, like any kitchen, has a lot "musical instruments": plates, bowls, cups, utensils, trays, pots, pokers. It all got utilized forming a wonderful orchestra! Ole. At this point, I couldn't hold myself back any longer. I blew everything else off: homework, piano practice, etc. (I finally followed your lessons and it turned quite well for me – next day I had no classes plus a free hour since I didn't have to take the physics test) and entered the kitchen door. And here my eyes lay on the following sight: Heniek is sitting down and playing on his comb wrapped in a paper tissue some sad tunes; Leonek accompanies him by pounding the wooden spoons on his chair and kicking his legs against some metal bowls and who knows what else on the floor; Eljasz beats the poker against our laundry tray; Mietek fiddles on the cups, then on the lamp, then on something else (placed on his crooked nose) to keep up with the others; and our meat ball is screaming on the top of her lungs in an attempt to be the loudest one among them all. Of course, I joined forces with Sarenka. Later, I danced with Heniek (who simultaneously continued to play on his comb). When everyone in the building had enough of us, the building keeper called asking to quite down as someone in the building was sick. We moved on to someone else's flat arguing all the way and having a ball at all times.

Our group is a very cohesive one and everyone feels at our home as it was their own. Mommy usually breaks our fun around 10 pm but we don't mind her at all. God bless her. We always manage to have some more fun. Today, I saw Danka Hagan. She got pregnant by some kid from our grammar school. Regards from Dorka Batz and Anka Brand (the later doesn't do anything at the moment). You chit of a girl, you took so much of my time. I should be doing some homework but I will find some excuse and, in the meantime, tell you about Srodborow. Though, I am not sure if you even have enough patience to read all this. My intent is to give you an example (you should write this much too). Even though our boarding house was designated for teachers, there were very few of them since it was not during the vacation time; actually it was immediately after vacation. Instead there were lodging some worker unions members and some relatives and friends of some teachers. I shared my room with some very nice ladies, two older ones and one younger, a sweet Palestinian, who kept an eye on me and was to me an ideal guardian, teacher, friend, mother, whoever you wanted her to be. Right across the wall lived three boys, big bulls, but super guys and very funny. They kept calling me and caused all kinds of row.

At the boarding house, there was a really sweet four year old boy, Izio, and a six year old Maria. Aside from them, there were Mrs. Kwas, Mrs. Bagno, Mr. Pentelka, Mr. Niedzwiedz (please note their last names). We had a ball.

Do save this letter since it will serve as a diary after I arrive to America. I will refresh my memory then about all the havoc I caused. Oh, I forgot to write you about the mess in Bojnowicz's sugar factory and other rows. But I have to say good-bye for now.

If you read it all to the end, you are quite brave. I am very proud of your grades. I kiss you, my sweet sister.

    Your Marcia

I didn't do the second shot for my vericose vein. I listened to you and wait. I feel great.

    Mania

February 19, 1939

Lonius!

I am taking advantage of a slow moment to write you a few words. For the past few days I impatiently await any news from you. I signed up for a course with the Methodists. I won't say that I am benefiting from this tremendously but, nonetheless, I do benefit some – that is I am familiarizing myself with the spoken language. I sit next to Halszna Kotlicka and Seniksmanowna. Besides that it serves also as a form of diversion. I actually know much more than most of the attendees; mostly the volume of my vocabulary is better. But my reading and writing skills are behind the more advanced group and I have no courage to sign up with them. I want to better myself more at this level before I move on to the higher one. Our assignments include writing newspaper briefs, short stories, etc. In any event I feel like I do benefit from all this – and, this way, the time passes by quicker. When do you plan to leave for the opening of the New York exhibition? Write more about yourself. The girls work hard; especially Marcia – very tired, as always. I wish she was already done with her school. Effective with the next year, Sarenka will stop attending school. Possibly, I will find a modern and comfortable bachelor apartment (own bathroom, central heating etc. in some newly built house for a higher monthly rent). This would allow me to eliminate a full-time servant. If that happens, I will not need any financial help and finally you all there will be able to start looking more after yourselves. The main thing now is to settle down with a good flat. Then, to find a job for Sarenka. She changed so much that you would not recognize her. She is lively and gay. She gained some good friends who she spends a lot of time with walking, going to the cinema and attending lectures. I believe that she has become mature enough to gain employment as well. Kisses and more kisses for everyone.

    Mania

Dear Loniuska!

I just saw your photographs and I am fascinated by them. You have warmest greetings and kisses from Rachela G. Also, greetings from Halinka. Did you hear that Ozia Welisler was resettled from Poland to Russia and no one has heard from her since then.

    (not signed but in Marcia's handwriting)

February 21, 1939

Dear Loniulko and Jack!

Yesterday, your double letter arrived. Since I waited for Sarenka to write a note from herself, I thought of some additional things to write you about. Also, enclosed you should find a separate letter to those sweet Sams. I am not naturally a funny person but I wrote it as best I could. I was informed yesterday that the apartment occupied by us currently has seemingly been sold. I indicated that there is no way I would move out before April. We shall see if they leave me alone for the time being. Nowadays it is very hard to find lodgings. It is quite possible that we will not have any choice but to move to Miedreszyn. But it will not be an easy undertaking and those constant moves. The primary problem will be the piano since it will first be moved to Miedreszyn – about 30 zloty – then to Michalin and finally back to Warszawa. I am still hoping to find something in Warszawa – but I have my doubts. To purchase something – I do not know if I will stay here longer than 3.5 years and a room with a kitchen runs approximately 1,500 zloty. Two rooms and a kitchen are even more. Thus, I am considering one room with a kitchen or a good bachelor apartment in a new house – the rent, in turn, will be very high. As I write this, Marcia has brought me your letter in which you describe the affair with my Yiddish. I know Yiddish quite well. On the flip side, I believe their knowledge of Yiddish is directly in reverse from mine. It doesn't matter. As long as they are concerned about me and try to do something to remedy our "situation". I am not overly thrilled about those 3.5 years. Kisses for both of you together and individually.

    Mania

"My lovely beautiful meatballs!

I will love you like crazy after I marry you."** All is well here. Today there was no biology class and, instead, I read a review of a play. Right now, Sarenka and I are lolling and pigging out on the couch. Everyone is healthy. Your "slim and fashionable"

    Marcia

 Translator's note: This sentence rhymes in Polish. It is an excerpt from a children's poem.**

My dearest ones!

I love you both no less than our sister and your daughter, Jack, but I do not say it out loud. We all are quite well here with nothing to be feverish about. Hearty kisses for the both of you.

    Sarenka

Translator's note: The letter includes a note from someone else - since a part of the note is missing the person is unknown.

Sweet Loniuska!

Lately I am very short on both time and patience but I am taking this opportunity to send you my kisses. Your mom shows me all your sweet letters with pride and I am fascinated (…)

March 4, 1939

Dearest Loniulko!

I write this letter still from Zelazna Street but, it appears, we will be moving on the 8th. I say "it appears" because we will be moving to a second apartment leased recently. Prior to March 1st, I leased a flat on 36 Sorczewska Street for 70 zloty per month. I put a 20 zloty deposit for it but later I decided to forego that deposit for a much closer and better flat on 25 Sorczewska Street, Apt. #1, with its own bathroom, hallway, on a high first floor (the other flat was on a 3rd floor) – but also more expensive since it costs 80 zloty per month. Also, I purchased a 3-month street car pass for line #9 which goes to my office. It will also serve Marcia to reach her conservatory and all of us with English classes (3 Sewerynow Street). I paid the 50 zloty tuition in advance which I do not intend to lose. The building is 3 years old (the other one only 1 year old). The apartment is dry, beautiful and in a new building which means there is not a surrender of lease clause. A tenant security has been eliminated to save monies which is good in our situation – maybe something will change and we will not have to wait the full 3.5 years. Overall, the cash outlay is substantial since, including the pass, it costs 102.50 zloty per month. However, Sarenka is finishing her school which will allow us to manage better during the next school year. Her school costs 30 zloty per month but I was awarded a discount up to 380 zloty. That means that I have to pay 38 zloty now and another 80 zloty at the end of the school year. I have 1,000 zloty with Wiktor which was designated for a flat. I will take from that amount about 400 zloty for three months of rent and moving expenses. It will carry us until the summer. Another 200 zloty will be used to pay our debt which will give me peace of mind. I feel great and am excited about our new place since it is both beautiful and will provide a place of "our own". But the past 2 weeks I walked my feet off. That flat on Zelazna Street has already been sold but I didn't want the new owners to move in before my time. Write, my love what's new with you. I will write from a new address in a few days. Also, I will notify the post office about the change in address. Would you like a picture from "studniowka"? I saw it at Gawronowicz's house.

Mania

Translator's note: "Studniowka" is a customary party in Poland arranged by schoolmates a hundred days before school exit examinations.

March 9, 1939

My dearest daughter!

Now you can, and should, write at our new mailing address even though I'm writing this letter still from Zelazna Street (10 pm). I paid 3 months of rent in advance and made arrangements with Minkiewicz for tomorrow. A part of smaller things was moved already and Janowa cleaned today and plans to finish tomorrow (after the painter). Maybe the room is somewhat small for our piano. Thus, we decided to move in only one large bed, settee, camp-bed, etc. Besides, all this is just temporary – what's important that the flat is clean, has a bathroom and hallway plus it is located on a high first floor. My splendid humor can also be attributed to the fact that I will not have to ride every day with Michalim. The trip from our new house to my school takes about 15 minutes by street car. We have 3 monthly passes for line #9 for 22.50 zloty. Our move coincided with the receipt of your last letter – my advice is: do not drive. Having just a room at somebody's house is an awful thing. I looked at a similar room on Alberta Street – a tiny room with an even smaller kitchen for 100 zloty per month. Here, it costs me the same 100 zloty with street car passes. And, after all, we used to spend a few zloty each month for street cars, I think around 10 zloty – so take your own independent apartment. Janowa will probably retire after August but will continue to come for a few hours only. I will change the kitchen into a second room. Write, my sweet child, what's new with you. You hardly write anything about yourself. When do you plan to see the exhibition? We are all healthy; the rest of the family the same. Grandmother is already some time after her surgery; the eyesight is good. She asked me to pass her kisses for you from afar. Berta also had some female surgery – she is healthy, works and lives in peace with her husband. Ida had an appendix surgery and is healthy now, as well. Rysia reads splendidly – she taught herself. On Saturday I went to see a choir at the theater performance called "The Great Variety Show". Kiss yourself on your pretty nose and regards for Raizens.

    Mania

P.S. Marcia is upset that I didn't leave her any room.

Dear Loniusiu!

You did not write us for quite some time. You are plain lucky that we got a letter from you yesterday. Otherwise, it might have ended bad for you.

Since we do not write you long letters too often (mostly postcards), I have to write you about everything in more detail. Well, I am getting myself pumped up for this project. First of all, the flat. I am sure this is the most interesting topic for you. The room is small; the hallway is narrow; the bathroom is nice; and the kitchen is sunny.

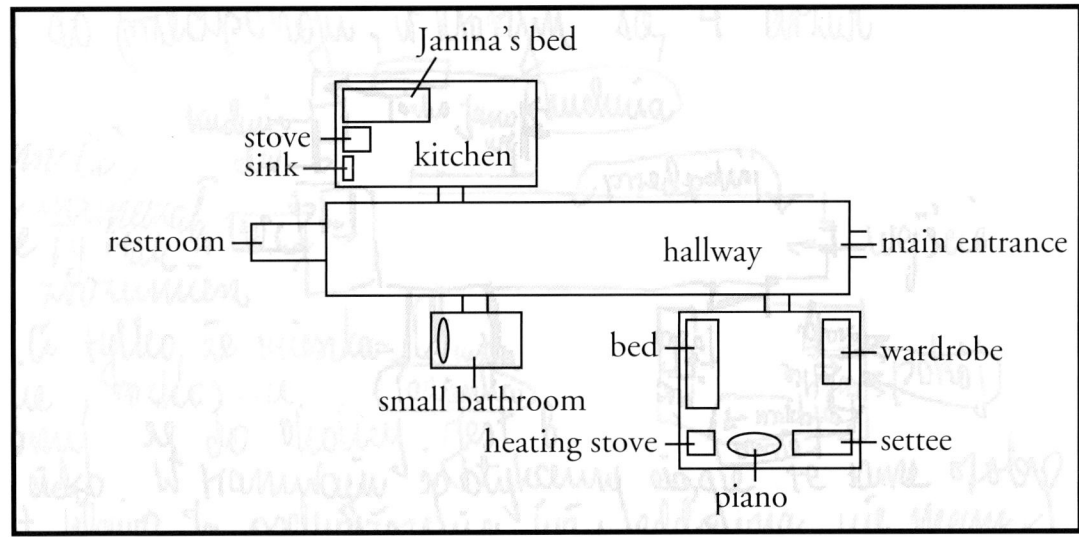

I drew it for you, scrawled is a better word, but I doubt you will understand any of this. Enough to say that the flat is nice and cozy. We got used to the area; it is very nice. We always meet the same people on the street car. Everything is okay. I do not have a raised temperature any more. Instead just lots of work. I am doing quite well at the Conservatory. Mommy pulled me out from theory classes in the middle of the school year; I attend only piano lessons. Lefeld is a wonderful man. He is a sweet and good professor. He changed the position of my hand and, now, I have no more difficulties with my technique. He has never told me so far that my playing is too slow. And what is even more important, he has never yelled at me (it appears that doesn't even know how to yell). I always leave my lessons cheerful, smiling and without all those flushed cheeks with Dabrowska. I have my exam already in May – I will play 2 etudes by Czernegi, 3-voice study by Bach, sonata by Hayden and one more, though I am not sure which, piece. I practice very little, even less than with Dabrowska, or maybe the same amount. I just cannot find any time. I hardly read anything besides some books. Let's face it, I hardly do anything. Anything I do has to be done superficially as the time passes by too quickly (that the way it has always been with me).

You may be interested to hear that I am going through some cadet corps training at the hospital. I represent my school troops with an official hospital title (erroneous as it is) of a "sister". We work there on Saturdays starting at 7 am (4 times 5 hours each time). We wash the patients, change their clothes, change their bedding, pass the food, give massages, check temperature, flirt, assist with giving shots, enema, pumping stomachs, surgeries, dressing the wounds. We work in two departments: internal medicine and surgery. How do you like all that? The last time I went there I fell in love with two guys, reciprocated by both of them. We have one more time to go (we go to Czyste).

Or, here is a better one, which you probably have heard already from the newspapers. We had a 3-day "gas attack" (a make-believe one, of course). It was just wonderful! Each house and institution was assigned someone in an overall commanding officer and also commanders for each type of service (security, fire-safety, medical, communications, etc. – six of them in total). All of them made sure than everyone follows the rules. There was a blackout of the entire city. The windows were covered with black paper and lights covered to dim them at all times. During the alarm signals everything had to be turned off. Upon the sound of alarm sirens all people on the streets had to empty them into the surrounding buildings (of course, I was assigned to the street) and a grave-like silence was falling upon the city. In the meantime, airplanes circled in the air and the attempts were made to catch them in the floodlights. The airplanes were dropping weak and fake gas and other bombs, etc. The news bulletins were passed on over the radio, like: some bombs were dropped on Ikerbednia Square, Praga was cut off from the rest of Warszawa without any electricity or water. It all was make-believe. The best time was while at school. We were ordered to make our own tampons from gauze and cotton wool, place them in metal cans which, in turn, were hanged from the ceilings with strings. We all frolicked around among those cans and waited for the alarm. It finally came during our physical education class.

You have regards from Pola and Szyfra. Regards from Giersztowa. Kisses from Marcin. The photo copies you requested are not available; someone has the negatives but I have no idea who. Everyone is healthy; everything is okay. Our regards for the old and little Rajcyns. Ciao.

    Tamara

March, 1939

Dear Loniuszko!

Yesterday, I received your letter along with a copy of the letter to the Consul written by Saul's wife. It's style appears to me to be a trifle. But, what's important, that it has an effect. It does not hurt to bother him – it just might work. Everything here is also "all right". I was starting to truly worry about a lack of news from you – 18 days – first time it happened. That letter from yesterday was forwarded from Zelazna Street to Sorczewska Street. Quite possible that some mail got lost. We live here at this address already 2 weeks and yesterday's letter was the first one from you. There was also no mail from Jack for about 3 weeks now even though he wrote quite often to us lately. In his last letter he mentioned that Rothman's sister will be visiting with you. He was somewhat embittered by this. He is afraid that his family is willing to help anyone but him. How is your school? Will you get any certificate equivalent to our secondary-school certificate? Your certificate plus a proof of additional courses taken, e.g. English courses, would allow you, I hope, to enter a university. I heard that state universities there, though just a few, are free to students. You should inquire into attending one of them. So far I did not ask you too many questions about your plans for the next school year. I assumed that I would be there and we would decide on that together. However, it appears that we must put our dreams aside and become realists. Thus, talking about next school year, I would like you to share with me your plans. Maybe you are not even thinking so far ahead yet and it may be for the best. But you know that I always prefer to establish a goal and conservatively direct my actions towards it. It is my wish that the time of our separation be filled for you with things that are both pleasant and advantageous. I try to practice it myself (since the year 1928). Now, I started quite seriously to study English. It will always benefit me in the future and for now it also brings me pleasure. I joined the 3rd class and, now, I am truly learning something. Besides attending classes twice a week, I also attend a biblical hour on Sundays at 6 pm (you may remember the song "God is my Love" – we sing, read from the Old or New Testament, etc.). Also, each Friday I have an access to so called "club hours" where one can read papers, converse or listen to lectures. Recently, I attended a lecture by Gitlin (Batysta) – I even understood most of his rubbish. Afterwards, I approached him, reminded him who I am, and asked about Elsa and Rosenberg. They have a son and live in Argentina. I am quite healthy. Same with Marcia and Sarenka. Aside from that both of them are quite gay and happy. I even forgot about my leg and feel very well. Lately, as I have already written you previously, I had lots of work and impatiently await Easter break. At this very moment I remembered your grandmother who's eyesight is excellent, continues to read a lot of books, does her embroidery and, again, invites us all for Seder. Kiss the Rajcyns from me. Did they receive my letter sent to them indirectly through Jack? I kiss you, my love, million times. Write more about yourself. All you doings and goals are of interest and happiness to me.

Tell the Rajcyns and yourself (Yiddish) which means "Happy Holidays". Also, give my best regards to other family members like Morris, etc. The weather here changes – I recall that you asked me about it – but hopefully not for worse. Other family members are healthy. Irusia is almost over with a pertussis. Eljasz finally passed his driver's certificate and searches for an employment as a chauffeur's assistant. Wawek works for Adam. He changed for better.

    Mania

Dear…not Leona (God forbid), and not meat ball, and not puppy (even the most beautiful one) – only my sweet doll and gorgeous angel behind the ocean!!!!!!!!!!!

We love you; you are truly a dear girl. You write us so many lovely letters!! My favorite pass time if there ever was one. It means so very, very, very, very much being able to read your "briefs".

As you already know we have a piano (for over 3 weeks now) and I practice at least 2 hours each time 3 times a week. I moved over to Lefeld; that is I filed an application to move over. We do not read any more literature (I did some at the beginning only). In turn, I relish beautiful works of Rolland, Sinclair, Gladkow Lindsey and others. You may write me that I became a very serious person – I do not want to disappoint you but, the truth is, I enjoy life too much to spend time reading. However, when I do read something, it is usually something good. Thank you for the information about clothes there. Personally, I prefer a blue outfit instead of a green one (of course, because no one wears that color here). What's new?

It is a truly stupid, formal question. (It reminds me of Urbanowa). But I read the same question 3 times in your last 4 letters and 1 letter from Jack.

You know, one of my friends, called Ajzyk, studies Yiddish for quite a long time now. We read together works of Perec, different stories and poems (extremely serious and intelligent boy and he happens to like me). We spoke to each other in Yiddish though not very grammatically. But, when I tried one day to speak German to some girl…it was just awful. Finally, I decided to skip any attempts to learn my beloved German language. Good-bye for now.

    Marcia

 Translator's note: The next note, from Sarenka, is missing the beginning.

(…) after all it can be molded to one's needs. I do just that. If I feel my effort are futile, I blow the whole thing off. After all, these is only a summer entertainment. All new acquaintances will end with the end of the summer. Therefore, no need to worry about it. I am doing the right thing, am I not? I am not sure which school I will attend now. After reading your letters, I am completely lost. Simply speaking, I do not even feel like preparing myself for any examination! (You know best that I have never been overly enthusiastic). We sent you 2 photos in our last letter. Since then we took some more but they did not turn out well. We will send you some more soon.

In the meantime, I kiss you my sweet Lonius-angel.

    Sarenka

Regards from Natek. Abram Bursztyn also asked to pass to you his regards.

    Sarenka

March 30, 1939

Dear Loniulko!

Your letters arrive now regularly but do write quickly. I just cannot wait any longer for your letter dated after March 22nd. On that day I read in the local paper about an airplane from Oklahoma City which crashed killing 7 passengers and the pilot. Also, I heard nothing from Jack for over 3 weeks now – I am worried. Everything is in order here and I mean it. Your letter received yesterday made me happy but I cannot believe that you continue to enjoy flying in the clouds. I would like to have received already your post-March 22nd letter. I do want you to have a great time but do not fly anymore. Those ground-level pleasures are so much better. Kisses.

    Mania

> **Translator's note:** Mania's letter is followed by a note in Yiddish. "Many regards and kisses for the family. I wish you a peaceful, happy yom tov. Mania" The next note is from Marcia. She starts it with a word "Dear…" but the ending of this word (in Polish) is directed to a male gender, instead of a female gender, as the case would demand. This explanation is necessary to understand the first paragraph of Marcia's letter.

Dear…

No, wait, I have to tell you what has just happened. I just returned home from the conservatory. In the street car, I met Finkel (sends his best regards; he wanted to know all the details about you). When I started to write you just now, Sarenka said: "What's with that smirk on her face?" and mommy responded: "From all that flirting with Finkiel." And, after that exchange, I started my letter with "Dear". I don't have to tell you what a wide smile that brought to that meatball's face. We have beautiful weather today. The sun shines and I am sun tanning. Yesterday, there was a parent-teacher conference (3rd semester). Mommy brought home my report card on which Hofmanka had written: "Don't worry. Everything will be okay." How do you like that? She is just to delightful. And, to begin with, I wasn't even worried – there was nothing to worry about. Her note "moved me deeply." Bye.

    Marcia

Dearest Loniusiu!!

Yesterday we received a letter from you – the one in which you describe the wardrobe of American ladies and preliminary work with evening parties of those ladies that seek some fun one way or the other. It is truly interesting. It brought to my mind a lot of funny questions. Alas, it has to be a terribly hard work to organize it in such a way that all present at the event have a great time. I cannot even comprehend how it can even be organized in such a way for "the wolf to be full and the sheep untouched". Regarding the garments, dresses and hoses – I fully agree with you; it is both very practical and hygienic. Kisses.

    Sarenka

My beloved, dear Jack!!!

Your youngest, though fully grown up, daughter is not neglecting her sweet daddy. Just because she writes very little and rarely, it has nothing to do with it. Mommy always leaves so little space or mails her letters without even waiting for us. However, not writing does not mean that one does not remember. One can write, pour out pages, shower with empty phrases, etc. but deep down having absolutely no interest in what is being written and mentally being somewhere else. Of course, it doesn't have to happen either always or often. But you know how it is with me. I think of you often. They say that I look like you. For instance, when I stubbornly practice an excerpt from a sonata or an etude, everyone complains of "swollen ears" and Mom claims that you used to work like that. I am very proud of the fact that I am like you but, also, I have to give Mommy credit for many other talents inherited from her (e.g. an aptitude for languages, etc.). Overall, I am a very funny girl which hopefully you will be able see soon for yourself. My face has characteristics borrowed both from you and Mom..

I am ready to go – you know where – but what will I do with that English? I have no time to study it. School and Conservatory – not a trifle. I am a quite important person. I attend the secondary school, advanced music (with sweet Lefeld) and study of instruments; solfeggio, harmony, basic theory and other "junk" are behind me. Bye!

    Marcia

P.S. "There, where the water is clear, the horses drink (2). Where a pretty maiden is, the boys fight".* I remember those days…

 Translator's note: It is a short poem rhyming in Polish language.*

Dear Lonka!

I have never written to you until now but I decided to write you. Please, do write me what is going on in America? What is the general atmosphere towards the present happenings here? Write me about your school and about your friends. What are the moods of the youth at your school? Are they also so narrow-minded? Do write me about your town and lifestyles of people living there. How do you spend your time? I kiss you heartily.

    Irusia

Dear! I'm rushing to school. I will write more some other time. Lots of love.

    Your Marcia

I am in even more rush than she is. But Mom refuses to mail you this letter without our notes. Well…I kiss you heartily and apologize for my horrible handwriting (I'm writing this on my school satchel).

    Sarenka

(…) Also, the Singers were next to us at this villa. Would you believe, Mrs. Bernard Singer leaves on April 22nd for New York to represent the Commerce Ministry at an exposition there. She will be there for about 6 weeks. Do see her. You can write her ahead of time from Duncan in care of the newspaper office or the consular offices in New York.

    Mania

> **Translator's note:** This letter starts with a copy of Mania's letter (in English) to Prof. Washburne at Winnetka and dated January 9, 1939.

Krynica, January 9, 1939

Dear Sir:

I am now in Krynica and have obtained your last letter from Warsaw. You are right, I must make up my mind and choice (sic) the one of the two ways. I don't know still if your information about my fitness to the College is favorable but I write now with the mind that it is. My plan was perhaps a little childish (a grown on child!!!!!) but I will end my writing to you as I have begun – in truthfulness. I think yet to drive out as an emigrant, than only in this way I shall can arrange my children in USA for constant, but I self have a great desire to study a year and then go back to Warsaw and make use from my training in work and perhaps writing and after about a year to sell my country house and go out to my children for constantly. Anyhow I must have a gratuitous furlough for a year or also two in USA. I will work, but I don't must. My hope is not a public school position. I know that it is a hard thing (also in our country), but my specialty – singing and also the languages which I know – perfectly: Polish, Jewish, Hebrew, Russian; less German and also a little English will help me to obtain a little work in private afternoon schools or perhaps courses. All this I shall see in the future. My relatives are rich enough and they will support me. And now, my dear sir, if you are unnightly(sic) to help me with a recommending letter to the consul. I beg your pardon. My request to you was in the mind to come in the due time. If it is impossible I shall wait on the quota and if you will not be able admit me, I shall visit the college if you please as a observator or a free student. Anyhow, after a immediate interview you will be able to decide what to advise me.

    I remain yours very sincerely,
    Mania

Dear Loniusiu!

It is so lovely here in Miedreszyn. On the whole, the entire view along our line between Warszawa and Otwock is very picturesque. That is when there are no vacationists.

We are having a great time. Kisses from afar.

    Sarenka

Jacks' letter arrived yesterday. I thanked him from my heart for sending you 40 zloty for clothes. I will bet that you don't have a single piece left from "our wardrobe". Kisses for the Sams and especially for your sweet nose.

    Mania

We are in Miedreszyn. The weather is pretty. Things start to bloom already. The birds sing. The sun shines pleasantly. I have here a tiny tot, Stefanek, and a little girl, Wladzia, who I take care of every now and then. Besides that I have a few books. I like it terribly here. This mommy of mine always comes up with something. I think somebody is supposed to come visit with us. Probably Hanka, Hala, Karola and who knows who else? Kisses. Are you still so beautiful? I will bet – even more beautiful. I kiss you my gorgeous girl.

    Your (silly cow) Marcia

Dear Lonius!

I do not remember if I have ever mailed you a copy of the above enclosed letter to Winnetka. Yesterday I received a response letter from Prof. Washburne which letter traveled to Krynica, from there back to Winnetka as it missed me there, then to Warszawa along with its original envelope addressed to Krynica. The route it traveled is quite interesting within itself but, which is the key subject here, is the appearance that the professor is quite interested in my persona. Otherwise he would not have bothered to mail again this letter returned to him from Krynica. And now, yet another brilliant idea of mine. You must reread all that correspondence. My letter from Krynica was written with an understanding that my response could be negative. First of all, the denial did not concern me too much since I would not have left without my children anyway. Second, My intention was to beat a negative response which, as it turned out, I found at home after return from Krynica. I felt a negative outcome – Prof. Ziemnowicz did the damage by demanding too much from the Inspector. But I am actually pleased with the outcome. Jack wrote me in his time, for God's sake, to avoid making efforts on both ends – it would only backfire. Thus, at the present, I am solely interested in taking advantage of Prof. Washburne's attraction to my "individuality" which, nota bene, should be quite obvious to anyone. Since you will be in Chicago soon, you must visit the college and meet Prof. Washburne in person showing him his own letter to me, enclosed herewith, as a form of an "introductory letter introducing you" as my daughter. Besides that, it would be a perfect opportunity to get better acquainted with Prof. Washburne. Ask Morris, Sam, etc. for some advice in this matter. You never know when such an alliance can become handy. Maybe one of your teachers' knows him personally. Show them his letter to me as an "access ticket" to Prof. Washburne. My dear, all is well here. At the present we are in Miedreszyn where we arrived yesterday for 9 days. We are staying with Mr/Mrs Woronkow (free of charge). Since I gave Janowa 8 days off, I have to cook. The girls frolic around the grounds of the villa. Kisses.

    Mania

Dear Loniusiu!

I am sending you my warm greetings and kisses. Regards from my mom, dad and Halinka.

    Irusia

Sweet Loniulko!

You will probably laugh at me for my latest "brilliant" idea. However, I do believe it to be a good one. First of all, I really do want you to do what is best for you but an acquaintance with such a professor, a school superintendent, who is a famous personality – a college professor; publisher of many, many pedagogical works; member of the Research Commission for Chicago Youth – a truly important person, could be very helpful at some point. He just may point you in the right direction. On top of that if the university was free of charge – it sure wouldn't hurt. And, if you indicated some interest in pedagogical studies, I am certain that he would help you. This college is designated for a truly small group of selected individuals but people graduating from there are in a very high demand – high job security. I sent Professor Washburne a small picture of you. What it's all about right now is only to maintain an acquaintance with him for a well known matter – letter to the consul – but we must pretend, at least, that what we really need is his advice what you should do with yourself. And, who knows, these pretenses may lead to something much more important and unexpected to us. You can always tell him that the money for potential studies will come from Sam. It would even be better if Sam went with you so you do not go alone for such a long trip – even though you are of age and high intelligence, I still fear for you. I am enclosing a copy of my letter to him so you can get acquainted with it and prepare yourself for a conference with him without causing any collisions. My dear! We returned from Miedreszyn sun-tanned and healthy. Marcia looks wonderful. Wiktor, his children and two friends (boys) spent 2 days with us – they all came down on bicycles.

After all this I forgot to thank you for your last 3 letters and a congratulatory scroll. Also, your letter from Wichita arrived. I am very happy that your time is spent in such a happy and care-free manner. Thank Sam for everything for me.

    Mania

> **Translator's note:** Mania sends Leona a copy of her next letter to Prof. Washburne. As usual, she encloses her own letter therewith which is missing except for its very end on the bottom of the second page.

Michalin, April 12, 1939

Dear Sir,

I am now in my country house for the Easter holidays. Several days ago I have received your letter which has traveled from America to Europe two times. I express hereby my thankfulness for your important consideration in relation to my person in spite of the unfortunate end of my dream about the College. I am sending your last letter to my daughter as a sign for a personal appointment and recommend her to make throughout our paper acquaintance a little more immediately. I believe that it will be possible because shortly she makes an excursion to the world fair by motor car and will visit Chicago. My daughter is an alive example of my own education method. She is like a sweet fruit of a tree, planted with my own hands, It is something, of that kind I want to have – an expression of my education ideal.

My request to you now is to have a little interest of her further education way through a reasonable and hearty advice – I am so far and can't do anything in this matter.

She is indeed a very interesting serious reasoning and in the same time joyful 21 years old girl, graduated from a high school in Warsaw (matura, in our studies), temporary a student at a Duncan high school. I enclose also her progress reports which she has sent me for a keepsake.

Please, my dear sir, accept a hearty shake of my hand, as a forever at far, but human friendship.

(…) in a newspaper office instead of friends or relatives. Remember, do not waste this opportunity. We agreed upon you meeting him there. He is not sure of an exact spot where he will wait for you – probably in the Jewish section. Call the editing room. Kisses.

    Mania

April 18, 1939

Lonius!

Today passes a week in our new apartment. We are very comfortable here – under our own roof. We have a very nice small room; clean everywhere. I took from Lusia one of our large beds for myself. Marcia sleeps on the camp-bed and Sarenka on the settee – she claims that it's great. We are taking our time unpacking our "junk" with an intent to settle here comfortably for some time. I bought new window covers for 8 zloty and our old curtains look here absolutely fantastic – I used them on one very large window as a double blind. We await impatiently any news from you. It has been almost 2 weeks since our last mail from you. I hope this is due only to our change of address. I did inform the post office but, so far, nothing has been delivered. I assume that all, my sweet child, is in order at your end. Today I saw Wisia. She received a letter in December – another 12 months. Simultaneously with our move, I had to take a 2-week L.O.P. training. I finished it yesterday by passing the required exam!!! I was so absorbed by all that transpired – search for a new apartment, the move itself, training course, a week earlier a splendid school-theater performance called "The Great Variety Show" that – in summary, I had no time to even think. Write, my love, what's new with you. Regards for the Raizyns.

    Mania.

Sweet Loniusiu!

It is truly lovely in our new place. It is small but very cozy. But we know how to make any place cozy and we will gladly leave this happy place for an even happier one. That is we listen to your promises and choose to believe in them. Of course, I am speaking about the future in "your" country. Everyone is healthy. Hearty kisses.

    Sarenka

Dear Loniu!

I write this from your family's new apartment; I like it very much. I used this occasion to see your lovely family and, now, I am writing you a note. Actually, it is a shame that it happened so late. But, as they say, better late than never. By the way, I follow your progress with an intense interest. Your debut in the newspaper was especially interesting. A moment ago I looked over you beautiful photographs for the second time in a raw. Well, I'm running out of space. Because of me poor Marcia cannot write anything. I truly apologize for that. I wish you all the best and send you my warmest regards. Marcia sends her kisses and asks why you don't write.

    Hanka

April 22, 1939

Dear Loniulko!

Yesterday, we received your funny card and today a letter; not as funny as the card, but including one very unique photo and another with you in a boyish outfit with that lovely smile on. You write that psychologically you do not feel very well – as if not prepared for the type of lifestyle you entered. Of course, a force of habit is our second nature. I think that you are doing much better now than immediately after your arrival. If not for the overall mess around we wouldn't even worry about things – we do have good papers and sooner or later we will arrive. Our hopes are increased now due to the initiative of your "host". Maybe things will turn around. Please, I urge you to be completely at peace about us, baby…Yesterday, we all went to the Zyngiers for a good-bye party. He leaves today on "Batory" out of Gdynia. I believe that the ship should reach New York in about 4 weeks. I would like so much for you to see him again but if you leave in June – I'm not sure if it will be possible. I would also like you to visit the Winnetka College on your way to New York. If, by chance, you manage to do all that, just maybe something will "hatch". I overheard that the Jewish-American press has already announced Zyngier's arrival soon – last year he was a chairman for the press syndicate or something like that. He has a lot of friends and is quite well known. If you can not coordinate your moves to his timing, at least you should write a double card to any better known Jewish newspaper in New York with a request to obtain an address for Bernard Singer who arrived with Minister Roman for the opening of a Polish Pavilion. Then write him a letter – maybe he will advise you something. During the summer, Benek must join the army. The Zyngiers are strongly considering moving for good to the USA if they only can. It is possible that Mrs. Zyngier will leave in about 2 weeks. Lots of kisses are passed on to you from Danka Iwonczyk. Also, there was a girl, Somptowna, who graduated from secondary school along with you. Afterwards, she went to Gdansk to specialize in international trade. She sends her regards as well. This past year was not only not wasted, but to the contrary, splendidly utilized. We wouldn't have thought of anything better or smarter.

    Mania

 Translator's note: The next note is started by Marcia but finished by Sarenka.

My dear!

I am waiting for the street car. I'm supposed to meet at 1…

At this moment the street car arrived and she couldn't finish her note. She promised to meet some boy from her school at 6:30 and it was already 6:20. She passed me the card back through the window – we live on the first level, street side. I kiss you mightily – no, double that for it's for Marcia too.

Sarenka

April 26, 1939

Dear Loniu!

How is your health? We are all okay. Did you see in America a negro or an Indian? If so, please do write us what they look really like. Do you like it there? We apologize for writing so little and having such ugly handwriting but the door bell is ringing. See you, bye, bye, 102 kisses.**

Pola and Halinka

 Translator's note: This sentence rhymes in Polish.**

Dearest Loniusiu!

We are including this short letter from those sweet callows. They are truly very sweet and smart girls. They both sing beautifully, dance and play mandolin. They were recently a part of the school's performance "The Great Variety Show".

We live without any changes. Unless you count the new flat. You must know that our room looks more like a bachelor's or maidenly apartment. No one would say that a family lives there. There is only one bed; beautifully made up and covered with a pink bedspread. On top sits, dressing it up, an embodied pillow with a matching pink ribbon, and on each side of it is a white curtain. The bed looks very innocent, doesn't it? Like a maiden. Actually, I meant to say a "virgin". Don't be too scandalized with what I write here. To the side stands the piano. On top of it are various handmade and other things (e.g. the framed picture of you behind a glass). On the other side stands the settee covered with an elegant tapestry and small pillows. Aside from all that there is a single venetian window covered with a netted curtain. The curtain presents itself beautifully from both outside (since we live on the first level) and inside.

In brief, that's what our little maidenly room looks like. Otherwise, one could spend quite a long time going into ecstasies over it. And that's how we live in it. The three of us are quite jolly here. We have fever visitors here that at our last flat. It's a little too far for them (Gorczewska is an extension of Leszna and has a total of approximately 150 blocks). But that's okay. Marcia appears to be even happy about it; she claims that no one will interrupt her in doing homework. I almost forgot to tell you that mommy got for me a super elegant outfit. It is made out of a gray British material tailored after an outfit you had on. Overall, it is great. Now we are just waiting for the summer to ride our bicycles and do numerous other sports. Hearty kisses.

Sarenka

P.S. Best regards from Marysia Gasior; I met her on the street car.

April 29, 1939

Loniusiu!

Sweet, darling, doll, marvelous, my beauty. It is so nice of you and America to be interested so much in music. When you see Paderewski, please tell him that I also play the piano and my technique is quite substantial. Do pianos look the same there? My teeth, considering where I live, are okay. Kisses.

    Marcik

Dear Loniusiu!

Spring is here! The weather is so nice that it makes me delighted. Talking about clothing, I didn't tell you that I have a beautiful Gray English outfit complemented by a navy blue hat. I will take a picture for you with it on outside on the street one of these days soon. Now I have to run to an evening party to Krynski.

    (not signed but in Sarenka's handwriting)

 Translator's note: The card continues with a note from Mania in English.

Warsaw, April 29, 1939

My dearest child,

Now I have received your card of April 12. In my last writing to you, I have not expressed my mind about your new proposals as it was my desire. Beauty shop – perhaps it will be good for you, but nursing it is very hard work and I should not like see you at this calling. Anyway, it is now a little too early too make up a mind, all this you will see in the near future. Don't judge Jacob in prejudices – simply the larger are our preparations to a profession, the better is the fee for our work and only in this way, we must make ourselves ready to the life. If a man can succeed without great preparations – it is a fortunate event. I am sure that you will succeed because such accidents are now in fashion. The more in America, the land of various opportunities (and with your fair face). Enough nonsenses! Take very much advices, but do as your common sense will teach you!

I have received a refuse letter from the consul, in which he says that about three years must last to my number for a visa. It seems to be in vain all our endeavors. We must wait on the quota. Now I think only about your health and future and it is all! We are all right, indeed. Try to see Bernard Singer or to write to him. I kiss you with love. My hearty greetings to Sam, Fanny, and their children. Ida sends her love.

    Your Mania

Dear Loniusiu!

You give us some very good suggestions and advice. You must not that take advantage of them to the fullest extent. If you remember the way I am, you know that I am a care-free person. Even when I do have a real worry (which almost never happens!) I talk myself into its nonexistence. Besides that what do I really know about true worries; I don't even know their true meaning. I just want to tell you that I can be a great follower of someone's suggestions. And what's more, I'm trying to teach this art to mommy and Marcia. I will give you an example so you can visualize this "hohmology": when I walk outside into the street and it is truly cold and I am cold because I didn't feel like putting on a sweater, I tell myself that in reality I am very warm and I become to feel warm. Marcia has already learnt this from me. Mommy is a harder case. Never-the-less, I am making progress with her as well. I do what I can… (…)

(missing ending; letter written by Sarenka)

(…) Following my own principles, I continue to laugh and make others around me laugh as well. Overall, it's a lot of around here. Besides that Marcia wrote you in detail about many events here. Based on those you should be able to recreate for yourself all the affairs and incidents taking place. And there are many of them. We have some wonderful friends to cause mischief with, go to the movies, sometimes to a theater. But the most fun we have at our house.

Besides that I attend an English course. I do not want to show of my knowledge of this language in front of you. I don't know too much yet. You probably don't even believe that I am studying it at all. To prove it to you I will write a few sentences in "your" language.

(Sarenka finishes her letter in English – not reiterated here)

I learn English 2 month. We have a very nice and good book. It call "tu everyday English course" for foreign students. It is import from London. The author it is Eskersley. I kiss you.

Your Sara

Warszawa, May 13, 1939

Dear Loniuszku!

It's Saturday. The sky is shedding tears. It started crying yesterday on J. Pilsudzki's death anniversary. We went to Belweder (there was no school!). In the evening, I went to Pilsudzki Square. It was beautiful. Three minutes of silence. Lighting of the ever-burning fire. Readings of Pilsudzki's thoughts.

We already had the examination for secondary-school certificate. All the chosen topics were very easy. The delegate delightful. Ipcio all smiles. What is new with you? What do you plan to do now? Greetings from the girls. We had a class party with Krynski. He was wonderful. I have an exam with him in a few days. Suspiciously, I am not afraid of it at all. Altogether, everything is okay. Mommy reads an awful lot in English. She constantly gets new books, newspapers, magazines from that club. I also went there once. I understood a little here and a little there. What's with Jack? What does he write to you about? Write more. The photographs sent by you are wonderful. But what a meatball you've become! Even bigger than our in-house meatball. None-the-less, our meatball is beautiful, fashionable and gallant. Too bad that are not here with us – you would admire her. She looks very lovely in her gray outfit and an impregnated coat – like a young chauffeur. When will we go to America? Do you know anything? Because I sure don't. But it's not so bad here. On the contrary, at the present it is quite nice here. I have here my friends, home, own life, and I really do not know what to expect there. None-the-less, I would really like to be already there. Just let it all end soon. Tell Roosevelt to take us away. What are those cousins of ours like? Do you attend the same school? Come to think of it, we really do not know anything. How is this admirer from a written correspondence? Those two characters on the photo look quite nice. Mommy likes especially the one closer to you. She claims that he tries to catch your attention.

All in all, that mother of yours reached the maximum level of perversion. She tells us such stories that even our backs turn red. What a hag. To top that, when Janowa comes over with her stories and we join them with jokes known to us (Sarenka and I continue to appear to be examples of modesty) we all laugh long and hard for hours. To the point of crying from laughter. We end up standing on our belly buttons underneath the chairs. We have to hold on to our bellies. We also go to see movies – we have plenty of fools who pay for us. We have fun

I go out with a little boy – a schoolmate from the conservatory who happens to be exactly my age. He is a terrible child but a very sweet one. His name is Czesiek. We see each other at the conservatory, and on Saturdays, and on Sundays.

What else can I write you about myself? … You see, I make a great effort and you don't write about anything.

How did you like Paderewski? Did you manage to reach him? We don't have any new photos due to a foul weather. Therefore, I enclose instead some really stupid ones taken at Rysienka's birthday party.

You know, your sweet "daughter" Irka, has changed. She reminds me more of Hala and Pola. Somehow she started to fuss and demand comforts. In summary – more like Pola. maybe she will change yet.

Ryska reads. Nobody taught her but she reads. In general, she is very smart. Halinka and Polcia are precious. Halinka attends some new ballet school. Polcia is her usual sweet self. Eljasz and Wowek became terribly tall and grown up. Eljasz is learning a new profession (he doesn't work any more for Wiktor). Wowek most likely will end up on the farm as he has no other work. Grandmother is healthy. Her eyesight is good. Wiktor didn't change any. Other family members are okay too, I think. (If you desire, you will do it all together…)**

And now for our friends. Danka, I believe, is studying to become a nurse. Tolka Fragman already gives shots in town. Polcia Lazer attends lessons with Sekulowicz. Scyfra does nothing. Kuba attends school and works. Moninta will be entering grammar-school. Alina is planing, planing and…still planing to get married. Mietek, any day now, is taking some entrance examinations. The candidates for secondary-school certificates furiously check around into their further options. Lena Eilstein plans to attend a Politechnical College.

Everyone lives, is healthy and in one piece. But enough of this. Good-bye.

    Marcia

 Translator's note: This sentence rhymes in Polish.**

May 14, 1939

This Marcia completely exhausted all the happenings around us in Warszawa; of course, with a slight exaggeration. Now it is my turn.

Your photographs are ravishing. I absolutely adore them. Especially fascinating is your clothes. I just love this dotted dress with a collar and a belt. You look lovely in it. But, by the way, I would like to inform you that I have a hat very similar to yours. It's shape is also cylindrical. I also look fabulous with it on. (At least that's what I am being told!) But talking about you – it is very stylish on you. The fashions here are the same as in America. At least this is my impression from your photographs. The same purses, coats, hats, even cars. Those Buicks can also be found in Warszawa. I was forced to write you about such "junk" since anything of substance was written about by Marcia. Hearty kisses.

Sarenka

May 14, 1939

Sweet Leonys!

Yesterday, I physically jumped up and down from joy after receiving a letter from you with enclosed copies of the letters from Mr. Washburne to you and yours to him. I truly did not except such an overwhelming success. Although, it was not an accident that I enclosed in my letter to him copies of your excellent grades to let him formulate his own opinion about you based something aside from my biased bragging. Also, I hoped for at least one of your present teachers to be his student. I also sent him a photo of my entire class and requested that he contacts a teacher at an equivalent level to mine there since my class would like to get a first grade photo in return. (It is very popular in modern days pedagogics). Apparently, he got your address from those copies of grade reports (the letter was mailed at the general school address). All that took place is good; what will come out of it remains to be seen. There is always a chance that something will come out and it never can hurt anyone. In the meantime, I am so proud of your praise that I am "the most intelligent woman under the sun" and I don't let the rest of my daughters to give me a hard time about what my Lonia said. But what good does it do me when I am quite lost regarding obtaining visas. I even thought of an attempt to start flirting with the Consul himself via mail but his kingdom here appears to be quite "closed" (please laugh). Nothing to do but wait. Maybe, in the meantime, the miracle that Jack awaits for over 10 years now, will take place – who knows. If not then those 3 years are guaranteed. Your first year there appears to be "beautiful" – it's just as you say – one shall see and hope for the best. California!!! What a cherished summer dream!!! After all it is similar to Italy. I am just choked up with emotions that you will see California. I am curious if this possibility will come true. Your pictures are wonderful – the only bad ones were in the negligée and by the car; the ones from inside the car are film-quality. Sarenka wears a similar hat to yours. Write, my love, what else is new with you; what language do you speak at home: English or Yiddish. How are your sweet Sams doing? Kiss all of them from us – they truly created for you a "fairyland". Of course, you will not manage to see Zyngier. Maybe Jack will be able to receive from him personal greetings from us. I asked him in a letter to see him. I appears that Jack considers attempting to start his own business. He asked for my advice – I told him that if he feels up to it, he should try. But what do I know? Maybe it is easier to accomplish it there. I am not sure where we will spend our summer. Maybe in Krynica for another 3 weeks. If I can rent again Michalin on good terms, possibly we will all go there. If not, we may go to Michalin and me, by myself only, to Krynica for 3 weeks. Kisses.

    Mania

Lonius!

Do not stint to spend the money for schooling. I have just rented another room yesterday elsewhere for my present one is just too expensive. Sarenka is finishing her school – there will be no more discount for her. Together with the street-car it will cost 110 zloty – it is not even sunny and quite cramped. I took a room with 3 windows on Leszno Street, corner of Wronia Street, with own bathroom and an access to the kitchen for an additional 25 zloty. I will be riding for another 7.5 zloty. If things will not work out there is no need to pay for the entire summer. I will go away but leave my things in this apartment – it will cost me only 80 zloty for 2 months. I will do anything to avoid Jack's financial help. Let him instead help you to stand on your feet. That's why I am willing to try a boarding home plus I will not have to pay for Sarenka. And who knows, maybe I can find some "Des". Enjoy yourself. Do not forget Winnetka unless something better turns out in this sunny California. If you weren't my own sweet one, I would envy you with all my heart.

    Mania

May 15, 1939

Sweet!

Yesterday I mailed a letter to you and today, imagine, I received a letter from Prof. Washburne along with a wonderful photograph of the first grade group, a copy of his letter to you (which I already received earlier from you) and his letter, as follows. (…)

 Translator's note: Mania copies here Prof. Washburne's letter (in English).

Dear Mrs. Zagranicia:

Thank you for your letter of April 12. I shall look forward with pleasure to hearing from your daughter and to giving her such help and advice as is in my power. Her reports indicate that she is a fine person and one whom it would be a pleasure to assist. With best wishes, I am sure of it.

P.S. I am enclosing a picture of one of our first grade groups, in exchange for the one you sent me of your class. You did not give me your daughter's address, so I cannot write to her. I assume, however, that she will write to me.

P.P.S. I have just noticed that the report cards indicate your daughter's American name and of the address of the high school. I am therefore sending her the enclosed letter in care of the high school. I am returning the report cards to you as you may wish to keep them .

(…) And what do you say now, my sweet one, wasn't it worth to send your mama your splendid grade reports? I am more than certain that something will hatch from this idea of mine. Do not neglect this idea which, in turn, doesn't mean – God forsake – that you should forego such a fabulous thing as a summer stay in California! I would never forgive you for that – not even when a job is at stake. A job is not a rabbit – it won't run away. But after California do your best to visit Winnetka and it would be best to do it before the start of new school year. This may even turn into a job in Chicago. Chicago has a Polish center. You can try to look for a job through them as well. You should be both as sweet as you already are but also as cunning as I am. Prof. Washburne returned to me both your grade reports and your picture. Give my regards to Jack. You can write him about everything. I will write him myself in a few days.

Mania

June 3, 1939

My dear!

I have just received your happy letter about the end of your school year as well as a letter from Jack. He informs us about his successes with singing and poor luck with business dealings. He also writes about your intentions to move to New York to help him with his business – and ironically queries what business – he doesn't have one. He writes a lot about his family members there whom he calls awful. I don't know whether that is caused by the present condition of his destroyed, for numerous reasons, nerves and worsened further by recent fiascoes in his business dealings but, it's enough to say, he is afraid that he will not manage at all with you around. The room rent must cost at least $20 and if I send this amount monthly to Sam it will enable you to study while living with good dear people and you will not get exhausted by this enormous unhappy New York. Talking about New York, I was told already a few tidbits by Zyngier. Everything is preserved and, immediately after eating, people take purgatives. If he was to live in the USA it wouldn't be in New York. He may still do in a year or so but after a 2-week visit to the USA it's hard for him to even tell if he would prefer to stay there or not. He spoke personally with Senator Stan Hullam. Rosfeld (sic – Roosevelt) patted him on the shoulder (at a press conference in Washington). Of course, for me personally it's not even a consideration for a second to stay here and he will also, most likely, leave but this first hand impression of this "boiling kettle" bewildered him. However, I do not pay much attention to what he says in this respect as he acts as there is nothing interesting to see in the entire world. He visited Niagara during this delegation – it also didn't impress him at all. Of course, we will never have the opportunities available to Zyngier therefore we measure life and countries with a different stick. I am happy beyond words for your trip to California. On the way back you just must stop by Chicago and get an advice from Prof. Washburne. Discuss everything with him openly (except about Jack). Tell him that you have good and wealthy relatives but you would like to become independent. That you love children but, until now, you have not thought about teaching. Besides, I am sure that you find things to discuss and he, I am also sure, will lead the conversation towards the appropriate topics. I am almost certain that something will come out of this. I don't even know if you know what kind of institute it is – ask for a brochure for The Graduate Teacher College of Winnetka – maybe he has already sent you one. This is not just a study course but an entire school to become directors, inspectors and for outstanding young teachers. Do not ask to be enrolled; just say that you want to get acquainted with their work, tour their school facilities but most importantly it was him that had invited you over for a "chat". I believe that this opportunity should not be looked over. Think hard about New York. After all, Jack knows somewhat more about it than either you or I. I assume that you will be there with Fenia and you should decide what to do once there. Needless-to-say, if they offer you an office employment – don't even think about it but you must have a protégé for that – just like anywhere else. And that's the main reason why I want you to take an advantage of this acquaintance with Prof. Washburne. Maybe this California will smile at you; that may be even better. Anyway, my dear, I trust you completely. You will see for yourself what must be done. I imagine that in the worst case you will find your way back to the Sams. They will not hold it against you and it never hurts to try. What do Sam and Morris say about this? What say sweet Fenia and that sweet "Miss Black" of yours? I received from her a heartwarming letter and I plan to respond thereto within the next few days. Yesterday I mailed a letter to Prof. Washburne. I sent him a letter from my class to the children a photograph of whom we received. I thank him cordially for an offer to help you in any way possible – I wrote that it was my hope that he won't be disappointed with his initial impression about you. Write, dear, about everything. Your letters are for me as always – happiness; Jack's – constant worry and anxiety. Kisses for yours, thus also mine, lovely Sams.

    Mania

Dear Loniusiu!

We also have a school-year end. The examination for secondary-school certificate went one-hundred percent – just beautifully. Within the next few days I have another exam. We are going to Michalin. Probably we will take with us a group of both youth and children and we will have a blast. Mom proposes numerous things: a trip to the sea, a new bicycle, etc. As usual, none of that will take place. I wish you to become Hollywood's most beautiful star and may it be that we see you on the screen soon. Have a great time, my dear, as you are at your prime and have the right conditions for it. Have a great time and be happy while you still can. Write us your impressions from all those beautiful places where you will end up. All is okay here. Kisses.

    Marcia

My dear!

I have just reread this letter in peace and quiet. Jack. He terribly judges his relatives there and says that, if you come, they will do everything possible in their power to diminish his earning possibilities. I do not understand what he means by that. Obviously, he wants to go on his own and they, of course, stand in his way either as his employers or – I do not understand this – enough that he says that there is still some time until my arrival and he hopes to accomplish something but he can't have any disruptions. That is why he wishes that you stay with the Rajcyns for now. Have a heart-to-heart talk with Fenia. Maybe she can think of some worthy alternatives locally. I don't know anymore…

    (Mania did not sign)

 Translator's note: The following letter was in Yiddish.

June 6, 1939

What is your opinion, Yakov? I am afraid she will struggle from place to place. It seems he makes a hard living. Maybe there is a possibility to come to your part of the country for a job. Maybe she should go to college, so Yakov, could you send her some money? Think well, and forgive me, give your opinion. For me, you will have to wait maybe three years. I am very sorry but I don't have any advice. It is very hard to be a mother from far away. Be healthy. Regards and kisses to all.

    Your Mania

Dear Shlanke,

I am obligated to thank you for helping my child. She writes such enlightening letters, that from every letter I gain life and health. I did not expect so much love from each word, that shines a light. She is obligated to thank you for her second home and the atmosphere she is in. There are no words to thank you for the will to live that you gave her. Now that Lonia is not there, I would like I would like you to give your opinion when she returns from vacation. I ask like a brother, what would your advice be for your own child? I think she would listen to you. This winter, she would like to support herself. I don't need her help. I want her to be independent. I want her to settle down, it will be easier for all. I would like to know if she still thinks about the man from Warsaw. She doesn't write and I can't ask her.

Translator's note: The letter is in English from Ida. It appears that she passed her letter on to Mania for mailing along with hers since Mania's letter is dated June 25, 1939.

June 12, 1939

My little, beloved Lonia!

Thank you very much for your little letter. I was very glad to learn that you are in good health. I beg your pardon that I didn't answer for a long time, but you know that I am always very tired. My Myshe(?) and Isaac are now in Nabhe(?) and the grandmama did not want to go there, that she feels faint for a long journey. I heard that you are very happy in America and when we'll be so happy all your family? It is a pity that you cannot be all together. Alas. I think it will be impossible to go to the World's Fair for I have no house and not so much money. But I think I shall be whenever in America. I cannot write more than I am afraid to make too many mistakes. I am hoping that this letter will find you in the best of health.

    Yours with love,
    Ida

June 25, 1939

My sweetest daughter!

Again, I have no idea of your whereabouts therefore I send this letter to Jack's address. I sent a letter long time ago in care of the Los Angeles post office but, just in case, I have also added the Duncan "home address" thereon. Hopefully you will receive it at some point. I received another distressful letter from Jack in which he writes that I just must influence you about New York. Independently of his worries, I wrote him back that the New York issue concerns me as well since your stomach isn't in a prime condition either and restaurant food will cause gastritis in you. He responded that my words are holy and I should not talk myself into believing that you would be able to dine at any relative's table; even aunt Bornsztejn cooks only twice a week – the 2 weeks you spent with her, she simply went out of her way to cook more often especially for you. Jack will have his appendix removed; it will not cause him any harm and he suffers from stomach problems. Talking about a stomach – I completely agree with him; talking about you becoming independent, which seems to be your goal, my dear, I do understand it very well, yet, if Jack is willing to pay for the college (maybe dentistry or pedagogics), you should not spurn it for some insignificant employment opportunity – unless he is completely wrong which I doubt due to his years of living experience there and knowledge of local conditions better than us. He says than you could earn 4 dollars per week (maybe he's exaggerating) but work like an ox day in and day out. If Duncan doesn't have a right college for you then maybe Oklahoma City, but truly, I can not help you in this regard as I am not familiar with the local conditions there. I would like you to seek Prof. Washburne's advice – maybe something can be arranged in Chicago. Or, maybe, he can recommend you to the New York College (with boarding) to save you from eating in the restaurants. But Jack continues to insist that you should not leave the Rajcyns' home – he is talking about the home environment. My opinion is not a deciding one. I believe that you are an adult and as such, without any "sentiments towards yourself" which we have as your parents, possibly you will direct yourself much better than any of us can do it for you. A human survival instinct usually leads to a self preservation from any dangers. Just do not rush into anything or you will only burn yourself. Choose a road which will give you a better future without a fear that it may be a longer one. So far there is nothing that I need from Jack and if a time comes that I do need something – I will write. Yesterday, Sarenka finished 18 years. She got from me an identical ring to yours plus I bought out her diploma from "Comercium". A week ago I introduced her to Engineer Sztoleman and asked him for a better apprenticeship (they practically give it to anyone). Imagine that she started work even before she finished her school year (3 days prior) in a large paper manufacturing plant in Rozenwajn, Graniczna Street 9. If I am not mistaken, it is 2-month training with some pay. We leave tomorrow for Michalin. Sarenka will be commuting. What do you think? She is happy that she didn't have to go to a secondary school. She feels great working (9 to 5) and work appears to agree with her. I have already started to inquire into finding a protégé for her and gaining a long-term employment. As you can see, I didn't do too bad of a job directing Sarenka. Stay healthy, my daughter.

Mania

P.S. Warmest regards from Janowa. She is still holding well – she goes with us.

Dear Loniu,

I am so happy that you are there and the fact that you are so happy there. Your mommy often reads to me your sweet letters. I kiss you with all my heart. Best regards for your family there and uncle Izak.

Your Grandmother

Dear Loniu!

You did not write to us for a long time. We have no idea what is happening to you. Everything here is fine. I moved on to the eighth grade and the fourth year at the Conservatory. I am an adult now. This meatball works and has 18 years of age.

Regards from Herman (every time he sees me he has to stop no matter what) and Rachela Gewiksmans. Kisses. Good bye.

    Marcik

Dear Loniusiu!

Did you know that I am starting my 19th year today? That is nothing to sneeze at! But that is not all. What is even more important that after finishing the "Commercium" I got a job; I work at an office on Graniczna Street not No. 13, like you, but No. 9. Mommy is already taking this letter away from me as she wants to mail it still today. Thus, I give you my hearty kisses.

    Sarenka

I took this letter away from them because they were being tedious and it was a shame to waste space here. Now, I am finishing it on the street-car. Both of you write more about yourselves.

Mina broke up with her fiancé and decided to forego marriage for a while; she claims there is no one worth marrying. They are going to Ciechocinek. Most likely we will be moving tomorrow to 99 Leszno Street to that flat I have told you about earlier. It has 3 windows and costs 75 zloty per month including the use of kitchen and bathroom. We shall see, maybe it will turn out to better than the present one. If not, we will have to do something after return from Michalin. Ciao.

    Mania

 Translator's note: The folowing letter starts with a note from Mania in English (not transferred here) and continues with more notes from Mania and others in Polish added over a span of few days.

Michalin, July 6, 1939

My most happy person in the whole world!

We have received your very sweet two letters with all the beautiful birthday wishes and one card from the way. We are all right. I have three children (only) for 13 st daily and also for a few dinners. So I think to pay this summer all the rest of my debts and finally to be free from this ugly thing. Perhaps to the winter holidays (if peace will be) I shall be able to go out to Krinica, according to your order. I love very much to be here as you know, my little dear child. I must be here also for Sara, because she works as I have written to you and must go to Warsaw every day. We are very happy to hear about your very beautiful trip and we wait for news. Sweet letters. Our best regards for all the Raizins.

    Yours with love
    M

Dear sweet Loniusia!

As you can see, I am again with your sweet mommy and sisters in Michalin where we will spend the entire summer together and in happiness. Though, I am certain, it would be much happier with you present here. But I am even happier with the knowledge that you are comfortable and joyful there. I can only wish that you all can be together next year. All of us staying behind will be sad but it's only right that your entire family be finally together with your father and, after all, we will be getting great letters from you. I kiss you heartily. And give my warmest regards to your uncle Izak and the family that you live with.

    Your Grandmother

July 12, 1939

Lonius!

As usual, I await my daughters to write their notes but it will be mailed today regardless whether they add them or not. The Post Office forwards to me all your letters mailed to Gorczewska Street. I received a card from Arizona and from Los Angeles the "oranges harvest". I live through all these wonders along with you. Kisses for Fenia. Stay healthy.

    Mania

Dear Loniusiu!

We are in Michalin. It's great here. We have the same company as last year and some new faces this year. Even in our villa live individuals who can be grouped in the "youth" category. We play, we take hikes (do not burst out laughing here). Kazik Gronek is our leader. He takes us to wonderful nooks and places. We play volleyball, tennis and ride bicycles. We read (now "Street Children" by Fink). Overall, I am very pleased. Oliwer is in Michalin. We apologized to each other a few days ago. You have regards from Mrs. Wyszomirska who claims that there is no other girl like Lonia. Regards from Herman (still from Warszawa) and others. There is a German woman here in Michalin (for a few days only then on to Switzerland) and Rebeka with her little one. I believe you are aware that she has something like that.

I still do not know what to do with playing piano, secondary school certificate exam and conservatory. I have to think about it some more.

I kiss you and wish you pleasant experiences.

    Marcia

July 13, 1939

How do you like this Sareneczka? She is holding this letter already the second day in a row and still didn't mail it (the mail goes out quicker out of Warszawa). Yesterday arrived your letter from Los Angeles. I am so thrilled that you feel so happy. I wish Marcia could end up there too; maybe her constant elevated temperature would go away.

 Mania

July 19, 1939

Dear traveler!

We demand to hear more about your travel experiences. They are exceptionally well done. Mommy rereads them endlessly and she plans, I believe, to have them published.

Our summer is very, very, good one. We have a ball. We have numerous and gay company. We play volleyball, tennis; we dance at different boarding-houses; cause havoc; take outings. I don't know if you are familiar with these territories. Most likely not. But seriously, too bad that you have left as you can not see this fabulous forest located far away past Michalin. Blueberries grow there. There are places to swim. We have gone as far as Wisla, Rycice, Swider. Swell, a rattling good time and just splendid! Just yesterday Wiktor was here. Ciao.

 Marcia

July 20, 1939

My dear!

A few days ago I wrote to you at Jack's address – this time to you with a request to mail, in turn, my letters to him and Sam – I'm saving money. I have not received anything from Jack lately. I have no idea what is new with him. What new with you I do know – gaiety and lots of hopeful promises after California. We will see what comes out of it. At least Los Angeles has a potential for great opportunities – if nothing else, good connections. Tasemka has a brother there; she asked numerous times if you would ever go there. Here is nothing new. I have with me here four children; among them Karol, Renius and Rysienka who, by the way, will most likely be sent to another boarding-house with a special care-taker. Keeping her is not worth it to me – she exhausts me, as well as, your grandmother who stays with me for the entire summer. The bulk of the first month of "vacation" passed by under a sign of work – move out from Gorczewska Street (to 99 Leszno Street Apt. 3) then to Michalin in the same day; shopping for groceries and supplies to take to the village. Here constant arrangements and many people to take care of – on Sundays as many as 17 people dining (including Janowa). I hope that I will manage to rest some during the second month – maybe even take a trip somewhere if I get a lady to replace me here temporarily. I am considering paying off the rest of our debts (about 100 zloty), buy Sarenka a winter coat, and possibly some new clothes for me and Marcia. Szydlowski has his girl again with me this year. He charged me only 20 zloty for tailoring a suit with jacket for Sarenka. I would like to take advantage of him some more. After all, I do what is in my power for him too.

Write what else is new with you. Write about everything. Kisses.

 Mania

Lots and lots of kisses for my sweet and intelligent Loniusia. I send my regards to your daddy as well.

Your always loving grandmother

Dear Loniusiu!!

After reading your letters, and especially one in particular (we received 6 of them all at once), I am in a splendid mood. And do you know what did make me so happy? First of all, because you keep on telling us what we take with us the following year. I do understand that that is your way of letting us know that soon, very soon, we will have to start thinking about it. In the meantime, I am laughing my head of and have to hold on to my sides. Not because I do not believe in any of this but because it is quite humorous. I practice living in an American way and do not refuse myself anything. The company in Michalin does exist though not much to talk about (anyone with more class goes much further out; at least as far as Kazimierz). But that doesn't bother me much. So far we do not send you any photographs as they do not turn out too well. We are waiting for the next batch which, hopefully, will turn out much better. Pretty soon the vacation will be over. It passed by very quickly with your wonderful letters. But no need to regret it. We wish to shorten the time to be with you as much as possible. I am curious if everything turns out as we planned it. Is Jack truly considering on settling down in Oklahoma? What would he do there? I believe that he would find some work. Besides that no need to worry ahead of time. In the meantime – we are happy for you. Write us, dear, is it really worth the hassle to get Sarenka into a secondary school? Let her attend her Conservatory and study English. What do you think? In my opinion, if everything goes well, our case will not take longer than one year. Taking this into the consideration, I am trying to follow all your advice. I thought exactly like you regarding the coats. I assure you that we will arrive there dressed very stylishly. That I fully understand its importance, I believe you have seen with your own eyes in connection with yourself. Kisses.

Mania

Michalin, July 21, 1939

Dearest sister!

I never did forget about you. I always, always, think about you and many times I tell myself what a pity that Lonius isn't here. She would give me a good advice for sure.

Lately, I have such moments quite often and I do not know why I do. After all, even though I have many friends, there are certain things I do not want to discuss with anyone else but you. No matter. I manage somehow and I am surrounded by many sincere and good people. Thus, everything will be okay.

I do not write to you often as there are no special occasions; we write too often on the postcards. Besides that I am too playful or busy – I have a hard time concentrating. I do have a first-rate time. Slowly I move my feet out into the world. My dear fool, you tried to explain to me what is "swing" and, though I am not sure how to write the word properly, I know very well how to dance it. After all, swing is what I do the whole day. I am almost as experienced as a professional dancer. We dance twice a day (after dinner and in the evening) at boarding-houses (Helena, Kratka, Zacheta). We attend all the local evening parties – mostly without an invitation (through the windows). Sometimes I play piano for others to dance to. We have the same fury here with both slow, sleepy and super fast dances. We have extremely pleasant boyfriends and girlfriends. But the best part is that the company comprises of last year's members increased by some newcomers.

Yesterday, I was given a birthday party shared with a male friend who finished his 20th year. What a beau, this meatball. He lives at our villa in a "bachelor's suite". We spent an exceptional time. The food was great. A lot of guests – over 30 people. We danced, visited different boarding-houses and, at the end, we climbed a hill. I got beautiful presents. Mommy and Sarenka bought me a pretty watch since I had lost the other one. Natek gave me a wonderful photo album and a chocolate box. Some stiff bought me an ink pen with a gold tip (I write this letter with it). I got a few more chocolate boxes, perfumes, pretty kerchiefs, etc. But all of those presents were topped by one, a most ingenious one, daring enough to be thought of only by that wonderful trio: Eljasz, Heniek and Leon. They brought "something" hidden inside a chocolate box. Then they created an artificial crowd and noise yelling at others not to push forward – everyone will get a piece. The celebrants stood in the middle and the rest of the mob stood around us with their eyes popping out. They started to open the box (with a sign "Lourse") slowly, to pull out two chocolates for the celebrants, and suddenly…

… suddenly appeared beautiful pink silk panties. It was so great, you just can't imagine. Of course, everyone demanded that I put the panties on in front of them – I did so unconstrained and modeled my new undies for them all. Then I read out loud a note included in the box. It said not to pee-pee on these panties as that person that was cold. I'm not sure if you know this joke so I will tell it to you anyway. A woman, walking into a toilet stall, overheard a man sitting in the one next to hers cussing from anger: "Damn it, she was cold, damn it!! Damn it, she was cold!" Intrigued, the woman stopped and waited until the man decided to come out of the stall. When she asked him what was the matter, he told her the following story: In the morning, he asked his wife what the weather was like. She told him that it was terribly cold and told him to put on another warm pair of long johns. And now he had a very unpleasant experience. He forgot that he had on two pairs of long johns and pulled down only one. That was the reason for all his cussing. Good one, isn't it? The note was signed "Preservation Committee over Young Cows" (the reference here is to the fact that after every evening party with them I had either a cold or was plainly sick). Talking about troublemakers, there are plenty of those around here. Lots of kisses for you, my dear.

Your 17-year old Marcik.

 Translator's note: The following card starts with a note in Hebrew to Jack. The rest of the notes are for Leona.

July 26, 1939

I received your letter today along with a picture of Lonia. A few days ago I sent Lonia's address, the letter of Shlomka (?) written to me. (The answer is on a postcard to him). You can know from this my opinion with regard to Lonia. Hence the possibility really exists to keep her in the university is good. All that need to be done now is to choose the correct faculty (college). I would suggest to her to travel to Chicago to see Professor Washburn and he promised me to help her in any way that he can. He is a famous pedagogue (academician). Please send this card to Lonia. (Two parts in one – ?)

Dearest Lonius!

Jack writes that he saved enough for your college tuition. Thus, don't even think twice – go back to the school bench. The key is to choose the right major from among so many; one that will provide a good pay, you will like, and make you independent in the future. I advise you with all my heart to go and see Prof. Washburne – if only you can talk your family to go to Chicago – unless something extraordinary happens in California. I do not believe that Duncan, itself, has a university and Oklahoma City doesn't appear to have a great selection of majors. Chicago has a very large university and (from descriptions) a very interesting institute for accredited teachers. Both his advice and acquaintance with Prof. Washburne can be very helpful to you. I hope that you saved his address (Winnetka, Illinois). Your account of the California trip is marvelous in Polish and a fairy tale like in English (I got it from Jack). I work a little studying some excerpts from English literature (XVII century). I manage now (of course, with a help of the dictionary) to read any average book in English. The summer is almost over – to tell you the truth, I do not regret it since there is nothing special for me here. I just kill time busying myself with work. You have warmest regards and kisses from my mother and your grandmother.

    Mania

I send you lots and lots of kisses.

    Sarenka

Kisses, best regards and good health wishes

    Marcia

 Translator's note: This postcard dated July 29, 1939, is written in Yiddish.

Dear Schlanke,

First I would like to console you for the loss of your brother, that I found out about from Lonia's letter. Each death from a close one breaks a part of our heart. I have read your last letter with much attention and tried to read between the lines about your opinions. But the closer you are to people, it's harder to give advice about what to do. I mailed your letter to Yakov through – (?) and she should give the woman. I believe that Fannie as a woman, can talk to her. I can't and don't want to ask her. I don't want to touch on a precious string. Yakov wants to support her in college. It's better she should study and in the future be independent. In this situation, I cannot refuse his help. For a half year, I didn't receive anything from him. I think I can go on without it. The main thing is to find the right course for the future that we can find in America. Dentistry is very good here or maybe teaching. I thank you for everything you are doing for my child and that's for me, too. Regards to all.

    Your Mania

August 2, 1939

My dear!

I am in Warszawa to collect my salary. I came here from Michalin with Saba Epelbaun who is a mother to a 5-month old baby, as well as, a rich and happy wife. This kind of stupid woman actually made an intelligent comment which, after a consideration, I decided to quote you. She was under the impression that you had become a serious movie star – such a gorgeous girl and so stupidly unable to take advantage of her own beauty. She sits in a podunk town and awaits Natek who, most likely, will not be able to leave, and when he does a few years from now, she will have to walk him through all the unpleasantness of immigration – playing the role of a mother to a son – while she should play a role of a child taken care of by an American – only to New York! If a college or a practical course has to cost, it should be taken only in New York. Lady, tell her – she is (no offense intended) a silly goose – someone has to open Lonia's eyes. She should not look back at the past but concentrate on the present. Lonius, is she so stupid after all? Did you get my letter mailed to you in care of the Post Office? Kisses.

    Mania

 Translator's note: The following card starts with a note in Hebrew to Jack. Then continues with a note for Leona.

August 9, 1939

Jacob!

Send my postcards to Lonia like you most certainly do with all my letters. I am waiting impatiently for the news about Lonia's decision. Anyhow she needs to be in a big city and among people. The thought about nursing is not a bad one. Almost anything she will learn as long as she will be admitted to the university. Her young man visited me the day before yesterday and he broke my heart again. I do not know how to relate this matter. She is still writing to him and she also sends her pictures – I do not know if this is really a serious relation or not. Good-bye.

    Mania

Dearest!

I have no clue of your whereabouts now. I am guessing that you are en route to San Francisco. Therefore, I am writing this letter to Jack's address who, sooner or later, will find you. I received your letter of July 25th in which you write that you do not have any definite news regarding school – followed by many dots. Please explain this comment – most of your letters are from so far away and are usually funny and, always, out of date. Nursing – good, possibly even a pleasant profession, definitely well paid but the work involved is very hard. If not 8 hours, it can also be an entire day for sure. Then again, you may be right. After all, you know that I will like anything at a higher level. But I do not understand why in Oklahoma City instead of New York. Does this result from Jack's wish, your own conviction or some other reason? Please explain this in more detail. You are full of new sensations – it is interesting how they influenced your outlook on life.

I believe that Winnetka institute offers nursing courses. The acquaintance with and recommendation from Prof. Washburne will count for something.

Mania

Translator's note: This letter appears to include two notes: one in Yiddish and another in Polish. Neither note is signed (or completed – portions of the letter appear to be missing) but a handwriting comparison to other letters provided for translation points towards Ida as the author thereof. The following letter seems to confirm this conclusion.

Michalin, August 17, 1939

Dear Jakubie!

Accidentally, I dropped by to visit Mania and I am just petrified by Lonia's decision to become a nurse. I work very closely with this profession and I hear nurses on a daily basis cursing the day they entered it. The pay is good but women age very quickly. While at the hospital in the morning hours, I often see nurses coming off a night shift with shriveled faces, pale and exhausted. In other words, this profession is just horrible. Simply a suicide. I don't understand how one can decide on something like that.

I heard that you also oppose this decision but you just must not allow this to happen. Simply refuse to pay tuition until Lonka gives her word of honor to choose a different major and, on top of that, insist on New York as her future chances there are much better. Remember that sometimes a single step can decide one entire future (...)

Dear Yakov,

I received a letter from Lonia. She is going to be a nurse. Ida was here today and told me that I should not let her become a nurse. She sees our young girls walking with swollen legs and with gray hair from the night shifts. She should better go to the university and study medicine. Maybe meet a young doctor. For nursing, women only study. Ida says it's sorry, her beauty would go for nothing. I would never let her go into nursing, to sit in the hospitals by the death beds and always think and be sorry that she chose that professions. I am writing to you again. You have to be a father and mother, like myself for eleven years. Be good. I am upset.

Translator's note: This letter was written by Ida around mid-August 1939 based on other translations done to date (see No. 39-29 and No. 39-30).

Dear Loniuchno!

I am petrified with your decision to study nursing. I am too close to this profession not to know all its dark aspects. The life in America is in many respects the same as here. People die the same as here. While doctors are asleep, the nurses have to walk at night from bed to bed, check pulses and wonder if a patient lives till the morning in time to see the doctor again. I see daily those prematurely old faces, wrinkles and gray hair on 22-year-old women; varicose veins and swollen legs on 24-year-old nurses. Every single one of them publicly talks with anger about 2 years of studies after the secondary school examinations. The studies where, like nuns, they had to sit in pews dressed every day in black hoses, black shoes, gray dresses buttoned all the way to the neck. Each one grieving over lost most beautiful years of their youth. And if America is different it cannot be too different based on the American school attached to our hospital. Remember that even after only 1 month of a night shift, your beautiful face will be left with wrinkles and pale coloring. Why are you so afraid of dentistry or medicine? If nursing takes 4 years, those 4 years will be spent much more happily with your family. Also, if after the 4 years of medicine you still insist in becoming a nurse, nothing will stop you from switching over to your "wonderful" profession. Remember, Lonka, that stars are smiling at you and it is you who wants to throw away both those stars and such a beautiful life potential laid out in front of you. I did not realize that choosing a profession can be so difficult for someone. Lucky for Sarenka, she still has some time to dwell on it. But you don't so think!! Love you always.

    Ida

Lonius!

Put your signing up for nursing on hold. I wanted to send you a telegram yesterday! Ida opened my eyes to all the dark sides of this profession. You just must wait for my letter sent yesterday, while being very upset, to you and Jack. Instead, enroll into medicine or dentistry. Do not even think about the 8 years ahead of you since after the first 4 years of medicine you will definitely be able to earn some money from medical procedures. You will never finish studying nursing, you will run away, as the grueling studies are the same as being in a purgatory. Afterwards all nurses regret choosing their profession.

Here medical studies also last 6.5 years (Ida). You don't know what will happen in 8 years but you will always have a profession acceptable all over the world. As a doctor, we will get a job anywhere. Lonius, do not reject medicine which, in the worst scenario, will aid your nursing. However, as a doctor, you will be truly free while nursing is a "slavery".

    Mania

Dear!

I am so upset by your decision to enroll in nursing. I just don't understand why you choose to disregard my pleas and explanations and, in view of your high respect for me, you choose to ignore my opinion. Ida sits next to me and is absolutely furious with your decision for the very reason that she knows that profession only too well. Young girls have swollen legs; swollen eyes; gray hair from overtiredness, night shift work and constant witness to human death. The years of studies are also 4 years of torture. In the initial years (based on the American school here as an example) one must clean the toilets and floors plus live in seclusion. I have no idea who talked you into this. Does a woman (and especially someone like you) have to have such a hard profession? Does she have to earn a lot of money? If you earn for your clothes – it is enough – you don't have to support the entire household. If you are required to work so hard like (let's not mention here any names) some other women, it is better that you stay single and earn just enough for yourself to cover you basic needs with a much easier job. It is my personal dream that you enroll at a university but to study medicine (or dentistry). You do not have to earn thousands (let your future husband earn it) and if you complete your studies you will get a good job. You do not want to go to Chicago, no one is forcing you to enter the field of pedagogies – but I do repeat that Professor Washburne's advice may only help you in your future. But, do choose any profession that your heart desires, as long as, it is not nursing.

One day you will stand shaking next to a bed of a dying person and remember my words. I am so upset…

Mania

Well, they since they let you have it, I will add my few cents too as an "experienced nurse". Practicing nurses tell us that they number less and less each day. Poor things try to escape from all those bed-pots and night shifts. But don't worry. Most likely you will drop out of the program before you even start it. If you wanted to study nursing, you could have done it in Poland. To achieve it, you didn't have to go all the way to America and look old being only 25 years old.

(not signed but appears to be Sarenka's handwriting)

Michalin, August 18, 1939

Lonius!

Today is Marcia's birthday. We will have a party for her on Sunday. Today is just a preliminary one. In the morning, I gave Sarenka an airmail letter to you but, due to the serious topic of a great importance, in my opinion, I am mailing myself another airmail card just in case Sarenka doesn't take care of the other one. Thus, my dear, it is very important to me that you under no circumstances enter the nursing profession but instead take up medicine. I almost sent you a telegram – that's how important this is. I just cannot visualize you in such terribly hard profession. Ida told me about young nurses twenty-some years old with gray hair, swollen eyes, having insufficient sleep and varicose veins on their legs from constant walking around and vigil over the sick people. I assume that the sole reason for your decision was that you didn't know what to do with yourself. Understand that it doesn't have to cost you anything and even if it does, I will never allow you to enter a drudgery. I really want you to enter the medical profession. If it isn't popular there now – it may become in 8 years and, as a doctor (even if you don't finish), you can always earn money from medical procedures. It's all God's willing. Understand that one doesn't even know what will be in 8 years and where one will be – and medicine is a true needed profession. Understand that even as a beautician, if you have a formal medical education, you will be more successful. Maybe you will work in a research field, who knows, but do not toss aside such a possibility. Listen to me! Under no circumstances are you to enter nursing! I will manage without anyone's help. Whatever the cost – Jack will manage to take care of it. You just must want to do it, says Ida. On the way to New York, stop by Chicago. Do not be offended by my other letter written while terribly upset. I spoke there words that were very bitter while under the influence of Ida's stories. Lonius – medicine! Kisses.

Mania

Michalin, August 24, 1939

Dearest!

We received your truly most wonderful pictures and a beautiful letter written in English. I am very happy that you missed the deadline and you will have an entire semester to decide what to do with yourself. In the meantime, I discussed this issue with many people. Everyone says the same. Wiktor was here. His joking comment on the subject – if you truly want to, after completing four year of medicine, you can still become…even a nurse. Alternatively, you will definitely be able to open up a beauty shop. I am concluding from your historical tuition payments for studies in America that only the very first year in medicine is expensive – or the first few years. Later…(Sarenka is back from Warszawa. Kisses from grandmother and Janowa.)…it gets cheaper plus one can earn some money by providing medical treatments – even with cosmetology which you can practice while studying. Within the last 8 years some women here also became quite successful as doctors – you will definitely be a good doctor and as a pediatrician you will be very successful. Listen to me, my kitty – you won't regret it. I assure you, my sweet. I have a lot of trouble here with the girls. All they think about are boys. Sarenka doesn't appear to be as bad but Marcia especially has a guy not even close to the commonly accepted standards. Do write her something about her attitude towards life – she doesn't listen to me any more – she took upon herself a mission, imagine this, to change that guy into a better person. Such an infant, isn't she? Kisses.

    Mania

Warszawa, August 29, 1939

Dearest!

We returned yesterday from Michalin. Everything is okay with us here. I think that the situation will clarify within the next few days. In the meantime Warszawians dig air-raid shelters in parks and gardens with humor and verve. Truly, everyone does it with no distinction. Sarenka continues to work till the 1st; we will see what's next. Wiktor claims that he will find her something. During this summer: I paid off 150 zloty in debts; supported both my mother and children; managed to return home with another 200 zloty and; on top of that, I bought Marcia and myself new outfits and for myself a black silk dress (not an evening one but very pretty) and other smaller items; and dried 13 kilograms of cherries and 10 litters of blueberries plus some juices. Of course, all that includes both my salary payment and what I got back for the last apartment. Well, I know you like me. Now, if there was only order in the world and you entered medicine. Kisses – kids are not home. Regards for the Raizyns.

    Mania

Dear Loniusiu!

I doubt if you remember me but I must write you and tell you what a wonderful mother and sisters you have. We are having a great time together. Bye for now! Kisses. Have a great time (though I hear that you are having a ball already).

Loniusiu, dear!

I am in a terrible hurry. Please forgive me for this but I have just arrived here from Warszawa and a bunch of friends are waiting for me since 5 pm to do something – it is already 7 pm. Hearty kisses.

    Sarenka

Lots and lots of kisses to you from loving grandmother. My best regards to Fenia and children. Send us your California pictures – we await them.

** *There are no letters received by Leona between September and December, 1939.*

SEPTEMBER

1
Germany invades Poland. World War II begins.
Three thousand Jewish civilians die in the bombing of Warsaw.

7
Masses of Poles – Jews and non-Jews – leave Warsaw, going East.

17
Red Army enters Poland. Poland is divided between Germany and Russia.

21
Heydrich, SS head of security, orders the establishment of the Judenrat,
Jewish Council, to be an instrument of German control.

23
Yom Kippur, a day of heavy bombing, especially of the Jewish Quarter.

27
Warsaw falls after weeks of bombing and shelling.

28
Poland surrenders to Germany. Jews establish a social welfare agency with
financial aid from the American Joint Distribution Committee (AJDC).

OCTOBER

1
German Army occupies Warsaw. Jews are immediately
subjected to attacks and discrimination.

3
Adam Czerniakow is appointed Chairman of the Judenrat
(Jewish Council) by the Germans.

10
Only Jews are taken for forced labor. Assaults begin on religious Jews.

12
Jews have to deposit all monies in blocked accounts.
All deposits of Jews in banks are frozen, Jews can only receive 250 zlotys
a week from their accounts. All jewelry has to be turned over to the Nazis.

NOVEMBER

22
Fifty-three Jews from Number 9 Nalewki Street are imprisoned and later shot on charges of rebellious behavior.

23
First anti-Jewish decrees are issued, such as: introduction of white armbands with blue Stars of David to be worn by all Jews; signs identifying Jewish shops and businesses; order to hand in radios; ban on train travel.

Census shows 359,827 Jews in Warsaw.

DECEMBER

22
Jewish education ends in Warsaw, Jewish teachers dismissed.

5 – 6
Germans seize Jewish property, including businesses, homes, household goods, currency, bank accounts.

8
Six Jews and 25 non-Jewish Poles accused of committing acts of sabotage, are shot in occupied Warsaw.

9
During Chanukah, a simple old woman asks, "Why is the world silent?"

12
Many of the Jews who were expelled from the Warthegau region of Poland, flee to Warsaw.

14
Unemployed Jewish teachers organize small groups of children to be taught for a few hours at the homes of the teachers.

30
More than 100,000 Jewish refugees have fled to the overcrowded and filthy conditions of Warsaw.

WARSAW 1940

JANUARY

Gestapo orders registration of Jewish property.

Wave of muggings and attacks on Jews launched by Polish gangs, encouraged by Germans. Jews are being arrested.

6
Freezing Jews in Warsaw are forced to burn Jewish books for fuel.

18 – 25
255 Polish Jews arrested by random in Warsaw, are shot in the Palmiry Forest outside of the city.

26
Congregational worship is forbidden; ritual slaughter is prohibited. Jews are forbidden to use the railways without special permission.

29
Jews are to receive reduced bread rations and no meat.

January 11, 1940. Mania writes Jacob that she and the girls are working sporadically.

June 14, 1940. Postcard written in German to Jacob from Mania, informing him that she is having money problems.

April 12, 1940. Postcard from Mania to Leona, sent through her cousin in Rome, due to Nazi restrictions on mail.

August 24, 1940. Mania writes Jacob that they received seven packages, but still need help.

October 20, 1940. Postcard from Mania to Leona saying some level of help is always necessary.

November 13, 1940. Mania writes Leona telling her to have fun on her approaching birthday.

December 20, 1940. Even though Mania sent this postcard registered, Leona did not receive it until March 7, 1941.

January 11, 1940

My Dear!

We are healthy and still waiting for any letters from you. What is Lonia doing? Your most important news did reach us but without any letters enclosed. All three of us work sporadically. I am working on a trial basis as a kitchen servant for the children; the girls also earn a bit. Wiktor stays at home – healthy. Eliasz Siedlinski remained with his firm in Rawula working as a chauffeur. The older Wawek left to stay with his sister and, yesterday, the younger Wawek found a kitchen job working as a type of janitor. Berta works as a hospital nurse.

    Mania

January 20, 1940

Dearest one!

I am not sure whether I should cry or laugh? How it all took place so suddenly. Did you have any symptoms? In reality it does not matter any more now. As you may know, I had my appendix removed as well some time ago. Please tell me how much did it cost. Do you need any help in covering it? Your proposal regarding sending mom your money is not a good one as "HIAS" advises not to send too much money to German Poland. Maybe $25 but not any more. Thus, hold on to your money for now. I am grateful to mine and your Mojsz for the care he provided you with during your sickness. His love fills me with happiness.

I did not answer your letter immediately as I wanted to enclose a postcard from Warszawa, 38 Muranowska Street Apt. 5 written by Hochberg family to aunt Zalcberg here in the US. It reads something like that: we are all healthy; reading your letter made us cry from happiness; signed by Grandmother Ida, Izak, etc.

I found out from you that you have a card from your mom and, therefore, I am not sending you that card to Zalcbergs. Thank you for your offer to pass your mom's card on to me – I am looking forward to getting it. How do you feel? Why didn't you write for so long – over 2 weeks? I wrote a long, "beautiful" letter to those lovely Raizyns – I am grateful to you for your help. I am so happy that you are my oldest daughter. And what a daughter you are! I couldn't have wished for a better daughter than you. There is no one better than you. But do not make any more surprises. Have some mercy on me since it is more than I can handle, my dear! How did your surgery go? What "famous" doctor performed it? I know that Mojsz is taking care of you but, who in turn, is taking care of his business? Do you feel all right? Do you…I know nothing about anything!

You do not have to write me letter if they tire you. Just drop me postcards. I am looking forward to seeing that card from mom. I hope that we will see each other soon. I miss hearing your voice.

    Your Dad

P.S. HIAS – for now, we have been told to wait until they establish their consulate in Poland. It may happen this week or the next one. I go there every other day. HIAS refuses to accept any money – instead they suggest to use the National Bank which will pay the money out on the other end in zloty. HIAS doesn't advise to send more than $25 at a time.

> **Translator's note:** The letter from Jack Zar to Leona starts in English and switches to Polish. It also includes another letter started on January 16th but, apparently, not finished. Letter from Jacob in English

January 20, 1940

Sweet dear – I am so happy. While at the bank, I experienced such tremendous emotions after finding out that Mania received the money so quickly – only 5 days after sending it. Even the bank clerk was beaming from pride as I kept coming the bank at least…75 times. However, he did not agree to release the original confirmation of the receipt of money by Mania without the original deposit receipt that I have sent you earlier. I had to copy the information but it doesn't make any difference. When you write your mother, do write short notes only and about trivial things only as anything else may not be "healthy" for them. Also, do use only postcards.

The value of zloty – there exists 2 possibilities. (1) That the zloty is practically worthless. In this case, and having in arrears about $300, I will send her all that money over a 3-month period: February, March and April. I planned to use these monies for your college but I will manage to save some more from my "cold earnings" from the ice cream business which amount to about $35 per week. (2) That the zloty has some value. We shall learn that value shortly from mother. In other words, we have nothing to complain about.

Listen, I just remembered something wonderful. Do you remember that relative of Bornsteins'? His relatives lived in Falenice. Last week he received a letter from them informing him that they are alive, need some things, etc. But the newspapers wrote that Falenice ceased to exist. Hias and its reports! One can sum it up as "empty promises"! Every day is exactly the same and we do not even expect anything new any more. A journalist from Paris writes that while taking care of business at Hias there, a famous music veteran, Paderewski, opened a piano and started to sing "Poland didn't perish yet"* and everyone inside including the Hias staff joined him while the journalist was forced to wait…

What about you, my dear, how are you? Are you sick but do not admit to it? Or do you have again – God forbid – more "secrets". Quite frankly, I have had enough of the latter. I am not saying anything…but I really do not want to have any secrets. On one hand, this is an honest and honorable way; on the other hand…Let's not talk about it any more, my intelligent and beautiful daughter. How is Mojsz? I will bet that this delicate and loving boy of yours is honorable and honest. But his greatest attribute, according to me, is the fact that he loves you. I am certain that there are many boys falling in love with "Leona" – "She Lion" – but the most worthy of them all is the one who receives my daughter's love in return.

Your Dad

* Beginning words of the Polish national anthem.

My dearest daughter!

Today, I received your surprise letter. I truly didn't know what happened there with you all. Almost 2 weeks passed since the last card written by Mojsh. I couldn't think of any reason for that. And now such a surprise! My dear, I don't know whether I should laugh or cry? But I believe that I cannot be angry with you any longer taking into the consideration your angelical kindness. (…)

January 26, 1940

My dear, little darling! I just received from the Public National Bank and Trust Company, through which I send the 14 December $75 by cable for mother the following statement:

Polish portion than switch back to English in plain English: They send by order of the National Bank and Trust Comp New York NY in accordance with the value of zloties of $75 – besides expenses the receipt of what I accept. + Mania Zagraniczna

Now lets talk over the whole business. 14 December I send by (speed) cable 19 December (5 only days later) our "stodka" received 370 zl in her very last card where she writes: (Polish) was sent Dec 5, 1939 – 9 days before I sent her the money.

The main question is how much is 370 zl. I think we'll wait for a letter. Will you think so?

January 31, 1940

DOCUMENT: Remitter's Receipt Cable

Money order #40220 of $103.25 (including commission and cable charges) sent

TO: Mania Zagraniczna   FROM: Jacob Zar
    Warschay   64 E 4th St.
    Muranowska 38.W.5   New York
    German Poland

Drawn on the Public National Bank and Trust Company of New York, Delancy Office

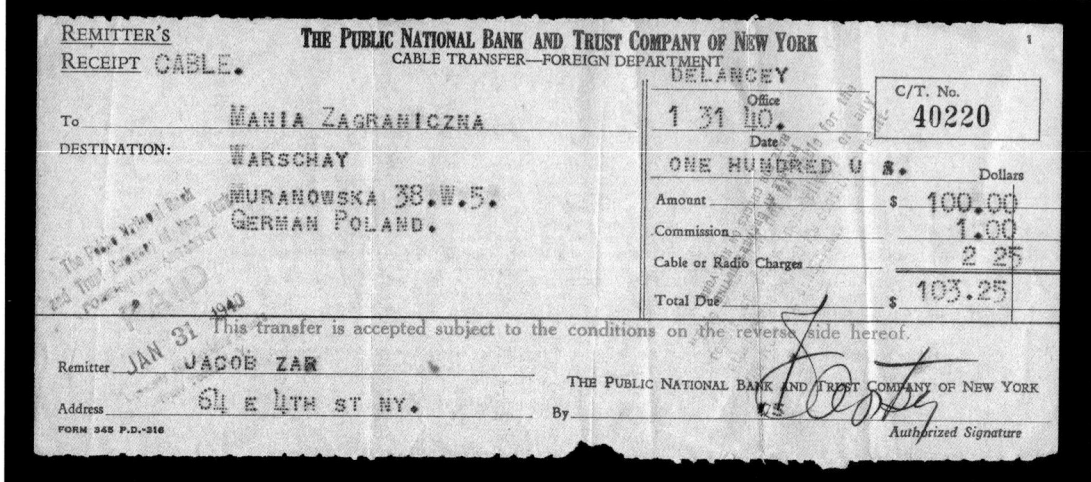

WARSAW 1940

FEBRUARY

The American Joint Distribution Committee (AJDC) is operating soup kitchens, benefitting tens of thousands of refugees and fugitives. Plans begin to be drawn up for the establishment of the ghetto.

7
Jews in Warsaw are banned from the city's public libraries.

18
Two teenage Jewish girls are raped in a Jewish cemetery in Warsaw by two German noncommissioned officers.

21
Nazis in Warsaw throw a Jewish woman from a moving streetcar.

26
Decree is issued ordering women to register for compulsory labor.

Translator's note: Jack starts his letter to Leona in Yiddish then switches over to Polish.

February 1, 1940

Dear children Shlomit and Moshe,

Only with pleasure I am to do according to your wish to write in Yiddish. Yesterday I have sent by telegram to Poland, Muranowska St. 5 No. 38 one hundred dollars for our dearest with lots of kisses. I want to explain to you why I sent $100 and not $25 each.

In HIAS, where I visit very often one hears all kinds of stories (different ones). But I have found an old man who works there and he explained to me what is going on, and usually he is right. So he tells me that he thinks that you can send to Poland as much as you want and they are not taking it for themselves. Sometimes when the Poles don't find the person, they send it back. And if Hitler takes everything away he could keep this, too. In short, I sent $100 and I am waiting to hear from them.

In short, I hope the mother (if it will be possible) will tell me how much she has received. I asked her to tell me if she has enough and for how long it will be enough the $170.

(…) Tell me, my dear, aren't you already tired of this reading in Yiddish? Next time there will be more. As you can see, I sent $100 for now until mom clarifies some things in her letters (or maybe something will change all together). Then, we should also establish a means of passing on money to her. Do not forget that the money did not reach them for the past few months! In my opinion, it would not hurt to send some more next week, however, I will hold myself back until your mom's letter. My dear, my happiness makes me speechless – it is all due to that last card in which the entire "trio talks" to me – they don't say much, yet they do talk to me. Try to imagine what it means to me when Marcia, while holding her pen, puts down her thought process as she sees it. "We live with Ida" truly requires a deep thought. I believe that Marcia can write something much better; especially under such circumstances and environment she is in?! Sarenka also writes some unnecessary, worthless things about mom. Sadness pours out of every single letter deep into my soul and, yet, I am happy. Do believe me, when I tell you, that it was an extremely hard moment for me when I read that Mother's tears went on each letter.

    We live with Ida.
    Kisses – Marcia

 Translator's note: The reference here is made to a common belief in Poland that infants coming out of the womb with their heads covered with a circle of placenta (looking like a kind of head covering) will have a lot of luck through out their lifetime. **

My dearest Loniusiu! You know what? I am truly beginning to believe that you were born with a golden galea.** Well…

I bought some stock shares 2½ years ago and in that time their value dropped from $12 to $3 per share. Do you understand? I paid $1,300 (thirteen hundred) and now they are worth between $300 and $400. Terrible, isn't it? Poor performance… But listen. I bought them in uncle Bornsztein's name. I would like to transfer their ownership into your name. If their value goes up, the money will be available for the needs of yours and mine "trio". What do you think about it? I think that you will agree with me, my oldest one! Thus, give me a kiss for that as an advance – the sweetest, truly, kiss in the world, my dear. I do love you though, my little Angel. The Jewish papers write that Germany does not permit any man-folk to immigrate to the US as they fear them joining a Polish Legion and going back to fight Germans hand-in-hand with the French and the British. There is no such prohibition regarding women; to the contrary, they appear to want to get rid of them, or so I hear… Which route do they leave the country? Via Italy or other countries. Kiss your "boy" from me (just not too hard) but do remember than you have a trio who begs your mercy… But jokes aside, do give him a hearty kiss from me. I thank you very, very much for your "card" and the information that you are healthy. You don't fully realize how much I love you, how much I love $, how much I love my wife – you know her, don't you? – but what good is it if you can not express it openly…

A long time ago, your mother took you to the country where she taught Hebrew. Once, I went to visit her there. She had only one broken bed too narrow for two people to lay in. You were only 9 months then. She wanted to put you in the bed but was afraid that you would fall out of it during your sleep. She didn't feel right to go to bed herself and lay you down on the floor to sleep on. In the meantime you slept cradled in her arms… When I came and saw your tanned body and that haircut a'la "Bob" – Mania's own design – I wanted to kiss you. But Mania would not let me kiss even my child's leg (what cute legs they were): "For God's sake, she will wake up." Okay, I agreed to wait until you wake up on your own. In the meantime we all are on the floor. While I was waiting for you to wake up, I kissed your mom (oh, what a mother!!). "Baby Jesus"…I point to you – my only child at the time. Mom doesn't let me talk and kisses me. The next thing we know, from all the noise we were making, my little "Baby Jesus" did open her eyes. Mania kneels next to you crying: "Oh, God, there is not a single dry diaper left" and keeps on looking for a single, clean one. I take off my shirt and offer it to her. We all laid together on the floor pretending to be in a barn on hay and you kept on rolling around. You slept across both of us with, at some point, your legs on top of me and your head on mom, just the opposite at other times. But it did not matter to me – I loved it all. It felt so good.

Your J. Zar

 Translator's note: Mania wrote this card, in German, to her cousin, Caterina Pacini. The front of the card includes a short note to Leona.

WARSAW 1940
MARCH

9

*From the Warsaw Diary of Chaim Kaplan, written in Hebrew,
"The gigantic catastrophe which has descended on Polish Jewry has no parallel,
even in the darkest periods of Jewish history."*

17

Registration for compulsory labor is completed.

24

*Mobs of tough Polish youths engage in Easter pogroms, not denounced by
the Polish underground. The pogroms last for eight days.*

**Mania works as a manager in a public kitchen.
Tamara works for the American Jewish Joint Distribution Committee (AJJDC).**

Warszawa, March 14, 1940

Dear Loniu!

Your letter dated September 4 arrived only yesterday. Write to Katia's address or Marysia Melamed's address. I am very concerned about your health; the same with Jack. We are all healthy; the same with the rest of the family. I trust that you will do all that is in your power towards us getting together again. Kisses.

    Mania

 Translator's note: Note in German to Katia in Rome

Dear Katia!

I received a letter from my daughter. It took six months. Send this card and she should write to me at your address. Maybe the letters will arrive faster this way. I am working in a public kitchen as a manager and live well. The 493 zlotys I received is possible to spend for my travel. I haven't seen my husband in 12 years and my daughter in two years. I was left here with two other daughters. One, 18, works for the American Joint and the other, 17, works at home. She plays the piano. Do you have children? Regards and kisses to your father and mother. The address for my daughter is Leona Singer, Duncan, Okla, P.O.Box 528 USA.

    Your cousin Mania

 Translator's note: Mania writes her letters to Leona in care of Caterina Pacini in Rome. The card includes also a brief note to Katia in German.

Dear Katia,

I thank you for everything you do for us. Many kisses and wishes for both you and your dear parents.

    Mania

WARSAW 1940
APRIL

9

Germany invades Denmark and Norway.

23

Eve of Passover (Seder).

28

The attempt of the Joint to set up a "Passover Project" consisting of food packages and not financial aid, was unsuccessful. The Nazis confiscate a large part of the flour and matzohs.

Warszawa, April 12, 1940

Dear Loniu!

We received your sweet letter dated December 16, 1939 and later a postcard from Marysia. So we know that you are already married. Do hurry up and write in care of Katia what is your chosen one's name, how old is he, what does he do, etc. What is the status of your and Jack's citizenship? I believe that maybe now something could be done for us to allow us to see each other after so many years – except that now there are six of us. Kisses.

Leona Singer, Duncan-Okla, POB 528, USA

    Mania

Dear Loniusiu!

We all share you happiness. You were born under a lucky star. My brother-in-law must be someone very special to be chosen by you. I am counting on you. Enjoy yourself.

    Marcia

I also enclose my kisses for you and your beautiful and dear husband.

    Sarenka

Translator's note: Mania wrote this letter to Leona in care of Caterina Pacini in Rome but the card was forwarded to St. Gallen in Switzerland. The card includes also a brief note to Katia in German.

Dear Katia,

Yesterday I received your letter to Ida. I thank you again for everything. I am writing to Lonia, she should send the letters to you. You should not have any expenses on my account. Hopefully we will see each other again, and I can thank you in person.

    Your Mania

April 21, 1940

Dear!

Yesterday your letter dated December 21, 1939, arrived. I feel rapturous with your happiness. It seems that I also had a small contribution in shaping your fate. The only thing left now is to rejoin us all. I don't need anything else in this world. The girls also enjoy themselves – they don't think about anything. They are joyous with your happiness. We would like to meet your dearest husband. You must know that I just had to spend a very small, but at least a symbolical, amount on cakes to celebrate your wedding – they wouldn't leave me alone. We had to drink to your health. Write us the name of your loved one. Are his parents still alive, etc.? Who is he related to? Morris' brother? Hugs and kisses to Morris, the Rajzins, and the entire family in general which, it would appear, likes me a little. I believe you caused enough commotion for them to benefit our case. Do send Katia some international postal stamps. She is not doing too well and want to continue using her help – this way I get your letters quicker and so will you.

    Mania

P.S. Why haven't we received a single letter from Jack?

WARSAW 1940
MAY

The Judenrat is ordered by the Germans, and at their own expense, to put up thick dividing walls at every intersection that did not have trolley tracks.

All normal conduct of business ceases – streets are filled with peddlers.

16

Nazis launch a plan, called the" Extraordinary Pacification Operation", to eliminate Polish intellectuals.

20

Auschwitz begins functioning as a concentration camp.

Translator's note: This postcard includes two notes dated May 9, 1940 (Warszawa), written in German by Mania and Marcia (Sarenka wasn't at home to include hers), and addressed to Morris Trachtenberg.

Dear Morris,

I received your letter today and feel that I know you a little. We saw your wedding picture. I am happy to have a son. I wish you both lots of luck. My need you must feel. I send you motherly and best regards, wanting to be with you.

    Mania

Dear brother,

I like you better and better. I would like to see you and your wife, my small Loniusa.

    Tamara

Sarenka is not home.

WARSAW 1940
JUNE

The Jewish Council is reorganized, limited to carrying out orders of German authorities.

10

Italy enters the war, as a junior ally to Germany.

17

France surrenders; Polish Jews are frightened.

> **Translator's note:** This postcard includes a note dated June 10, 1940 (Warszawa), written in German by Mania, and addressed to Leona Trachtenberg.

Dear ones,

About you I know everything. I thank you for all you have done for us. We await with impatience. Maybe it will work. We live well. If possible, we ask only to send food packages. See if Katia could be helpful. If it is not too much trouble, we ask this little help. We work, but we don't earn enough.

With many kisses, Mania

> **Translator's note:** This postcard includes a note dated June 14, 1940 (Warszawa), written in German by Mania, and addressed to Jacob Zar.

Dear Yakov,

I need a little help from you. We're good but together we only make 300 zloties. I have not received my salary since May. Good-by.

Mania

The whole family lives well. All work is more or less in order. Also Berta works as a nurse.

M

WARSAW 1940
JULY

8

*Edict is issued to close printing houses owned by Jews.
Trade in books is forbidden to Jews.*

27

*Order is issued forbidding Jews to enter city parks
or municipal promenades and certain streets.*

30

*News reaches Warsaw that the entire Jewish community
of Kracow is to be expelled.*

WARSAW 1940
AUGUST

13
Edict is issued concerning forced labor.

The shipment of Jews to labor camps begins.

The Judenrat is obligated to furnish the Germans with 8,000 working youths (up to age 55) every day.

Translator's note: This postcard includes a note dated August 24, 1940 (Warszawa), written in German by Mania, and addressed to Jacob Zar.

Dear Jack!

I write more often to Lonia, but I think you get those letters, too.

We need a little help. We received the seven packages. They were good. We live well.

Write.

    Mania

WARSAW 1940
SEPTEMBER

*A 7:00 pm curfew is imposed on the entire population,
for Jews the curfew begins an hour or two earlier.*

13
*Order is issued that the Judenrat must support schools for
academic and trade education for Jewish children at its own expense.*

19
Order is issued forbidding Jewish doctors from treating Aryan patients and vice versa.

28
*Jews can only ride on certain streetcars. Jewish streetcars
bear Jewish stars and signs. "For Jews Only."*

Translator's note: This letter was mailed via Registered Mail by Mania to Leona. The date of mailing in Warsaw is not readable. However, it passed through New York on September 5, 1940, and reached Seminole, Oklahoma on September 7, 1940. The letter itself appears to be missing.

September 17, 1940

DOCUMENT: Money order receipt #5993745

This shows that Mania Zagraniczne, 38-5 Muranowska, Warschau, received and signed for 100 zloty from the American Express office in New York issued thru the American Express Office in Berlin, Germany.

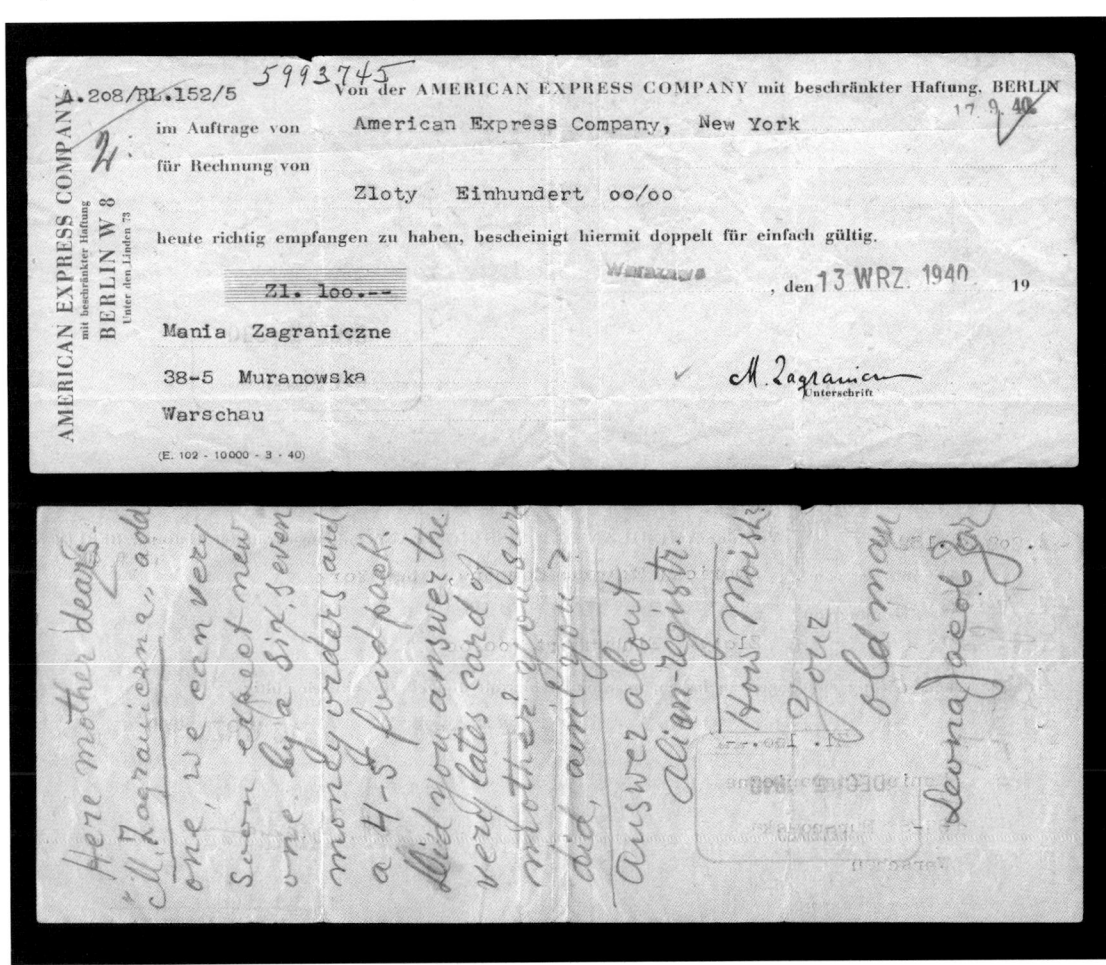

 Translator's note: The back of the document bears a message to Leona from Jacob after he got it returned from Mania:

Here Mother dear's. "M. Zagraniczna" add one, we can expect new one by a six, seven money orders and a 4-5 food pack. Did you answer the very latest card of mother? You sure did, ain't you.
Answer about alien register.
How's Moish?
Your old man

Leona Jacob Zar

WARSAW 1940
OCTOBER

9

*Jews must make way before every German,
both soldiers and civilians.*

12

*Yom Kippur (Day of Atonement) Jews are informed of the
decree establishing the Warsaw Ghetto. A map is published
a few days later, indicating the streets assigned to the ghetto area.
Jews are forced to pay for and build a wall around the Warsaw Ghetto.*

30% of the population of Warsaw is packed into 2.4 % of the city's area.

*The daily food ration allocated to the Warsaw Jews consists of 181 calories.
(Germans are allowed 2310 a day; foreigners 179; Poles 934).*

14

*Nazis move non-Jewish Poles out of a designated
section of Warsaw, and move Jews in.*

October 20, 1940

Dear!

We are healthy and working little by little. A few weeks ago, we received 100 (hundred) zloty and one package via Kowno (number eight in total). Thank you so much – some level of help is always necessary; please, keep that in mind. So far, we live at Ida's. Wiktor moved to Pawia Street #38.

    Mania

WARSAW 1940
NOVEMBER

5
Jewish children begin to peddle in the streets.

16
The ghetto, in the heart of the Jewish quarter, is sealed off by a high wall.

There are 445 deaths in the ghetto this month.

The population of the ghetto is 380,740 people.

Translator's note: Please note that the return address on this postcard is for someone named Jadwiga Bednarska.

November 13, 1940

Dear!

Keep on thinking positively about us. We are managing somehow – especially with your help. This month alone we received 100 zloty twice. Your help is needed. Especially with the winter almost behind the corner. Lonka! Your birthday is almost here. Have fun.

We received your letters written in August. Some better wishes would be preferable but you have no control over them. I have more hope.

    Marcia, Mommy and Sarenka

P.S. Continue writing to the old address.

 Translator's note: Please note that the return address on this postcard is for someone named Stanislawa Jaworska (but different building and apartment numbers).

Dear!

We received your postcard dated October 20 – strange that there is no word from Jack. In November we received 100 zloty twice (2-3 months earlier also a 100 zloty) earlier four packages through Kowno – eleven packages in total (seven through Ryga). We are still in dire need of your help; especially now that the winter is here. Hugs, kisses and best birthday wishes for Lonka from us all. We are healthy. Kisses from grandmother. We continue to live with Ida.

    Mania

WARSAW 1940
DECEMBER

*Inside the ghetto, the Polish-Jewish historian,
Emanuel Ringelblum, begins writing a secret diary of ghetto life.
Smuggling becomes a means of survival.*

20
*The Jewish Hospital begins preparation for its forced move.
Twelve to fourteen Jews are dying daily.
Beatings of Jews by the SS are becoming more common.*

26
Chanukah is celebrated in the ghetto; parties are held behind closed doors.

December 10, 1940

DOCUMENT: Foreign Money Order Receipt #7020028
Issued to Mania Zagraniczna, Muranowska 38/5, Warsaw. Poland, from Jacob Zar in New York, for 100 zloty ($17.82). Sent from the American Express Company Broadway office.

December 20, 1940

Dear!

We are healthy. We are working but your help is still required; especially now due to winter. We received 200 zloty in November and 100 zloty in December. We could use some more packages even if only one of them was with clothes (stockings, underwear, etc.). We need approximately 200 zloty each month. Our work is practically enough for food only – I still have not been paid for July. Berlin informed me quite a long time ago that we are registered. The registration is valid for only one year – after that we will have to renew the documents. You have to check into it there.

    Mania

WARSAW 1941

JANUARY

The Jewish Council census shows 378,979 Jews in the ghetto.

Jews in the ghetto are freezing to death because they are denied fuel.

Beatings and atrocities towards Jews continue.

8
Jews are still required to pay taxes, even back taxes.

31
3,000 exiled Jews from Pruszkow and other Polish cities enter the ghetto, without any personal belongings.

February 13, 1941. *Mania writes to Leona that she received her card from her wedding anniversary.*

March 28, 1941. *Mania writes Leona that she received the money through the Dresdner Bank and a package through Subotice.*

May 15, 1941. *Mania writes Leona that they just got paid for last September, they need help.*

June 29, 1941. Sarenka wrote that she celebrated her 20th birthday that week.

July 19, 1941. Mania tells Leona that Marcia left with a youth group, protecting her from the truth – that her sister had died.

November 11, 1941. This was the last correspondence Leona received from her family in the Ghetto.

January 28, 1941

DOCUMENT: Money order receipt (in German) # 1256/17 EE
Mania Zagraniczna, Muranskowa 38/5, Warschau, received 100 zloty (less expenses) from Jacob Zar, New York, sent through the Bank of Cracow. Mania signed for it on Feb. 12, 1941. A copy of the receipt was sent to the Dresden Bank in Berlin. Receipt was also stamped with the name of the Trade Bank and Trust Company in New York.

WARSAW 1941

FEBRUARY

Poles caught selling food to Jews in the ghetto are automatically sentenced to three years of hard labor.

The daily bread ration for Jews in the ghetto is reduced to 3 ounces per day.

Food parcels from abroad for Jewish recipients, whose value is more than 50 zlotys, are banned.

15
Nazis are seen giving candy to Jewish children in the ghetto and then photographing them for propaganda purposes.

There is one post office for 500,000 people.

20
It is forbidden to hold parties with music and dancing. Germans become stricter in separating the ghetto from the Aryan world.

February 2, 1941

Dear!

I received four packages almost simultaneously. We are healthy. Everything is very useful. Please, do write your uncle letting him know that mom, and Berta plus Dyncia also need their help.

   Mania

February 5, 1941

Dear Loniu!

Today your birthday card arrived. This month we received two packages. It would be very hard to do without them as we still do not get paid our wages. It is especially hard due to the winter season. Also I received 100 zloty in early January. Make sure to write both your uncle and your aunt that your mom is in dire need of their help since her brother-in-law has been gone for over a year. Hearty kisses.

   Mania

P.S. Lusia L. Sends her greetings.

February 13, 1941

Lonius!

I have just received the card from your wedding anniversary. Your and Jack's happiness fills us with joy. Somehow, we manage to take care of ourselves with your help. All of us work. We received four packages almost simultaneously in January – apparently some were delayed. In spite of all of us working, we would not be able to manage without your help since we are very poorly compensated. Besides that it was only the last week that we finally received our pay for July. Kisses for Moris and Jack. Marcia goes to a new, good professor.

   Marcia

February 28, 1941

Dear!

The card from your wedding anniversary did reach us. Recently, we received four packages almost simultaneously – three through Copenhagen and one through Yugoslavia. Thank you so much for everything. We stay healthy and all of us are working – however, continue to keep us in your thoughts. Lonius, your and Jack's happiness feels us with joy. If only we could share this happiness together. Hugs and kisses from us all.

   Mania

WARSAW 1941

MARCH

*Since January 70,000 displaced Polish
Jews are forced into the ghetto.*

*The number of dead is growing every day.
There are 400 deaths the first week.*

People are dying on the street every day from hunger.

10
The Judenrat decides on an 8 P.M. curfew in the ghetto.

18
*The horses of Jewish drivers are taken away,
depriving them of their livelihoods.*

March 28, 1941

Dear!

A little over a week ago, we got 93 zloty 90 groszy through the Dresner Bank. Yesterday, a package through Subotice. It the seventeenth one in a row, the smallest one. I do not think that I should write you this but that is exactly the type of help we require, despite the fact that we all work and earn money. Sarenka wrote you last week. We had some extra expenses due to flues. But we are all healthy now. Kisses. We received the card dated February 5, 1941.

    Mania

WARSAW 1941
APRIL

*More than 40,000 German and Belgian Jews
are deported to the Warsaw Ghetto.*

24
*One hundred Jew are seized in the ghetto to dig
canals and drain swamps in Poland's Kampinos Forest.*

26
News from labor camps is very bad – very little food and much abuse.

30
*No newspaper will be allowed in the ghetto
except the Gazeta Zydowska (Jewish Gazette).*

April 4, 1941

DOCUMENT: Money order receipt (in German) #80184

Issued to Mania Zagraniczna, Muranskowa 38/5, Warsawa for 100 zloty from the American Express office in New York through the American Express Office in Berlin, also bearing the stamp of the Trade Bank and Trust Company in New York. Mania signed for it in Warsaw on April 4, 1941.

April 10, 1941

Dear!

We are all healthy. We continue to work and, so far, the pay didn't improve any. They still owe us for September. That's why it is so hard but your aid saves us – we would be in bad shape without it. Recently, we received ten small packages from Lisbon each weighing approximately 4 (four) kilograms. Grandmother was thrilled with your uncle's card. Jack added a note thereto. Sarenka sent them a letter as well. I'm not sure why you didn't receive it. The money also reached us but very good packages are most crucial. If possible, we could use a good package with clothing. Hugs and kisses. Tomorrow is my birthday. Accordingly, let us wish each other the same thing – that is to see each other.

Mania

April 21, 1941

Dear Loniu!

We all are healthy and working. They just issued us remaining pay for September. We manage to survive with your help. It has been quite a long time since I got any letter from you – the last one was dated February 2nd. Continue to do things as you were.

    Mania

Lonik! How are things going? You are so lucky.

    Marcia

My Dear! How are you doing? We are healthy and, so far, and continue to feel well.

    Sarenka

Warmest regards and kisses.

    Lusia L.

WARSAW
1941
MAY

Census shows 430,000 Jews in the ghetto.

*1,700 ghetto inhabitants die, mostly from starvation,
but also from typhus, TB, and heart attacks.*

11
Jewish children in the ghetto are seen tickling a corpse as they play.

Kitty!

Write mom a few words on a piece of paper and this response letter by "Air Mail".

    Lonia

May 15, 1941

Dear!

Yesterday, I received 97 zloty. However, the packages announced in received cards dated in March – never arrived. Before the holidays, we received twelve packages weighing 40 decagrams each and nothing else since then – neither to us nor to grandmother from your uncle (he also sent two packages).

Please, lodge a complaint as there is hardly anything left from our salaries – they hardly even pay us (they paid for September only a month ago). We are healthy. Kisses.

    Mania

P.S. Make sure to send your letter via "Air Mail" – properly paid postcards travel very quickly.

WARSAW 1941
JUNE

9
*42,625 lunches are served to adults and
25,372 to children from the community kitchen.*

10
Trial air raid alarm.

12
*Tamara dies of typhus in the ghetto and
is buried in the Gesia Cemetery.*

23
First air raids on Warsaw (from the Soviets).

24
Order to register foreign Jews in the ghetto.

25
Baths are set up for 1,000 per day at Prosta Street.

June 16, 1941

DOCUMENT: Receipt #1875 from Polish Atlantic Shipping Co. of America issued to Jacob Zar for $9.10 for the purchase of one food package for Mania Zagraniczna, Warshau, Muranskowa 38/5, Germany

June 29, 1941

Dear!

We received your card dated April 24, 1941. We are healthy and working. I do not understand why Jack has to go all that way to see his brother. Is it possible, that nothing can be taken care of locally? Besides, almost everything you write about is moot for now. I sent Lusia your address in connection with the information issue – if anyone can do anything it has to be at your end. Though, the way things are, I have doubts. During the past two months I received seven packages in total – probably the ones you wrote about in March, plus twice money (100 zloty each time).

    Mania

Kisses from me.

    Marcia

My Dear!

All is well here. This week I celebrated my 20th birthday.

    Sarenka

WARSAW 1941
JULY

4
Number of lunches distributed is 117, 481.

7
*Polish teenagers are trapping Jewish teenagers
who are caught smuggling rhubarbs.*

8
Adult and child beggars are everywhere in the ghetto.

July 19, 1941

Dear!

We received your card dated May 30th. On June 19th Marcia left with a youth group to Chaim. I have not heard from her to date. Two weeks ago we received a 4 kilogram package from Lisbon. Kisses.

    Mania

Marcia's trip did cost me a lot of nerves and health but I was not able to stop her.

    Mania

My warmest greetings and kisses for you all.

    Sarenka

WARSAW 1941
AUGUST

18

For several days, the ghetto is receiving up to 4,000 refugees from Nowy Dwor, Polish territory incorporated by the Reich.

20

Meeting with grocers about the reserves for the winter, food substitutes, etc.

28

Residents of Krochmalna Street are ordered to prepare to be bathed and disinfected.

August 18, 1941

My dearest child!

I just received your letter from June. I am very happy for you. I hope that everything will turn out well – what's important that you have such a wonderful friend which is extremely important at times like this. I am in terrible pain due to our separation. My life now consists of only one dream – there are no others. I still have no news from Marcia.

    Mania

WARSAW
1941
SEPTEMBER

Germans announce reduction in ghetto rations.

**Ghetto post office forbidden to handle foreign mail.
End of parcels from neutral countries.**

The director of HIAS is arrested and the organization is liquidated.

September 16, 1941

Dear!

Yesterday your postcard arrived via Air Mail. Unfortunately, I am not capable of not worrying. I am doing all that is humanly possible to improve my health. I eat well but even your departure during more normal conditions made me very sick. There is no news from Marcia and no news is permitted – I do know that and that is why I suffer so much. Sarenka is so dear; there is absolutely nothing to reproach her about – she is an adult in the full meaning of this word. Along with the postcard, I received a notification from Berlin about a wire transfer for 500 zloty – I will have it within a few weeks. I sent back to Berlin the notice confirmation. So far I have not received that last 100 zloty.

    Mania

WARSAW
1941
OCTOBER

Germans drown 30 Jewish children in clay pits near Okopowa Street in the ghetto.

Seventy children are found frozen to death outside destroyed houses after the first snowfall of the season.

5
Death edict for any Jew leaving the ghetto without permission. Any non-Jewish Pole who aids a Jew will be executed.

23
Liquidation of the Small Ghetto. Streetcar lines are abolished.

WARSAW 1941

NOVEMBER

6
Proclamation for death penalty for Jews leaving the ghetto.

17
Execution of eight Jews, including six women, caught leaving the ghetto without permission.

20
Paper and linen are no longer available for burying the dead. The bodies are left naked in holes in the ground.

November 11, 1941

Dear!

Today, four weeks have passed since I got sick and two weeks from getting past the critical point. As you can see, I rush to write you and calm you down. I didn't expect to survive such a terrible sickness, especially due to my mental depression lasting the past four months, but fate wouldn't let me leave Sarenka alone. She took care of me day and night for three weeks. At the critical point my blood pressure was 60 and I showed some cerebral symptoms. They put leeches on my back, gave me intravenous shots and other things. Wiktor and Dyncia were going out of themselves doing everything in their power – Jola also helped. Luckily, there still was a few hundred zloty available at home from the money just received from you. Also, we sold a few items. It's already the fourth day when I dress for a few hours and walk over to the table on my "wobbly" legs. My recuperation depends now on the proper nutrition and on my mental balance which has been shaken lately. File claims for missing packages.

    Mania

This was the last letter Leona received from her family.

WARSAW 1941
DECEMBER

The Jewish cemetery is walled off; coffins are used for smuggling. Free soup kitchens support 100,000 people.

Fifteen Jews are shot to death in the courtyard of the ghetto prison on the first night of Chanukah.

1
Receipt of food packages forbidden, under pretext of danger of epidemics.

7
Pearl Harbor leads to withdrawal of American relief organizations (JDC).

10
United States declares war on Germany and Italy, providing hope to Europe's Jews.

16
2,500,000 Jews in Government Central must be "gotten rid of."

17
German post office refuses to accept mail out of the ghetto and uses excuse of epidemics again.

WARSAW 1942
January

*The use of Zyklon-B gas for mass killings begins at Auschwitz.
Jewish workshops in the ghetto make products needed by Germany.*

Leszno Street becomes a center for smugglers, black marketeers.

*The ration of black bread is 2 fi kilos per month.
Butter and meat are not available.*

FEBRUARY

Thirty-three Jewish doctors in the ghetto begin a study of the effects of starvation, as they themselves slowly starve to death.

2
Reports reach the ghetto of Jews being taken from towns and shot to death.

Residents go for a long time without gas and electricity.

MARCH

Five thousand Jews die of starvation in the ghetto.

7
Size of the ghetto is diminished. Free access to the Jewish cemetery is strictly forbidden. No one may enter without an admission ticket, new income for the Germans.

APRIL

More than 4,400 Jews die of starvation in the ghetto.

18
Wave of terror in the Ghetto, "The Bloody Night", when the Germans drag 52 Jewish men from their beds and kill them, wounding others. Among the victims are people suspected of being involved with the ghetto's underground paper.

German and Czech Jews are brought into the ghetto.

MAY

60% of the ghetto residents are starving; more than 3,600 Jews die of starvation.

5
Jewish teachers and educators in the ghetto create a special day for the children. They treat them to games, plays, and special rations of sweets.

10
Nazis force their way into Jewish apartments in Warsaw, shoot and club the residents, throwing their bodies out of the windows.

15
Nazis take pictures in the ghetto to use for propaganda purposes, to show the "abundance and good fortune" of Jews in the ghetto.

29-30
914 men are taken from the ghetto to an unknown destination.

JUNE

Four thousand Jews in the ghetto die of starvation.

1
Liberty Barricade, an underground newspaper in Warsaw, published by the Polish Socialist Party, reveals that Nazis are gassing prisoners at the Chelmno death camp.

2
Information is smuggled out of Poland by the Jewish Bund in Warsaw and is reported by the BBC. The report states that 700,000 Jews have been exterminated.

3
Nazis shoot 110 Jews in a prison on Gesia Street, including ten Jewish policemen, women, and children.

7
A Jewish woman who had escaped from the ghetto is dragged back into the ghetto and shot.

JULY

380,000 Jews in the Warsaw Ghetto.

19

Himmler orders the SS to complete the resettlement of the entire Jewish population by December 31, 1942.

22

Mass deportation of Jews begins (regardless of age or sex), continuing until September 12.

300,000 Jews are expelled or murdered; 265,000 to Treblinka. 55,000-60,000 Jews remain in the ghetto.

Members of the Judenrat are taken as hostages.

23

Adam Czerniakow, chairman of the Jewish Council, commits suicide rather than having to choose 6,000 Jews to deport each day.

The activists of the underground begin to meet.

28

The Jewish Fighting Organization (ZOB), a resistance group, is created.

AUGUST

5

First week of August, Janus Korczak, his staff, and 200 children from his orphanage are deported from the ghetto and murdered at Treblinka.

An extermination squad descends on the ghetto. The operation lasts a week.

7

Blockage of every street and house begins.

15

Third stage of deportation (lasting until September 6) – total evacuation. Jewish policemen are compelled to bring in daily quotas of five Jews per day or their wives, mothers, or children would be taken away.

SEPTEMBER

*From September to January, Polish Jews trapped in the ghetto
construct more than 600 fortified bunkers.*

12
More than 4,800 Polish Jews are deported to Treblinka from Warsaw.

21
*Yom Kippur – ghetto area reduced by more than half. More than
3/4 of the population has already been evacuated.*

2,000 Jewish policemen deported.

22
SS and SD take over formal administration of Jewish affairs in Warsaw.

OCTOBER

*Jewish ghetto leaders ask Jan Karski, a Polish Catholic working
for the underground, to tell the Polish and Allied governments
"…Our entire people will be destroyed."*

*Ghetto was reduced to 45,000 able-bodied men and women
employed for slave labor in German factory complexes.*

20
*Coordinating Committee of resistance movement, the
Jewish Combat Organization (ZOB) is formed.*

NOVEMBER

15
*The Soviet based Jewish Antifascist Committee releases a
report entitled, "The Liquidation of the Jews in Warsaw."*

**Mania and Sarenka are murdered in the
Warsaw Ghetto. (Exact date unknown.)**

DECEMBER

According to the Judenrat, 65 Jews were shot in the street during December, down from 360 in October.

4

On the initiative of a group of Poles, ZEGOTA (a secret name of the Rada Pomocy Zydom), Council of Aid to the Jews, was established in Warsaw. It was run jointly by Jews and non-Jews.

9

German Governor-General Frank, although a vocal supporter of the extermination program, complained that a "significant work force" was being depleted with the liquidation of the Jews.

WARSAW 1943

JANUARY

18
After a four month break, Germans resume deportations of Jews from the ghetto. Jews react with the "January Revolt", the first act of overt, armed resistance.

One thousand Jews are executed on the streets.

Six thousand Jews are deported to Treblinka.

19
Germans raid the ghetto for a second day.

19-22
6,000 Jews are murdered at Treblinka.

21
SS men are met with Jewish resistance when they fire into windows and throw grenades. They withdraw, leaving 12 dead.

FEBRUARY

Himmler secretly instructs the High Command to destroy the Warsaw Ghetto, while confiscating all valuables.

MARCH

21
Three orphaned children, ages 14, 12 and 9, escape through the city's sewer system.

APRIL

19
Eve of Passover. Final liquidation of the ghetto begins. 2000 German troops entering the ghetto (of 40,000 inhabitants) are met by 700-750 poorly armed Jewish resistance fighters.

Beginning of the Warsaw Ghetto Uprising, the first urban uprising in German-occupied Europe.

20
Germans set fire to houses in the ghetto, block by block. Jews hiding in houses, bunkers, and sewers continue to fight.

End of the month – Jewish resistance is weakened as the German artillery bombardment continues.

MAY

3

In the Aryan section of Warsaw, Germans arrest and kill 21 women who are Jewish or suspected of being Jewish.

8

Germans take over the headquarters of the ZOB on Mila

18

Mordechai Anielewicz, Commander of ZOB, commits suicide.

**Shortly before his death Anielewicz wrote:
"My life dream has come true. I have lived to see
Jewish Resistance in the ghetto in all of its greatness and glory."**

16

Germans blow up the Thomackie Synagogue.

End of the Warsaw Ghetto Uprising.

The Jewish resistance movement, ZOB, held out longer against the Germans than the country of Poland.

JUNE

3
German troops in the ghetto destroy a bunker on Walowa Street where 150 Jews are hiding.

29
Outside of Warsaw, five Poles are shot, along with the four Jews they were hiding.

AUGUST

Fifty Jewish men and forty-seven Jewish women hiding in the Aryan section of Warsaw, are discovered and executed.

SEPTEMBER

Germans send a Polish labor battalion into the ruins of the ghetto to flatten any structures left standing. Most of the Jews who survived the uprising are killed.

WARSAW 1944

MARCH

7

Ringelblum is among thirty-eight Jews captured by the Gestapo in a bunker in the Aryan section of Warsaw. He and his family are tortured and killed.

WARSAW
1945
MAY

Germany surrenders. The war in Europe is over.

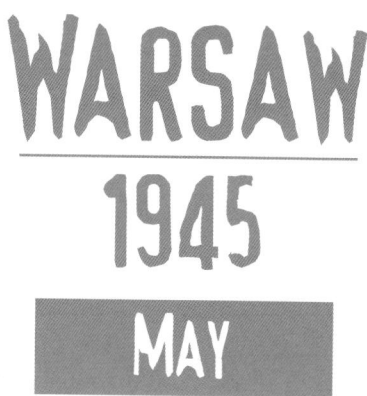

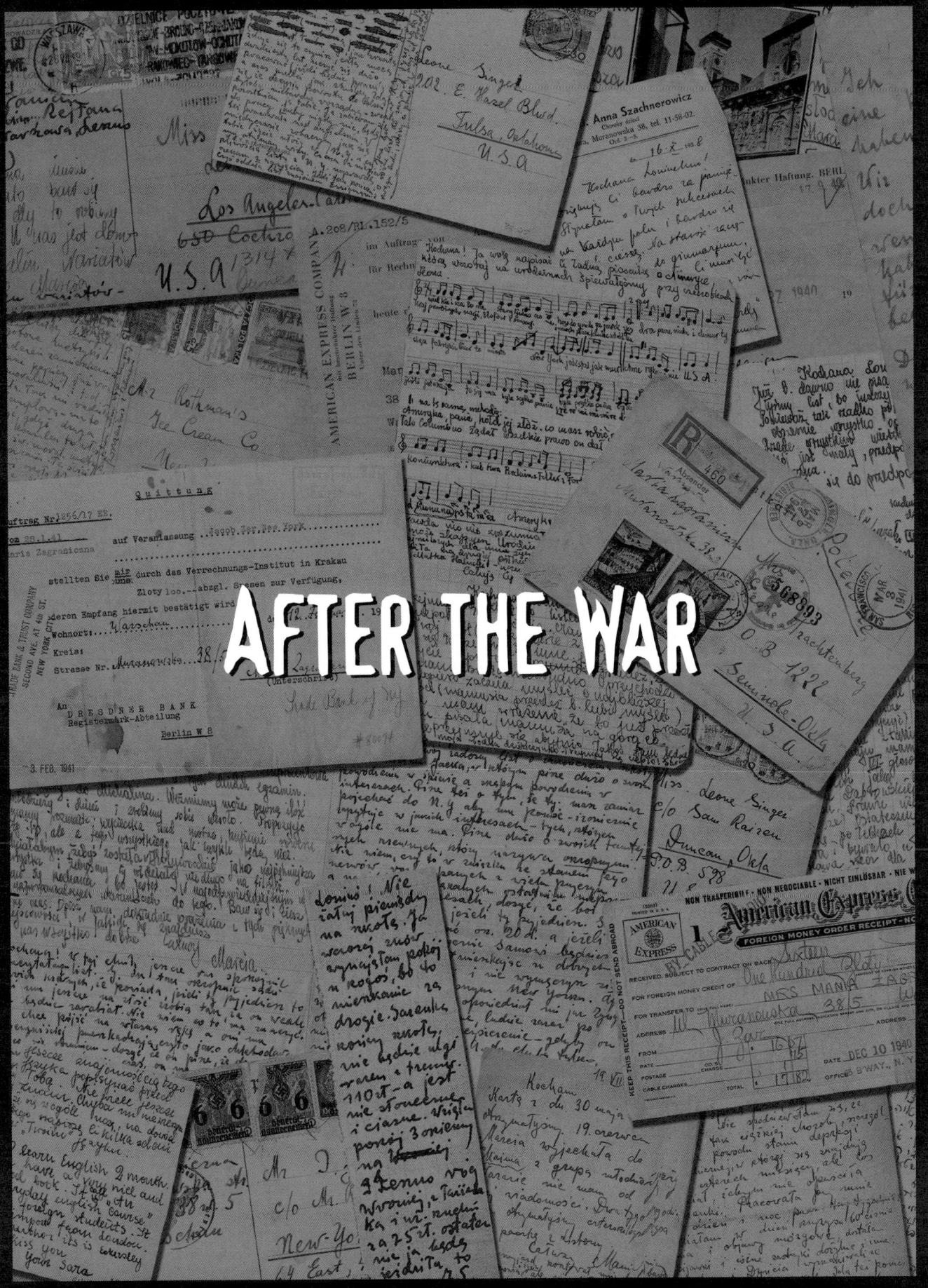
AFTER THE WAR

September 8, 1945

Dear Loniu!

We are vacationing at Cote d'Azur which is unusually beautiful. I will write you a longer letter from Paris. Everything is okay with us. What about you? How are your children? For now I send you kisses from Ed, Pierre, Jean-Claude, Jasmine and, naturally, from me.

    Marysia

Lodz, June 13, 1946

My dearest Loniuchno!

Your every letter is like a holiday for me! Every photograph alleviates sorrow and longing for close relatives like yourself! You write that it will be the happiest day for you to see us with you there! My darling, you cannot even imagine what happiness and relief it would be to be able cry openly in your arms and tell you the entire story. Yesterday, along with your letter, I received a return of my own letter to you written in May 1945. It had the wrong address. It traveled to Oklahoma and back after 13 months en route. If you would like me to I will pass it on to you but it is the first letter after the war and so full of sorrow that I probably should not? Your parcel arrived. So far just one. All these beautiful things you sent me affected me in such a way as if the cemetery never existed in my heart and the recent events never took place and as if I was 16 again! I cried like a little baby. These socks, gorgeous sweaters, fabulous dress with a cover over it – absolute wonders. And this night dress for me? There is so much heart in each piece here, so much love! I touched each piece, laughed and cried. I cried remembering the never leaving me memories and from the sorrow that others did not survive to experience this happiness. I will try to let it go, Loniuchno! Nowadays, in that new life of ours, there doesn't exist a moment of happiness without swallowing the tears of sorrow for all those that died in those murderers' hands. I will never find the pleasures of life as those known before this horrible Hitler era. He took it away even from those who survived.

All these dresses are not good for me. They require a lot of alterations as I gained a lot of weight during the pregnancy. I kept the slimmest cream colored dress eventually for Halinka and a light brown outfit with a white blouse for Danuta. But I did not give them yet as, please do not understand me wrong, my dear Loniuchno, but I am afraid of some family quarrels resulting from this. It would be much better if you were willing to send them something directly from you. After all, I have Pola to think of too and, no matter what I choose, she will never be pleased and resentful towards both me and you. There is no need to destroy the relationship with the only brother that I have left over this. However, if you believe that I should pass these clothes on, the dress and that blouse outfit rest untouched. I await your decision.

This package with your sister-in-law's clothes, that you wrote about in your letter in English and listed clothes added thereto from your wardrobe, never did reach us. And I do not expect it to show up.

Loniuchno! Do not send us any more food parcels. We are not hungry. Working people receive food allocations. Clothes are very important since they are a necessity for a working person and are not available here. Especially now, as you can guess for yourself, since I stopped working to take care of the house and my newborn. Until the child was born, we all dined at my work place; the apartment was locked up. Now, things changed completely. Feliks has to earn living for the entire family.

Yesterday, I received some photographs from you. Your entire family looks so sweet – just as you always were and are to this day. Who knows, with time, you may have become even sweeter and more lovely.

Pola informed me yesterday that Wawek Hochberg was found in Haifa and works there as a biotechnician. What a happy piece of news! We, in Warszawa, were told that he was in Moskwa along with Sarenka. As it turns out, he is searching for both Sarenka and his parents. It is too late to find his parents but Sarenka may still be alive somewhere!

Now, Loniuchno! What should be done with your family's villa? The deadline to claim it is through the end of 1946. After that deadline the government will claim its rights thereto. In my opinion, it should be sold. Thus, either mail me a power of attorney to act on your behalf, or a moral approval for me to claim that none of you survived leaving Wiktor and myself sole beneficiaries. That will allow us to sell it but I am not sure how to exchange the money into your currency later on. Just remember that the deadline to claim its ownership is the end of 1946. Maybe you can write to an attorney directly from America and engage him to represent you? Do what you think is right. Talk it over with Jacob, who, I hear, fell on some very hard times.

Now, please let me know something. If I send you some of my poems from the occupation area, would you be able to publish them in some Polish paper? I wrote a lot but most of it got lost. I believe that I will start writing again after our life stabilizes again.

Please, do write your letters in English which I treat as language lessons. I have no other occasions to practice. I correspond with an uncle in English. Point out my errors which will help me to learn the language.

I overheard that it is all over with Sweden but I am not sure whether it's true or not. Most likely you or my uncle in New York can find out for sure. It's being said that presently the best thing to do is to mail an affidavit to Paris. From there a French consul requests specific persons out of Poland to Paris and further on from there. Anyway, I am very grateful to your friend, Morris Singer, for wanting to do something like that. It is absolutely astounding!

Dearest Loniulku! After all, I do feel that you do all that is in your power to get us over there. And if a person wants it really badly it just must happen. We live like on a ship. Awaiting. Impatiently looking for the shoreline.

We kiss you and your sweet children whole heartedly. Warmest greetings and many thanks from me for your Morris and Feliks. I will try to take a photograph of the three of us including Joasia. We named her Leokadia Romualda Joanna.

    Your Ida

8 Sivan, 1948

To whom it may concern:

It is appropriate for the bearer of this letter who is Yakov Zar, he who for a period of one year was the assistant of the conductor of the choir in my community and very often substituted for the teachers in our Talmud Torah (Bible Learning Institute) and distinguished in his talents as a teacher and to my opinion he deserves this post.

    With the Torah blessing,
    Rabbi Chaim Porille

Warszawa, September 29, 1949

My dearest Friend!

Dear Lonius, forgive me, please, that I am responding to you so late. It happens not be caused by my own fault. I was absent from Warszawa for quite a few months. Upon my return I found such a wonderful surprise – 2 letters from you. I am writing back to you immediately and, once again, beg your forgiveness. First of all, I want to thank you all for the holiday greetings. It was so sweet of you to remember, as I must honestly admit, I forgot completely about the holidays due to my work. Unfortunately, Lonius, I never did receive your letter in English. Maybe it was returned to you under my absence. If true, please send it again to me. Dear Loniu, I vacationed in June by Baltic. I had a great time. The sole activities occupying my time were swimming, rowing a boat, fishing, hunting and, mostly, sun tanning. As you can see, a complete repertoire of a vacationist and a loafer. I came back tanned "black" and wonderfully rested. How did you, Lonius, spend your summer? Did you go anywhere? How is yours and your family's health and overall well-being? Everything here, Lonius, is normal. My wife and children feel well. I continue to work in my specialization. Recently, I received a letter from Tolka. You can imagine my total surprise. I exchanged some letters. She sent me some pictures of herself, her husband and children. Any day now, I plan a trip over to visit with them. Also, do imagine that Wawek finally got hitched. He lives and works on the outskirts of Warszawa. We do not see each other too often. I did see your aunt and uncle a few times. Very nice people.

Talking about my work, I will send a copy as soon as it is published with a personal dedication inside. Let it be an expression of my warmth and feeling towards you cherished in the past which continue unchanged to this day. Dearest Lonius, please accept my and my family's warmest wishes of abundance and happiness in the new year. They are, of course, late but coming from deep within my heart. Please, give your husband my regards and kiss all your children from "uncle" Natek. You all have best regards from my wife, Ania. Is there any reason why your husband doesn't write us at all? Do pass my personal greetings especially for him. I await your hasty response and promise not to be the one holding back the response letter in the future.

I hug you warmly as always.

    Your Natan

Translator's note: Letter written in German from Mania's cousin, Katia in Rome, to whom she had sent letters out of the ghetto to mail to Leona in the U.S.

June 18, 1952

My dear Leona!

Your loving card received on May 1, 1952. I have not written in a long time since I am very sad and always lonely. Being alone is the worst, especially if one was used to a family life. But when the loving G-d decides no one can do anything. And so I am getting used to my loneliness. I am happy that you and your loved ones are all well. I had hoped, that Ida could travel overseas. But I see she is still in Lodz. I am sorry I can't read Hebrew, therefore I can't read the book from Pnina Halperin. Next month G-d willing, I will be in Paris. From Motele Wlostowice (?) I have good news. The whole family is doing fine. My health, thank G-d is good. Write me soon my dear, and greetings to your husband. I miss you very much.

    Your,
    Katia

Photo Album

Family gathering before Leona's departure to the United States in May, 1938.
Back row (L to R): **Victor Gora, Anna Hochberg Szachnerowicz, *Ryscenka and *Izaak Szachnerowicz, *Mania Zagraniczna, Jehiel Halperin, Wowek Hochberg** *Second row (L to R):* ***Helena Gold, *Dyna Hochberg Shedlinski, Leona Trachtenberg, *Ruchla Bornstein Hochberg, Paula Halperin, * girl Gold, *Bertha Hochberg Ziberman Gold, *Sarenka Zagraniczna, *Volvek Shedlinski, *Gusia Ziberman, Danuta Gora, *Tamara Zagraniczna, Yossi Shedlinksi.**

*those killed in the war

Leona's great-grandparents, Eleazer and Feige Borenstein, Warsaw, 1820.

Leona's grandmother, Ruchla Lea Bornstein Hochberg.

Leona's grandfather, Woolf Hirsh Hochberg, age 41.

Mania Hochberg and Jacob Zagraniczny on their wedding day, Warsaw, Poland, 1916.

Mania Zagraniczna, 1930's.

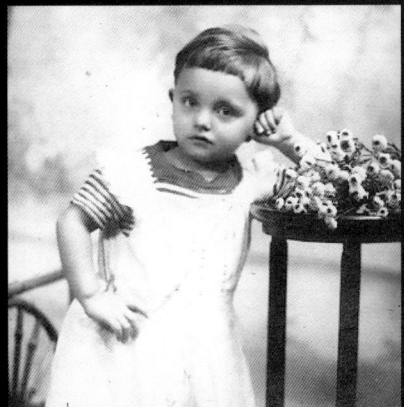
Leona as a little girl.

Tamara, Mania, Leona, and Sarenka in Michalin, Poland, July 11, 1934.

Sarenka and Tamara, Poland, 1936.

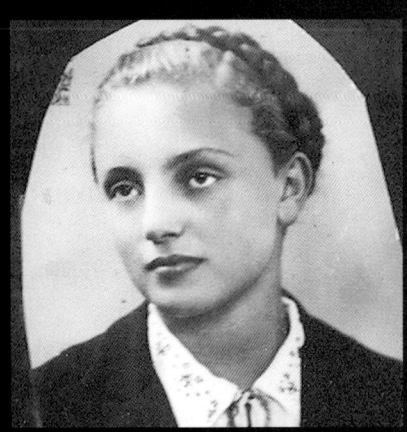
Leona as a young woman.

Leona and her friend, Marie Melamed, walking down a street in Warsaw, 1938. caption here

Leona and her boyfriend, Natek, enjoying a bicycle ride. Back of the photo reads," To stubborn Leona, as a souvenir. Adek", Poland. August 31, 1935.

Tamara, a student at the Warsaw Conservatory of Music, performing at the Hotel Zacheta. Summer, 1939.

Tamara Zagraniczna, sister of Leona, as a young woman 1939.

Fanny and Sam Raizen, cousins of Mania. Leona lived with them and their children Ben, Harold, and Becky (Raizen) Hayutin in Duncan, Oklahoma, 1938.

Leona, Polish "cowgirl" in Duncan, Oklahoma, summer, 1938.

Leona in California on vacation with her American family, while Germany invaded Poland, September, 1939.

Leona and Morris Trachtenberg, before their wedding on December 24, 1939, Oklahoma.

Morris and Leona attending a wedding with Leona wearing her wedding dress, Oklahoma, 1939.

Bertha Hochberg Ziberman Gold, Mania's sister, who died along with all of her children.

Mania's sister, Paula Halperin with her three sons: Dr. Ouzi Ornan, Ouri (Halperin) Shelach, and Dr. Svi Rin, Palestine.

The ship, M.S. Batory, from the Gdynia-America Line, Inc. which brought Leona to the United States.

Leona, on board the M.S. Batory, sailing to the United States, May, 1938.

Leona and her father, Jacob, when they were re-united upon her arrival in New York after a ten year separation, June, 1938.

Tamara, Nathan, Sarenka, Leona's grandmother Ruchla, Ryscenka (daughter of Mania's sister, Anna), and Mania, in Michalin, Poland, June, 1938.

Tamara and child, on a bicycle in Michalin, Poland, summer of 1938.

Sarenka, Nathan, and Tamara, being playful in Michalin, Poland, August, 1938.

Mania Zagraniczna at a ski resort, 1939.

Mania's sister, Dyna Hochberg Shedlinski, with her sons Yossi and Volvek, Warsaw, Poland, 1937.

Victor Gora, his wife, Paula, and their daughters, Basia and Danuta, Warsaw, Poland, October, 1956.

Mania's siblings, Paula Halperin, Victor Gora, and Dr. Anna Meroz, Israel, 1966.

Victor Gora by the tombstone Leona had installed in the Gesia Cemetery in memory of her sister, Tamara, buried there in June, 1941.

Leona, holding her first born child, Leonard, in Seminole, Oklahoma, 1942.

Leona and her children, Lenny, Marcia and Dan, on vacation in Colorado, 1957.

Lenny Trachtenberg, 1965.

The Raizen family, Oklahoma City, 1948.
Back Row (L to R): **Harold, Ben** Front Row: **Fanny, Sam, Becky**

The Raizen family, Oklahoma City, 1948.
Back Row (L to R): **Sam Raizen, Evelyn Trachtenberg (Leona's cousin and sister-in-law), Jack Trachtenberg (Morris's brother), Fanny Raizen, Ruchla Turner (Evelyn's mother and Fanny's sister).**
Front Row: **Larry Trachtenberg, son of Jack and Evelyn**

Morris Trachtenberg, Leona Trachtenberg, Sylvia Trachtenberg, Marcia Trachtenberg, Ellen Trachtenberg, Oklahoma City, 1972.

Lenny Trachtenberg, his son, Randy, and Dan Trachtenberg,, Oklahoma City, 1974.

Wedding of Marcia and Bruce Strongwater, New York City, October, 1977.
(L to R): **Dan, Marcia, Bruce, Ellen, Leona, Sylvia, family friend Mark Shekter, Morris**

Oklahoma City, 1985.
Back Row (L to R): **Ellen Trachtenberg, Evelyn Trachtenberg, Jack Trachtenberg** Front Row (L to R): **Mark, David and Barry Trachtenberg.**

Marcia and Dan with their beloved great-uncle, Victor Gora, Tel Aviv, Israel, April, 1987.

Leona and her aunt, Dr. Anna Meroz, a pediatrician, Tel Aviv, Israel, April, 1987.

Leona and her best friend from Warsaw, Danka Zdunska, and her Uncle Victor (Hochberg) Gora, Tel Aviv, Israel, April, 1987.

Yossi Siedlecki (Leona's cousin), Leona and Morris in Israel for Leona's 50th anniversary of her high school in Warsaw.

Leona (third from left) with some of her high school friends at her 50th high school reunion. best friend, Danka Zdunska, is on her far left, Tel Aviv, Israel, April, 1987.

Leona and Morris at the Bar Mitzvah of their grandson, Barry, Houston, Texas, May 5, 1990.

Wedding of Leona and Morris' grandson, Randy to Yvette Sidon, Denver, 1993.
Back Row (L to R): Bruce Stongwater, David Trachtenberg, Ellen Trachtenberg, Dan Trachtenberg, Randy Trachtenberg, Yvette Trachtenberg, Sylvia Trachtenberg, Leona Trachtenberg, Barry Trachtenberg, Mark Trachtenberg
Front Row (L to R): Marcia Stongwater, Candice Strongwater, Leslie Strongwater.

Wedding of Leona and Morris' grandson,
Mark Trachtenberg to Stefanie Shoss, Houston, Texas, June 7, 1998.
Front row (L to R): *Leslie Strongwater, Candice Strongwater, Barry Trachtenberg, Leona,*
Dan Trachtenberg, Ellen Trachtenberg, David Trachtenberg Back row (L to R): *Bruce Strongwater,*
Marcia Trachtenberg Strongwater, Sylvia Trachtenberg, Yvette Trachtenberg, Randy Trachtenberg

Candice and Leslie Strongwater,
Houston, Texas, April, 2003.

Marcia Strongwater and
Dan Trachtenberg, 2004.

Barry, Mark, Jacob, and David Trachtenberg, Houston, Texas, 2003.

Megan, Taylor, and Brandon Trachtenberg,
Oklahoma City, October, 2004.

Sylvia Trachtenberg and Ellen Trachtenberg with Ava,
Leona's fifth great-grandchild, Houston, July 16, 2005.

Leona's grandchildren and great-children, Oklahoma City, August, 2002.
Back row (L to R): **Taylor Trachtenberg, Barry Trachtenberg, Brandon Trachtenberg, Randy Trachtenberg, Mark Trachtenberg, Jacob Trachtenberg, Stefanie Trachtenberg, Candice Strongwater, David Trachtenberg**
Front row (L to R): **Leslie Strongwater, Megan Trachtenberg**

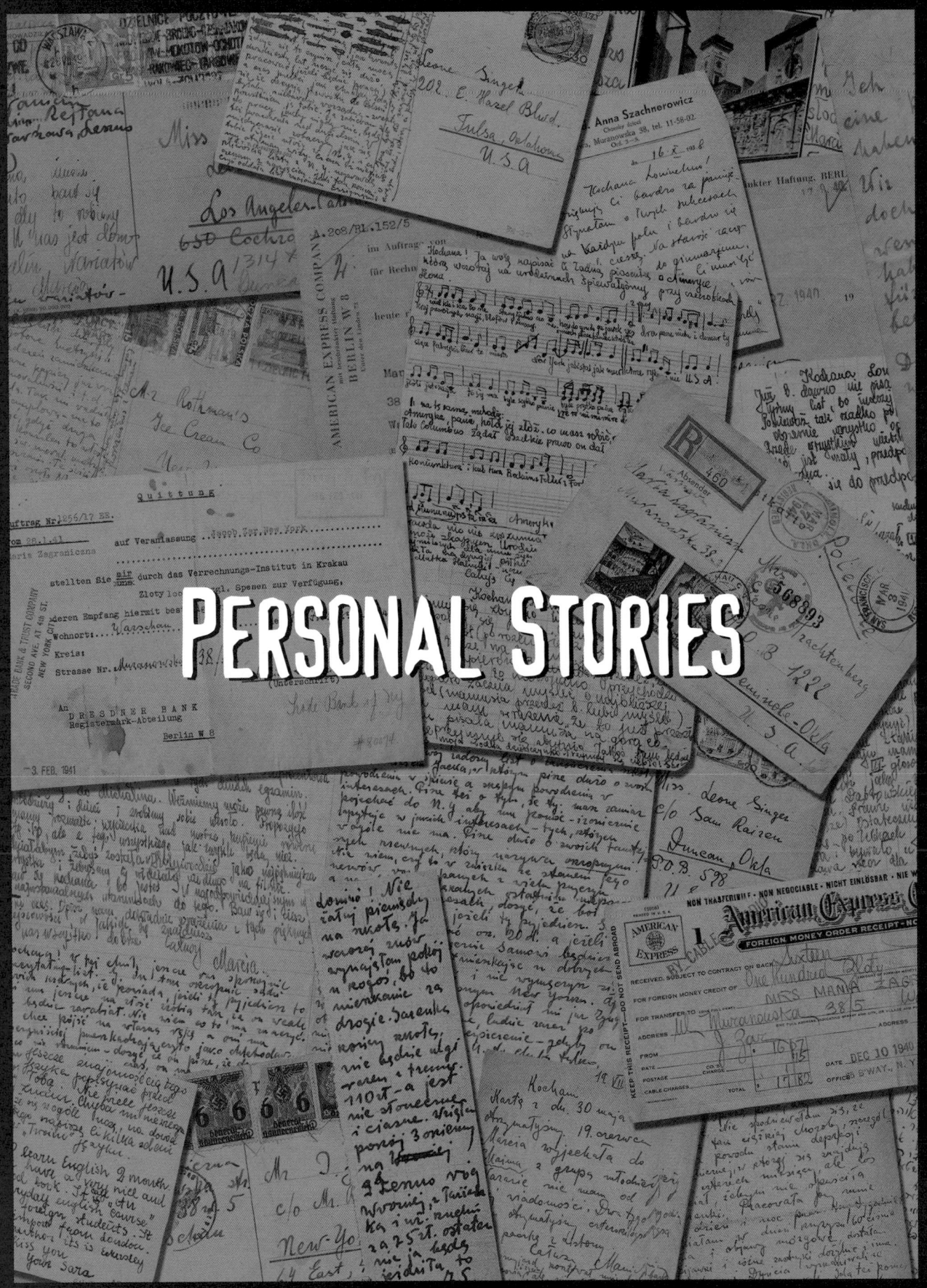
Personal Stories

LEONA'S STORY

Our Forefathers

Marcia, you keep asking me over and over again who you are. Perhaps if I set you straight about your forefathers it may help you in this search for truth.

I shall try to the best of my abilities to put on paper some of my recollections. They may not be one hundred percent accurate. Some will be things which I remember Mother mentioning, others I may remember from my own observations.

I will try to be as objective as I can though I know how easy it is to idealize certain happenings and people from the past. My Mother was born April 13, 1898 in Warsaw, Poland, one of eleven offspring of Ruchla Bornstein Hochberg and her husband, Woolf Hochberg.

Her father whom she worshipped, must have been an unusual man, loving husband, devoted father, and very idealistic man. Unfortunately he died when Mother was only eleven years old, something she could never forget.

In time, when my grandfather was growing up, Jewish children didn't get any formal education besides Hebrew School or "Cheder". Being a very bright young man, he decided to study alone and put himself through grade school, high school, college study and medicine. When he felt that he was ready to show the world what he had accomplished, he went to Geneva, Switzerland and took both oral and written exams and received diploma of doctor of medicine. It really takes a great deal of discipline to be able to study that much alone, no wonder the family was always so proud of his achievements.

However, on the return home, he never set up a regular practice of medicine. He hated to profit by people's suffering and illnesses and he did help some people but gratis only. Later on when he married, he inherited his father's shoe factory so that's how he made his living.

These were years of much unrest in Poland and somehow by mistaken identity he was arrested on political grounds. Anti-Semitism, being as rampant as ever, didn't help to clear his name in time and while waiting for a hearing in jail ("PAWJAK") he caught pneumonia and shortly afterwards died at the age of forty-six. His condition was complicated by the fact that he had pernicious anemia for which there was no cure at that time.

What a nightmare it must have been for my grandmother and her children. Grandma was one of the first liberated women I knew. She was left alone with nine children (two died in early childhood) to support and care for. It was lucky for her that she had profession of a midwife-nurse, well-respected and thought of, so that she could take care of her brood.

Of course, the older children had to help her when they could. As a matter of fact all of them got education, vocation, or profession and became self-sufficient people. The oldest, Motek, I never met as he was forced to run away to Russia, being a journalist with communistic ideas. The same fate met the youngest, Heniek, who followed in the same footsteps. Their children are still alive in Russia but I never met them. Mother's brother, Yacob, I never met either, he was the "black sheep" of the family, a policeman, despised by everyone because of the fact that he married "some ordinary, uneducated shiksa".

Then there was Adam who was so bright, self-educated and obtained a degree of electrical engineering in Geneva, Switzerland. He was eccentric, wrote poetry which was published in the Polish newspapers. His son, Wowek, is still alive in Warsaw, Poland and teaches political science at Warsaw University. He is well-known in his field, published many books and won many special prizes. He was one year younger than I and we used to be very good friends during our childhood and growing up times. However, he is a communist and doesn't want or is afraid to have any contact with any family abroad.

Wiktov was an electrician, very sweet and outgoing fellow, my favorite one. During World War II, he was captain in the Polish Army, changed his name to Witold Gora (Polish) and that's how he survived with his whole family intact. Later on after the war, he went to night school and got degree of electrical engineer. He lives with his wife in Warsaw, will soon be 74 years old. His oldest daughter is a professor of pharmacy at Warsaw University. She married a Greek man when she was almost forty and has a lovely daughter. Basia is about forty-two, never married and has good job (degree in agriculture) and loves to travel. We correspond for years.

Now for Mom's sisters, only the oldest (86 years), Pola, and the youngest, Anna (70 years old) are alive and in Israel.

Bertha was a teacher. She had a sad life, her husband died from TB and left her with one daughter, Gusia. Later she married widower who had grown daughters and she had two children with him. He died soon afterwards leaving her with three children to support. Dyna was so sweet. She was a nurse and her husband deserted her for South America, leaving her with two sons to raise. Yose survived the war and loves also in Israel. Wowek got killed in the war.

Returning to my Grandma, I'll always remember her with loving tenderness. She was very special to me somehow. I loved to visit her in spite of that anaesthetic smell of her nurse's bag and the smell of iodine in her apartment. I remember the Seders we had in her apartment, when all the daughters helped with the cooking and my Dad conducted the services with such precision and singing so beautifully. Walking back home after midnight, hanging on his sleeves half asleep from the wine and the late hour…what pleasant days were these.

How saddened I became when Grandma got sick from a heart attack and was obliged to stay in bed. I used to "baby sit by her" after school. It was sad when she had to retire because until then she had led such an active life. Then she made her home with her daughter, Anna, who in spite of the Jewish quota, was accepted to the medical school because of the fact that her late father had a doctor's degree.

Summers, Grandma always spent with us in our cottage. Everyone loved her because she wasn't old-fashioned like most older women I knew. She kept up with world affairs, with literature, was a free thinker and very intelligent. No wonder Mother grew up such a wonderful person and such a great human being.

Mother married when she was nineteen years old. She fell in love with her then piano teacher who was nine years her senior. They met in what was then the only seminary of Hebrew Kindergarten teachers. It was organized by her oldest sister, Pola, and her husband, Jehiel Halperin. When they decided to leave Poland for Israel in 1913, they sold this seminary to my parents. (In Israel, they began the same type of institution later on.)

Dad was born in then Rowno, Russia in 1888, the son of a cantor well-known for his fine voice and education in Hebrew. (Dad's name was Jacob Zagraniczny). Dad didn't get formal Russian education but received excellent education in Hebrew, Talmud, Gemara, Mishna, etc. He became a teacher of all those subjects but music was his love. When he came to Poland he applied for admission to the conservatory of music and to his pleasure and surprise he was accepted. This was unusual achievement for a young Jewish man.

He studied there nine years taking piano, voice, harmony, composition, counterpoint, etc. This helped him to become music teacher so he earned living by that as well as by teaching Hebrew. Later when Dad and Mom purchased that seminary they added to it Hebrew kindergarten and this way they supported themselves and their three children.

I do vaguely remember the kindergarten days there. I liked especially arts and crafts and singing. The Hebrew somehow didn't appeal to me. I didn't like to concentrate on "abc" so Dad used to get on me. I rebelled and never really mastered that language. The same was with piano lessons. Dad shouldn't have tried to tech me piano. He should have hired a stranger. Of course he couldn't afford one, so it frustrated him because I was musical. Dad was a wonderful story teller, therefore getting ready for bed was fun time. Almost every night he kept us fascinated with his imaginative tales. Til now I never found out if they came from Bible or were the original stories. I know how much we enjoyed them because they were enchanting.

After Dad left Poland in 1928 Mother realized that she couldn't keep the kindergarten so she gave it up and enrolled in Polish Teachers Seminary. Upon receiving a teacher's certificate, she learned that government jobs were still difficult to obtain, unless one had some specialty. That's when she made her mind to apply to the Music Conservatory and she began her musical studies. Only then was she able to get position with the government so that she could support us and keep out of debt.

She became outstanding teacher and was recognized in her field. Radio was rather new I these days and she was often invited to perform with her choir on special occasions. Her students loved her. She was good psychologist. They minded her because she made her classes interesting and fun. She even organized a small orchestra and the whole school was very proud of this achievement.

As to my Dad, he had terrible time in Canada where he first landed after leaving Poland. He wasn't able to get a visa to USA so he finally crossed the border with a false passport, under an assumed name of Jack Zar. That was a big mistake because he had to keep working in New York City for his sister, Sara Rothman, being afraid that he may get deported if someone found out his secret. He didn't like his work, he was out of his element and he never got adjusted to this country. Sara had a candy and ice cream factory.

He dreamed of going back home until he realized that war was inevitable and Hitler meant business, when he wrote Mein Kampf. Not being a citizen he couldn't send for his family so he turned to his cousin, Morris Singer in Tulsa for assistance. Morris knew my Mother well because he visited in Poland twice so he finally agreed to send the affidavit for me. After I was brought here it would be my mission to reunite the family.

I arrived in New York on June 7, 1938. War broke out so soon afterwards with such a fury that my dreams and hopes were ruined unmercifully. Dad didn't become a citizen until after the war, but it was too late for that. He was finally able to leave the ice cream company and become free man not afraid of deportation. When I got married he came to the wedding. He sang the appropriate songs. He was happy about me but yet so upset about the unknown fate of my Mother and the girls.

He visited me twice in Seminole, the last time when Marcia was six months old. He had concealed from me the fact that he had a heart condition or I wouldn't have let him leave me. Soon afterwards he died from a heart attack which struck him on the streets of New York. As soon as I was informed of this I flew there to be at his side for five days. How I hoped that he may pull out of it and that I cold bring him home with me. He was fifty-nine years old and looked ten years younger, but he somehow lost the drive to fight for his life, he died of a "broken heart".

My Childhood

I remember my childhood memories as pleasant ones, but summer time I liked the best. As you know, we lived in Warsaw which was a big metropolis of Poland with over two million population. The summers there were hot, dirty, the cement paved streets oppressive. Everyone who was able, rented a cottage in the country and fled there with his wife and children. Some husbands commuted for the weekend to swim in the river and bask in the sunshine on the sand-covered banks surrounded by the evergreen pine trees. I can still smell that aroma. Other men spent a week or two of their vacation in the cottage reunited with their families.

This kind of lifestyle was rather expensive proposition; one had to pay sizable amount of money in advance for the season. There was additional cost of transportation of one's belongings such as kitchen utensils, beddings, clothing, and small pieces of furniture. All of these items were sent on a day or two ahead, loaded on a large horse-drawn wagon. The family traveled to its destination on trains which often took several hours.

My parents could never afford this luxury so they devised a plan to start a "summer camp" which could provide us all with a summer of fun and healthy activities in the country and began laying plans for the camp.

Dad stayed in the city enrolling his kindergarten students, while Mother and we girls went on to the village to begin preparations and cleaning for summer of fun. Mother was the director, the cook, chief bottle washer, nurse, etc. She did the marketing, planned recreation, worked hard, never complaining. She seemed to thrive on all the goings on, and really enjoyed it a lot.

At times when things would get hectic, she would get some help from some relatives or friends who were always ready to pitch in, in exchange for free room and board in the fresh air. Later on, as the camp became better known somehow it took a form of small family pension. At times parents of some of the children became guests for a few days at a time. When the house would become pretty full my parents hired extra help to help with different activities. We made excursions to other towns, went to carnivals, fishing expeditions, swimming in the river, hunting for wild flowers, berries or mushrooms. At times we played croquet, volleyball or soccer. I remember being a real tomboy, borrowing boys' clothing and playing with them just like I was one myself.

We had little theater programs, sold tickets and invited people from town. I liked to climb fruit trees and stuff my mouth with fresh cherries, apples and pears. On the fence of our villa grew currants and other berries begged to be picked.

What fun it was for us city kids to watch the farmers toil their field, watch wheat, oats and other vegetables to grow and be picked. When it rained which it did sometimes we played checkers or dominoes. Best of all I liked going with Mom to the farmers' market by the depot. It was always very early in the morning on Friday when the selection of fruit, vegetables and poultry was the best. The chickens were sent to the "shochet" for inspection and slaughter, not because we had kosher kitchen but because it was more sanitary and merciful. The farmer woman brought freshly churned butter, sour cream, milk and cottage cheese three times a week. They brought homemade sausages also and the unused items were stored in the cellar.

Mother was inventive and ingenious cook if ever I saw one. No matter how many unexpected guests would sometime show up she always managed to have enough to go around. Actually, the guests of our pension were either people who were friends to start with or they became such soon after arrival. Most of them were so-called "intelligensia" people, interesting teachers, journalists, editors, doctors, etc. We had discussions, singing, mandolin playing, storytelling times, and hikes in the woods. When I think of it now it seems like a beautiful dream which happened a long, long time ago.

When later on, due to existing world circumstances, Dad decided to leave Poland (1928) for USA, it was thought by all of us as temporary arrangement. He planned to return to Poland and to his family and many friends. He had a dream of building his own large villa in the country where he would have a permanent place for a "Summer Camp". In this matter he could save on the big expense of rent and would build a more professional and profitable institution.

He worked very hard sending Mother large enough checks to help with the tuitions for our high schools plus separate money for the building fund. After several years we built that summer villa in Michalin and named it "MILANOWKA" on Rejtana Street.

I remember when we first broke ground. Mom laid the first brick, I the second, followed by my two younger sisters, Sarenka and Marcia. The fifth brick was placed by our Russia friend, Piotr Woronkow, who helped us with the building process. It took long time to finish it, the price of the material kept going up and that slowed us down.

It turned out nice, six rooms, two verandas, red brick house with tin roof. We helped Mom plant grass and several birch trees, flower beds and vegetable gardens in the back. The whole yard was surrounded by pine trees so common in this part of the country, and always smelling delicious. We used this house several summers while renting out the back part. By then, Mother was teaching in public schools and she was too tired to tackle the job of Summer Camp alone. Besides, by then no one had money for summer camp, the clouds of war were slowly gathering on the horizon.

Few close friends who still wanted their children to enjoy a carefree summer in the country would send their kids to us for a few weeks. Marie Melamed (Parreau) was one of them. We were happy to have her and enjoyed her stay a great deal. When we graduated from high school, she left Poland for Belgium to study medicine. I lost contact with her until WWII ended. She was desperate, lost everyone and asked me for help which I gave her. Later on when she married I heard from her again and was so happy for her. We corresponded on and off for years and renewed our friendship when Marcia visited her in Paris in 1968 and the following year when Moish and I visited her there. Since that time her son, Jean-Claude Parreau and later his sister, Jasmine, visited us in USA.

My Sisters

My sisters, Sarenka and Marcia – what can I say about my sisters? Only that they both were lovely girls, wholesome, happy and really beautiful human beings.

Sarenka was three years younger than I but somehow I remember when she was born. It was in June and Mother and I were in the country when one morning she was rushed in a hurry to Warsaw for the delivery. I was left with the landlady which I didn't like much but was promised to see my new baby soon. I do remember seeing my sister and wondered why her eyes were so big like dark cherries.

Sarenka grew up to be a lovely looking creature with large eyes, dark lashes, tiny nose and small mouth. Her hair was brown but her complexion in contrast very fair. She was tall, walked straight and had lovely posture. Her legs were shaped beautifully and her pretty hands had long tapered fingers and nails. She developed the last three years or so weight problem because she had to become a vegetarian on doctor's orders. Mother had always worried she didn't get enough nourishment so she stuffed her with extra food.

Sarenka was sweet, good, bit shy and somewhat reserved. She was musical and had a beautiful soprano voice. We had fun harmonizing with Marcia, accompanying us at the piano. She was always ready to help when something was in need of repair. She was our "handy girl" around the house, could sew, cook, etc.

Sarenka and Marcia were one year apart, so they had many mutual friends. In fact many of their friends were younger sisters and brothers of my girl friends,

Marcia was blond, had large green eyes with dark lashes. Her skin was dark with a bit of golden shade especially during summer. She had cleft chin, high cheekbones, dimples when she smiled. Her figure was perfect, she had good coordination. She was "holy terror", witty, bright, good in school, in sports, fine pianist with absolute pitch, real extrovert. She had great sense of humor. She liked fun, she loved life. The three of us had great relationship. There was never sign of jealousy. We really adored one another and couldn't wait to be reunited in America.

My Jewish Identity

Marcia, dear, you never could understand what caused me to have that ethnocentric feeling, which had bothered you for some time. I shall try to explain as well as I can.

Growing up in Warsaw I suppose had a lot to do with it. We lived in the north part of town, which was the "Jewish" side. Most people I knew were Jewish. From the time I began kindergarten 'til I finished high school I lived segregated life without realizing it. My parents spoke perfect Polish without any "Jewish accent". So did I. My Dad, contrary to many fathers of my friends, wore so-called western clothes, while they were easily identified as Jews by their Kapoles and caps and tzitzes.

The Jews were looked down on, spat on, terrorized by the Poles, called dirty "Yids". The Christian University students from their fraternities, with their fancy caps were no good and they persecuted Jews merciless. Very few Jewish students were ever admitted to the University or Politechnic. If they were they had to be almost genius types. I had never dated boys who weren't Jewish because I didn't know any, in spite of the fact, that I looked more like typical Polish "shikse" than some Christian girls.

The only gentiles I knew were the night watchman to our apartment building or the maid who worked for us and they were never too friendly.

Sometimes during the summer months we came in touch with some Christians from whom we rented a summer house. In the city we shopped in Jewish groceries and supported mostly Jewish establishments, restaurants, etc. As far as I can remember the only good Christian friends were the Woronkows. They were nice and kind people. He helped Mother with building the summer home and his wife did our sewing. Mom's political views were opposite to theirs, but just the same we were on good terms and Mother had opportunity to refresh her Russian while visiting them.

The only other gentiles were again minority there, coming from Germany. We used to rent a summer home from them and we became friendly (in Mrozy).

Their children visited us often in Warsaw in winter and that gave Mom a chance to polish her German. They often stayed with us overnight. Their ages ranged from twenty to thirty.

Of course with her "Hebraist" friends, Mother spoke Hebrew, with Jewish, Jewish. She could switch from one language to another without batting an eye. Something I always admired so – when she talked to peasants she used their slang, returning to school, back to her perfect literary Warsaw Polish.

What kept her sane in the first few years after Dad left was her attending classes at the Warsaw Conservatory of Music. When she walked in that place there was a special aura about it, no doubt. It was almost like some religious experience. She loved it and there listening to music, concerts, choir, she could lose herself and forget everyday tribulations. She was almost as transferred as to another world – a world of music which she loved and of peace which came within these walls.

I remember going to visit her there and later my sister, Marcia, when she was accepted there as a serious piano student. When Mother had become better recognized as a teacher of outstanding abilities, she had applied to the government for a housing project and soon was granted permission to move to a lovely duplex on the edge of the city in the back yard of a Polish school house. We had three rooms, bathroom, and maid's alcove fenced in lovely yard. It had trees, vegetable garden and flowers in the back which was most unusual to be in city limits and not too far from Mother's school and our high school.

It had become favorite place for our friends to meet after school and especially on weekends or holidays. With the first sign of spring everyone came to get a sunbath and we had company constantly.

High School

My high school years I shall always remember with joy. I had lots of good friends, few very special like Marysia and Danka. We had good times, fun in the spring and summer. Our school was small private gymnasium "Landau". We stayed with the same students five years and it made closely knit society and teachers' association. It was girls' school but we had lots of boyfriends from a nearby boys' high school chasing us.

In winter we would meet in the park for skating on the ice on the lake or sledding down the hills covered with snow. We had school dances, attended plays, concerts, movies etc. Made many excursions to different parts of Poland like Danzig, Krakow, Milno, etc. We dated in bunches, meeting boys in coffee houses for pastry and tea. Often we would change out of school uniforms which was not allowed, put fancy hats and veils on and a little make-up and acted so daring, hoping not to get caught.

I was a bit of a tease, and boys liked me and they kept following me. I was kind of naughty but nice girl, absent-minded and very likeable (I was told). I tried not to embarrass Mother due to her position and because I cared for her a great deal. Really all of my friends loved her, often came for advice. She was frank and sincere and just great. My sisters and I were subject of envy of many of our girl friends because of that fact. Few have such a relationship with their mothers and they missed it.

There was never a generation gap between Mom and us and everyone who knew us wondered how we developed that natural trust. I always knew that I was lucky in that respect and hoped that someday in the future I may be able to repeat this with my own children.

Natek was my steady boyfriend for about four years. We had good times together, taking long rides on the ship on the beautiful Vistula River, dancing in the moonlight, drinking seldom anything stronger than orangeade. He was always willing to take me anywhere that I wanted to go, even to an opera though this wasn't exactly his cup of tea. He preferred light musical reviews, comedians and other less intellectual entertainment such as nightclub reviews. I went because I enjoyed dancing. I had good time with him.

During the summer he would spend lots of time close to our summer home. We took hikes, went swimming in the river, boat riding in the lake, dancing to what was called "5 o'clock affairs" at different pensions where we usually meet some of our friends. It was happy and carefree time and I wouldn't let anything too serious spoil my mood.

You may wonder how my friendship with Danka Zdunska has survived all these long years of separation. First of all, a friendship which a person makes during his youth is usually stronger than one made in adult life. From the time we began high school we shared many interests. Also the fact that soon afterwards I began going with her brother, Natek, brought us even closer together. Their parents approved of this friendship and they often invited me to their family gatherings which I always accepted.

I had great admiration for Danka's logical mind and her intellect and I always appreciated her sincerity. She was an excellent student and a genius in math in contrast to me. She was always ready to help me with my school work and took great interest in me. As a matter of fact, if not for her able assistance I may have flunked math and would never have gotten my high school diploma "Matura" which in turn would have prevented me from receiving visa to the U.S.A.

After the war, ever since I had gotten in touch with Danka I tried to show her my appreciation by helping her in varied ways. She knows how I feel about her and she told me many times that she feels closer to me than she does to her two sisters and brother. We have a very special relationship and always will. I suppose the fact that she knew my whole family has a lot to do with it. The reunion in Israel in 1969 has strengthened our bond even more.

The last year of my winter in Warsaw I took an office job for some electrical company on recommendation of my uncle. I hated to do nothing while waiting for my visa. Natek was working and his job took him out of town on trips often so I accepted dates with different people because I wanted to break our relationship off gradually. When it was getting closer to the date of my departure, Natek began to worry and wanted to marry me. I refused, not seeing any sense in such an arrangement. What sort of marriage could that be? Why be tied down to the other when we were so uncertain of the future? I began to seriously doubt my feelings toward him and really didn't break the truth to him until I was sure of it.

Of course this didn't dawn on me until I met Moish. When I first met him, I just knew he was my man and so at once I informed Natek about this fact. The rest you know. I married him and have been living with him happy ever since. We had our differences but in the big things in life we were always one. I care about him more than about myself. He is my friend, my love, father of my children.

He never had to prove his feelings for me with gifts or flowers. I know he loves me and that is all this life is about. I hope he stays well and we may have many more years together. As for our children, we love them each in an individual way because they are three different individuals. We hope we did right thing by them and gave them the right upbringing so they know right from wrong, that they treat people right with no malice to anyone, that they judge them for what kind of human beings they are, not for their material achievements, that they have integrity, walk with justice and treat their fellow human beings like they wanted to be treated themselves. We hope that each one is at peace with himself and in this way he will be in peace with his fellow man. I hope they have good health and good spirits because they go hand in hand.

The Summer of 1936 – Jaremcze

Early this spring, Mother and the principal of her school, Mrs. Lublinerowa, decided to organize a Summer Camp for their friends (mostly teachers) and some young people. This time they rented a large size cottage in south of Poland in the beautiful valley of "Jaremcze" which was surrounded by the "Tatry" Mountains and they made plans for a small camp which turned out beautifully.

First of all they hired some kitchen help so this way they could also have a well-deserved vacation. This was summer before my matriculation from high school, so being week in math I got a tutor twice a week and worked hard at my studies. The rest of the time I had carefree time and together with my girl friends we had a ball.

There was mountain hiking, mushroom and raspberry picking, swimming in the river and dancing at nearby pensions every afternoon at 5 o'clock. Jaremcze was a resort town, full of tourists from all over Poland. I remember my boyfriend Natek, was in one of the pensions for few weeks and he took me to all their activities. After he was gone there were other fellows whom I happened to know from Warsaw and some I met there.

We planned attendance at mountain festivals and fairs which were most interesting and enjoyable. These peasants wore such colorful costumes, they danced their heels high up. They had displays of their handiwork, women's beautiful embroidery and men's lovely handtooled articles and whittled wooden objects. I remember being fascinated by their speech, which had that musical twang to it.

Every county in Warsaw had its own national costume. They all were a little different but very colorful with ribbons and beads streaming on the women's necks and shoulders. These peasants dressed that way only on Sunday, for holidays, church processions and festivals. They were in general simple people with very little education, very religious devout Catholics like most of the Poles. None of them like Jews, because that's what they were taught by the priests from childhood. They didn't bother us, all they knew that we were tourists from Warsaw and talked better Polish than they.

This valley of Jaremcze was really most beautiful place. It sort of reminds me of Jackson Hole in Wyoming. We could hear at nighttime, small rocks falling from the mountain tops straight to the river bottom. The water was clear as spring water and it had such a brisk flow. It was very cold and foamy at times and it was fun to swim there and frolic. Our cottage was just in front of it, we often bathed there, washed hair and had picnic lunches.

Evenings, a bunch of us would meet at the depot platform. It was a "drag walk" where we walked there and back many times, meeting old friends and making new ones. That's where the "action" was. Boys teasing girls, flirting, joking, and maybe going for a ride on a horse-driven carriage for a while.

Yes, this was a good summer, carefree and fun. I made up my mind then not to think about future but enjoy each day as it came. I am glad I did because in spite of everything that happened in later years I shall always remember it as most enjoyable summer.

Epilog

Reminiscence of my arrival to USA, my voyage which took ten days on the Polish ship, Batory, was a most pleasant experience. Dad provided me with best accommodations, tourist class. I enjoyed myself very much, met some interesting people, liked the food and other activities, movies, dancing. Went to the library when I felt like it, wrote there "thank you" notes to friends and sent post cards home everyday.

There was a kosher section for people who wanted it, but I and the other young people sat together. They both were Jewish, but not observant like me. They each left their mates home, hoping to send for them.

I was lucky not to get seasick like many people on the ship, so I really had fun. There was a well-known polish hero from the air force, a flyer, on board and when he asked me to dance at dinner time, I was really nervous (I wore my first long evening dress). When my sisters heard later on that I danced with him they were so excited. They knew he was on the boat because they read it in the paper. He told me how beautiful I was. In fact, he pointed to some German girls there and said, "Look how fat and vulgar they are". He hated their guts and said Warsaw women were the prettiest from any women in the world, and I was good example of this fact. Ha ha. If I had had the nerve I would have told him, yes, but I am of the Jewish faith. I hated to make a scene at the dance floor. His name was plastered all over the papers for some specific flight. His name, I believe, was Skarzynski.

We stopped in Copenhagen, Denmark and went sightseeing there. It was my first time abroad. I enjoyed every minute of it. Our ship arrived in New York City on June 7, 1938. My Dad, all dressed up in a suit and tie, came to meet me together with his nephew, Jack Rothman. Dad hadn't seen me in ten years, but he recognized me at once. Just as I did. How touched he was. What a reunion! He couldn't get over my change. I was just a ten year old tomboy with bangs and buster haircut and I had become "all of a sudden" a young lady. He took me to all the relatives to show me off and to his pleasure, I made a great hit with them. They thought I looked like a beautiful Polish "shiksa" and they approved the way I dressed, like a big city girl, not like a "greene" (which was Jewish description for newly arrived emigrants from "shtetel", small village in Europe).

Dad hadn't changed much, his hair had touch of gray and he gained few pounds. We took a photo together to send to mother and the girls and they were so glad to have it.

I remained in New York two weeks, staying with the Bornsteins because Dad had just a bedroom in someone's apartment. While I was there I saw quite a bit of the city, was impressed with all of the skyscrapers and visited the highest one to get a bird's view of that big city. I went to the NYC Library which I thought a fascinating place, to the zoo, aquarium, etc. Since we had relatives on both sides of the family I got to do lots of visiting in different parts of this big city. I really had fun, but Morris Singer was anxious to see me so he wired me and wrote asking me to come already to Oklahoma. Finally,

Dad took me to Penn. Central Station and I was on my way to unknown fate, to land of cowboys, Indians and oil wells.

When I first came to Oklahoma City, no one greeted me with more concern and friendship than my cousin, Evelyn Trachtenberg. She was really instrumental in my decision to accept the Raizen's invitation to stay with them in Duncan. Before I even had a chance to meet them she told me of their generosity and sincerity so it was easy for me to accept their kind offer. Evelyn and Jack were very nice to me from the beginning. They often invited me to their cozy duplex and made me always feel at home. Later when they heard Moish and I were getting serious they were very pleased, especially Evelyn because now we were going to become relatives second time around. She helped me with all my shopping and we had great times together. When the Raizens began to make preparations for the wedding they had previous experience because Evelyn and Jack were married in their home five years before.

Evelyn and her mother pitched in with all the arrangements. They helped with cooking, making gefilte fish and their famous "strudel".

In time when Lenny was born, Aunt Evie came to Seminole to help Dad with the "Bris" and she did the same when Danny came. When in later years time came for the "Bar Mitzvahs" she was again first to offer helping hand. I will always be grateful to her for her support in time of joy as well as in time of illness and sorrow.

As for her mother, I learned to love her soon after I met her, which came easily. She was a gentle and sweet creature and so was her husband. No doubt your children remember them with affection.

The first summer visiting in Morris Singer's home was most difficult. I was new there and everything seemed strange. Their lifestyle didn't appeal to me at all. They really didn't have normal home life. They treated me well and were hospitable but I guess I was just homesick even if I tried to conceal it. Addie and I just didn't hit it off from the start. She tolerated my presence, which I resented. I could tell she wasn't happy at home and couldn't wait till she goes back to college. Somehow she always managed to make me feel ill at ease. I am not sure if it was intentional but I wasn't used to this kind of treatment.

I was confused, didn't know should I go back to New York and try to make a home for Dad 'til Mother and the girls will join us. When I met Moish, about whom I heard many nice things from my cousin Evelyn T., my decision became more complicated. I liked him because he was more serious than the boys I met that summer, not so overbearing, more interesting, had that continental charm and was very appealing. If I would go to NY I may never have a chance to get to know him better.

The Sam Raizens came to my rescue. They invited me to spend the winter with them. They opened their lovely home to me and I accepted it. They were the best-natured people I ever met, they treated me like a daughter and so did their lovely children. They became my second family and their home became my second home.

I enrolled in Duncan High School to learn English better and I enjoyed this experience no end. The following summer they invited me to join them on a two month vacation trip to California which I will always remember with pleasure and gratitude. Returning home from summer's fun, we heard on the radio news the terrible message that Germany invaded Poland. To describe my feelings then would be impossible…all my dreams went up the chimney. I worried about my family all the time. Talking about depression – I had it, naturally. If not for Fannie's understanding and moral support I would go mad.

Dad wrote me that if I wanted to go to O.U. he would send me money for tuition, books, lodging, so I enrolled there. I tried not to think if home. I accepted dates but my mind wasn't on studying or other school activities. When M. T. (Morris Trachtenberg) came back from Wichita, Kansas where he worked for the Singers and settled in Seminole, he called me and we began dating. Being with him helped me to bear under the pressure and when he asked me to marry him I didn't hesitate a minute.

We were married December 24, 1939, in the home of the Raizens. I shall always be grateful to them for their help, their love and devotion. They all made me feel so welcome.

Dad attended the wedding and "gave me away". He sang under the "chuppa" and it helped to have him there at least since Mom and the girls couldn't be with us.

Just for the record you may like to have the following information:

LENNY – was named after his paternal grandfather, Leib Trachtenberg and maternal great-grandfather, Woolf Hochberg. His godfather was cousin Sam Raizen and his godmother was cousin Ruchel Turner.

DANNY – second name Stephen meant to be for my sister Sarenka. His godfather was cousin Morris Singer and his godmother May Singer.

MARCIA – was named for my mother Mania (Miriam in Hebrew) and for my youngest sister, Tamara whom we called Marcia for short. Her godmother is cousin Fannie Raizen and she is sort of adopted grandma to all three of you.

* Written in 1974.

Anna Meroz's Story

How the most awful war started for me…

It was a warm September night. September 1, 1939. During my sleep I heard a noise. I was lying on the couch beside my husband, Isaac. The noise kept getting louder. What could it be? Like…the noise of the sea.

When we were college students, my husband and I traveled to an academic retreat in Karwa. On the first day my friends took me by the hand, told me to close my eyes and led me to what turned out to be the coast of the Baltic Sea. "When you hear the roar, open your eyes, you will be standing at the edge of the sea." This was exactly the noise I was now hearing.

Slowly and quietly, so as to not wake my husband or my mother, who was sleeping in the next room, I slid off the couch and approached the window. Darkness. Only the moon lit up the streets of what would later become the ghetto. The noise became clearer and gradually I realized that it was not the sound of the sea, but the steady steps of thousands of soldiers. They were already beneath my window. Green uniforms, with eagles on their hats. They marched in groups of six. One, two, one, two, left right, left right. Terror gripped my throat. In my mind it all started to make sense. I recalled the slogans that had recently appeared on walls in Warsaw: "Away with the Germans! Let Poland live", "We will not return anything", "Citizen beware! Spies are listening", "In Warsaw we have a fifth column".

So we were at war! They were moving towards the Gdansk railroad station. Who among them would return? Today courage was no longer important. Machines were doing the fighting! Yesterday my dear brother Witold came over to say goodbye to mother. "I'm going to war! Who knows, maybe after the war we will meet as two pieces of soap on the shelf at Maida's!" It seemed like a macabre joke, but people were already saying that the Germans were melting human fat for soap production. I crept back into bed silently. It was good that they did not hear this march of death.

Shortly thereafter, the signs of war were everywhere. The lines at the grocery stores kept getting longer. Mothers tried to get their hands on milk powder. Flour and rice were disappearing from the shelves. Groups of people started to gather on street corners asking each other about the latest news of the war. The radio was playing war marches. Marshal Rydz-Smigly was calling on people to act calmly. "Don't panic, don't hoard food. Poland is ready." Every day however he delivered distressing news.

Mothers were notified that their sons had died on the battle field, honorably defending their country. Each day it became clearer that Hitler's great war machine was brutally trampling over Poland's territory. Then came Umiastowski's orders: "Citizens capable of using weapons should escape to the east. The enemy is approaching the walls of the capital." Modlin fell.

Thousands of people with packages in their hands left their possessions behind and escaped across the green border to the east. Apparently a new army was being created in the east. Soldiers left their units. People were killed by bombs dropped from German airplanes. The government was escaping to the south, over the Romanian border.

I sat up all night talking to Isaac. I begged him to escape. They won't touch women; they can't mistreat a small child and an old mother. "You want to get rid of me! Are you crazy! Either we go together, or we stay here together." He could not be persuaded. In the morning I found my mother in tears. She had overheard our conversation from the next room and was convinced that we would escape to the east without her. I had never seen my mother cry, even when her own son came to say goodbye before going off to war. Now she was crying. We all stayed.

You could already hear it in the distance, like an approaching storm. Then it drew closer and became clearer. The cellars at 38 Muranowska Street, like all the other cellars, were cleared out on the orders of the Air Defense Department. We would have to seek shelter in the cellars if the alarm was sounded.

The bombing started in Warsaw. The noise tore the air apart. We bowed our heads because it seemed that the ceiling was about to fall down on us at any moment. Houses started to burn. Even though it was September, there was not a single drop of rain to douse the fire. People cracked their knuckles; they said that Hitler had made a pact with the devil. The wind howled through the capital, carrying the fire from one house to another. The city had no fire department anymore. The fires turned night into day. Tall buildings fell like a child's building blocks. We ran to the cellar. Isaac held me and shouted: "This is not war, this is torture". Rysienka, who on the first day of the war sat down on her little chair and started to cut out paper angels, finished off her work in the cellar. She gave everyone an angel. "Take care of this angel, mother, it will save you from the German bombs". And it did. Later, when she was no longer there, I would wake up from a dream and shout wildly, why did she give me that angel?

The cellar was humid. My daughter wanted to return to her room, to see the shelves on which Miss Henia had created scenes of the four seasons. The first shelf represented spring. Colorful flowers, green grass, birds. Oh, what golden hands Miss Henia had. The little one also helped to cut out those flowers. At the bottom was winter, with snow, a Christmas tree and Santa Claus with his presents. Rysienka looked at mother, at grandmother, she tried to read their faces, she wished that the good old days would return, but in her mother's eyes she read fear, and in her grandmother's eyes a silent, stony tranquility, a tranquility that cast shadows that gathered together in the little heart of a child and created a deep sadness.

Daddy's patients came to the cellar. "Doctor, save me! My husband is in the army and I have four children at home. What shall I do about this pregnancy?" Isaac did not pay any attention to our protests: "Don't go upstairs, a bomb will kill you!" "I am a doctor, my duty is to save these unfortunate women." Between one bombardment and the next he would rush upstairs to get the instruments ready. Some explained that they had no money. But money was not important. The important thing was to save lives. They kissed his hand. "He's not a doctor, he's an angel." They blessed the child: "May the Lord protect you because you have such a wonderful father."

There was hardly a house left on Muranowska Street that had not been burned down. The nights were especially hard. We could not even leave the cellar to cook something. We decided to leave Muranowska Street and, taking some food with us, we left for Czacki Street where a good friend of Isaac's lived, Dr. Szwarc. On our way we saw many people who, like us, thought that things might be better in a different neighborhood. They went to their friends, only to die in the rubble.

We had only been at Dr. Szwarc's home for a few hours when a horrible air raid forced us to seek shelter elsewhere. The six-story building was struck by a bomb. Dr. Szwarc, in a panic, left a suitcase full of valuables, his entire fortune, in the house. He ran back to get the suitcase but he was killed in front of his apartment by a beam that fell through the ceiling and struck him in the head. We waited in vain for Dr. Szwarc to return. Suddenly the cellar turned as black as night. A loud noise filled the air. A second bomb had fallen on our building. Beams started to fall. The dust was unbearable. All six stores could collapse at any time. People started to run out of the cellar in the one direction where a little light could be seen. Rysienka was in her father's arms, she was almost unconscious. Isaac ran with the others towards the stairs, and from there to the store above the cellar. I could not see Stasia. I jumped out of the store window and pushed my mother in front of me.

A wild, hoarse voice escaped from my throat: "Where is the child?" At that moment Isaac threw my daughter whom I caught in my arms. She had changed so much she was unrecognizable. Her beautiful long blonde braids had come undone. They were full of rubble and ashes, dirty, gray and tangled. Her face was as white as a sheet of paper and her large pensive eyes grew even bigger in silent awe as she looked in front of her. The whole of Czacki Street was in flames. There was not a single home that was not engulfed by fire. The air was filled with the stench of burned flesh and poisonous gas. Breathing was almost impossible. We ran across the street and stood beneath the arched entrance at No. 1. The eight-story building had disappeared from the face of the earth. My daughter nestled into my dress, her whole body trembling. We could not see Stasia. Every so often the noise of an engine could be heard before a bomb was dropped. "Mother," asked Rysienka "is that an airplane?" "No, those are wasps" said Isaac. I smiled through my tears. I hugged the trembling child and tried my best to calm her down. Once again the air was shaken by falling bombs. Rysienka twitched and cried: "I don't want to die. I want to grow up to be a lady. I want to have a mother, father, grandma and Stasia!" The people around her began to cry when they heard the lament of an innocent child.

In the breaks between one bomb and the next people raided the store and took loaves of bread, butter, sugar, whatever they could find. They ripped the flesh from a horse that had been killed just a few minutes earlier. Rysienka could not bear to watch this. She turned her head away: "Such a poor horse!" She had always been sensitive to the suffering of animals. She also loved nature. At that moment, when we faced a constant threat of death, I thought back to certain Sunday afternoons in April. I would take walks with her. She saw a flowerbed with primrose buds on Bielanska Street, near the Bank of Poland. Her blue eyes, covered by the dark curtains of her long eye lashes, brightened. A smile bloomed on her face, "Look Mommy, spring is coming, the flowers are blossoming and soon the birds will return from the warm countries and will sing to us! I'm so happy!" And she was barely four years old!

One time Stasia came running in, terrified and restless. We started to run away from Czacki Street which was entirely on fire. We reached Mazowiecka Street through openings that had been made in the walls between houses during the war. The walls seemed strong to us and here, in the front hall on the first floor, we spent the night. When the horrible noise of the bombs began in the morning, Rysienka laid her head on her grandmother's knees and waited with resignation for death. She had no more tears. Her eyes were dry; her lips tasted bitter. Although she hadn't eaten for three days, she no longer asked for anything. She would be woken by the moans of the wounded, which Isaac tended to. Unfortunately we found out that we had come to a house that was requisitioned by the army. One of the many soldiers smiled at my daughter when he saw her poor face and said: "Don't be afraid little one; we won't give you up to the Krauts." Then he placed a chocolate bar in her hands. The others followed his example and soon Rysienka didn't have enough hands to carry all the sweets and chocolates. We only had flasks of water because all of our supplies were left behind in the rubble on Czacki Street. In the morning they chased all of the civilians out of the house on Mazowiecka Street and the five of us started our journey again through the burning capital.

We were looking for shelter. Many people were walking here and there, looking for shelter. We held each other's hand. From time to time Isaac would take the child in his arms. Meanwhile, Stasia and I dragged mother along because she no longer had the strength to walk on her own. The smoke hurt our eyes. The tram lines became obstacles. Glass breaking beneath our feet made a sound like the screams of injured people. People fell down before our eyes and others trampled over the dead as they fled from the bombings. The little one closed her eyes; she did not want to see all of this. She let us lead her blindly. We dragged my mother and daughter in turns, because any delay could result in death or permanent injury. We stopped to take shelter in the entrances of apartment buildings, if they were still standing, trying to protect ourselves from shrapnel. Where should we go? Where should we hide? Maybe in the hospital on Czyste Street, where Izaac used to work? But will they let everybody in? Anyway, it is too far away. Or maybe the Berson and Bauman Hospital where I worked? The road was covered with ruins and ashes. On Grzybowska Street the Church of All Saints lay like an injured giant with fiery flames carrying his lament to God: "Look, I was not spared." Is the children's hospital still there? People say it's a safe place, but they are not letting anyone in.

Three days, since we had left the house on Muranowska Street. Suddenly another trrrach! The crowd shoved us into the gate, where the destroyed pillars were looming. Suddenly something pulled, jerked Rysienka, causing her to nearly fall down.

It was Stasia, falling and still holding Rysienka by the hand. But Isaacs's strength was visibly greater, because he snatched her away from Stasia's hand and then she was found together with us in the gateway. "Stasia, Stasia," shouted Rysienka, "Where are you?" Stasia is gone. A thought like a dagger penetrates her consciousness. Stasia was killed! She has already seen so many corpses on the way. An hour ago on Krolewska Street she had stepped on a dead little boy's leg, who was wearing dark blue velvet clothing. She did not see his face, for he was lying face down, with arms outstretched as if he was hugging the stone. This was near the Saski Garden. At the shelter on Czacki Street that lady in an old grey costume, who jumped after father from the window, but on the road something fell behind her and Rysienka soon after saw her dead on the street. Farther and farther, we walked in the hopes of reaching Sienna Street. The air raid had ended. I walked out of the gateway. Stasia is lying on the street, her eyes are open. "Get up Stasia, we're going to the hospital," the child cries out, "quicker, quicker." She kneels by Stasia and kisses her cheek, but runs away with a fearful shriek. Stasia is dead! Isaac feels for her heartbeat. "She is dead", he announces. Rysienka wants to say something but her voice dies in her throat. Suddenly – bzzzzz. Once again we seek shelter at some gateway. My daughter constantly repeating: "Stasia, Stasia, Stasia…" She hung her head and started to fall asleep on my shoulders. In her dreams she sees her father burning, his shirt is already burning. Everyone is running to help. Rysienka brings a cup of water. No one can put the fire out. "Daddy!" she cries hysterically, daddy's face changes into Stasia's. Stasia's face becomes bigger and bigger, her eyes full of horror, until the child wakes up screaming…in the hospital.

In the dark basement bags of sand are on the windowsills. On the floor there are straw mattresses one next to another. Rysienka and I are work personnel; we are allowed to eat in the hospital. I steal two plates of rice from the kitchen. "Eat it quickly, so that the nuns won't see." My daughter is talking with the son of doctor Minc, Jurek. "What kind of orders are these in a hospital?! I will not eat rice with sugar again." I tell them, "Eat, eat." If only this could last us throughout the war!

The Berson and Bauman Hospital is no longer a pediatric hospital. Everywhere, in the hallways, the offices, in the laboratory grown-ups are lying stretched out, taken from under the rubble. At a glance of a white coat they shout, "Help, it's been three days since I've had any water!"

The hospital is short on doctors. Izaac was accepted to work. His mood changed immediately. The little one does not want to hear what her parents are talking about. What does amputation mean? A sixteen year old girl has gangrene in both of her legs. There is no other way, we will have to amputate! Rysienka thinks to herself, that she too will be a doctor when she grows up. But no! Better to be a nurse. The hats the nurses wear are so pretty!

How good it is to not be able to hear the bombarding! At 5 AM the hospitals director's phone rings in the basement. "They have hit the water pipes! The hospital is without running water!" Doctor Braude-Hellerowa grasps his head. "Terrible!" But we put up a gigantic flag with a red cross! We are operating without washing our hands! Who survives, will survive! There is nothing to sterilize our equipment with. The doctors are shuffling around as if they are unconscious. They work in a trance. The whole building is filled with the smell of pus and rotting flesh. Rysienka cannot understand how the beautiful world so suddenly became such a living hell. Not too long ago Miss Henia sewed for her a little goat's costume and she was a real artist on a real stage. She was the youngest goat. Mother goat went out and forbade her children to open the door to anyone. But the wolf came and opened the door, and the little goats ran away in every direction. Mother goat returns home, she desperately looks for her children and that is when Rysienka, the youngest goat, jumps out and says, "Mother, I'm alive and the others too!" How many times afterwards have I dreamt of her words and woken up crying, realizing that I will never see her golden smile neither hear those words.

Suddenly everything went quiet. The silence hurt our ears. Warsaw has surrendered! What we did not know, was that the most terrible war was just only starting. Let anything happen, only no more bombarding! For a long time we still bent our heads forward, as if the ceiling were to fall upon us.

We still did not know what Oswiecim, Treblinka, Palmiry and Brzezinka were. We did not know that the Germans would shoot at children who were thrown out of a burning house by their own mothers. That they will drown newborn babies in buckets of water like cats. This was still all before of us. It all started when Hitler's armies marched onto the streets of Warsaw.

They decreed that all windows were to remain closed. Soon we were ordered to wear a Star of David. It was now that the most horrid war commenced.

From the Hospital to the Palmiry

Friday, January 14, 1940. We were sitting at the table, my mother, my seven-year old daughter and I. "Why aren't they letting Daddy come home for the night?" Rysienka asks. It is so lonely without him! She did not know about the recent typhus epidemic and the doctors on duty had to stay in the hospital for three weeks without returning home to their families. I had just returned from that three-week duty at the children's hospital (Berson and Bauman on Sliska Street) and my husband, a gynecologist, went on duty to the hospital on Czyste Street. "And Mommy," she went on, "why can I see so many German soldiers through the window, and why are the people afraid of them?"

A soldier's silhouette was imprinted in Rysienkas mind as a symbol of kindness and honor.

She remembered how during the bombarding of Warsaw a Polish soldier with an eagle on his hat came up to her and handed her a bar of chocolate. She did not have time to enjoy it before a second, third and fourth gave her more sweets until Rysienka ran out of hands to carry all this chocolate and candy. It is impossible that a soldier would want to kill children!

But she had also heard, that a few days ago the Germans came and asked for the neighbor's son, and when they answered that he is taking a bath, they entered the bathroom and shot him, and the mother upon seeing her son dead, went to the fifth floor and jumped out of the window. The day after, they came to say that it was a mistake.

The doorbell rang. I opened the door. Two metallic helmets, two pairs of wicked German eyes. "Wir haben einen Auftrag an Ihren Mann." For many years I had thought, what this "Auftrag" meant. Apparently they had instructed Czerniakow, president of the Jewish Commune Council, to hand over a list of doctors, and the Germans at random took every fifth and Isaac must have been one of them.

With satisfaction I replied, "My husband is not at home." "Where is he?" During this time they plundered the whole house. They searched through every room, the restroom, even looked under the table. They opened the cabinet and cupboard. My daughter who stood up when they greeted and nicely said, "Good evening." (She was told beforehand that she was not allowed to shout or cry, if an incident of this kind were to happen, because they could shoot.) Now she looked frightened, as they took out the new table cloths, bedding, the beautiful, big crystal, the wedding present from our parents, and many other things. "But those are Mommy's and Daddy's, why are they taking them?" We did not dare to open our lips. "My husband is in the hospital," I blurted. "Which one?" the dry question followed. "It is an isolated hospital. There hangs a gigantic sign, 'Seuchengebiet'." I knew that the Germans are terrified of typhus, although they claimed that only Poles and Jews are diagnosed with typhus, which is carried by infected fleas, never the Germans. "What is the name of this hospital?" the German blurted out with anger. Fear had taken its toll. "Czyste Street" I choked. They left.

A look of lightening came upon my mother's face. "Why did you betray Isaac's location?" she screamed. "They'll go, take him and kill him. He is dearer to me than a son. Remember, after my cataract operation he would come everyday from the gynecological department to the eye section. How he would sit next to my bed and feed me with a spoon, like you feed a child, as to not infect the eye. The sick would ask me if he was my son. Or at home when my nimble would fall, he was able to run from the fourth room. Sorry, Mrs. Hochberg I didn't make it on time." I laughed at her somber thoughts. "You talk of him as if he were already dead!" I went on Wilcza Street to buy some buttons for my new dress. Mother did not sleep. She did not eat or drink.

On Wednesday I prepared a package of food, because it was known that hunger prevailed in the hospital. What they did not have! Mother fried calf's cutlets; I took sandwiched with ham and Swiss cheese, a jar of sour cherry compote and headed for Czyste Street. I was happy, if there was still food to buy in the ghetto, my Isaac will not go hungry. The journey from Muranowska Street to Czyste was not easy an easy one. The tram lines were destroyed. The broken glass was still everywhere. Overturned trams lay on the streets in many areas of the city. The telephones were still not in service. Warsaw still has not recovered after the three-week-long air raid.

Right before the hospital I went into a shop and bought half a kilo of halvah, which Isaac likes. Loaded with these wonderful things and in the best mood I entered the hospital.

The first person I ran into at the hospital was the midwife who worked with Isaac in the same department. When she saw me, she turned pale like death. "Can I see Doctor Szachnerowicz?" She was speechless. She wasn't in a state to say a word. "Doctor Szachnerowicz? Doctor Szachnerowicz?" The package fell out of my hands. "Four days ago…" she lost balance and fainted. I understood. Mother was right. His friends assembled. My friend Jadwiga, a gynecologist as well, ran up to me. She handed me a pocket knife, a watch and a wedding ring. "Give this back to Anna, I don't know if I will return, and she had begged me to run away to the south. I did not want to leave her alone. Send her my love." I stood there like a stone. I could not even cry. Why him, such a dear husband and father? What will I tell mother? What about my daughter? I sent out the malefactors myself! Oh my God!

My friends assembled. That day ten doctors were taken from the hospital. Among them doctor Bern from the department of surgery and Doctor Rakower from the department of internal diseases. Isaac was conducting a C-section, when they came. "We are not barbarians, let him finish." His friend Kon gave him his warm pants and shirt. "Take this my friend, we have such frost. Be warm at least!" The words stabbed me in the heart like a dagger. The wedding ring burned my fingers. I rode over to the prison. January 19, it is very cold. The prison was surrounded by many women, each one with fear in her eyes and a package in her hand. I gathered up my courage and asked, "Excuse me sir, within the last few days they brought my husband here, Doctor Szachnerowicz? Please sir, I am worried about him. They took him straight from the hospital, he was operating on a patient." The worker was Polish; you could tell he pitied me. "I'm sorry Ma'am, in the last few days they have not brought anyone in. People are disappearing; you hear a lot of things. I cannot speak for long, the Germans are watching."

How can I go back home? Fear had silenced me. "People are disappearing," he had said. I will never see Isaac again! Why did I tell them the truth? I wished to die. I had potassium cyanide, but how could I leave my old mother and small child? At one point I thought of poisoning them both and myself. I stood in front of the prison.

No, I will not go home. I will not look into mother's eyes. I sent the malefactors myself. I did not feel my hands swell from the cold. I will not tell Rysienka the truth, let her be deluded!

I stood in front of the prison for a long time. The tears froze my face. Slowly the women disappeared, the suffering of a tragedy apparent on their faces.

At seven in the morning I took my doctoral briefcase and went on Powazki to give people shots against typhus. These were the new orders; Jewish doctors were to be registered to give shots to the Polish population. Izaac rebelled. "I will not be ordered around by Germans." But he assisted me unofficially. "So the doctor will not be assisting today?" These words wounded my heart. Walking on the street, a grown woman, a serious doctor, I was walking on the street and crying. The devil, I cannot find a tissue for my nose. People are staring at me. Maybe the director of the factory, volksdeutch (Germans abroad), can advise me? Lately I have been giving shots to his workers. I should try!

Then we found out that same day, 14th or 15th of January, the intelligentsia was executed: 200 Jews and 600 Poles. This was the Germans' revenge for the radio broadcasting-receiving found in the basement on Wilcza Street.

Home was like hell. It is cold and there is no more coal. My daughter is sick. Isaac was resourceful with everything. Mother wore a black dress, as a sign of mourning for Isaac. She walked back and forth at home like a qualm of conscience.

During opening hours from five till seven, crying, the patients are losing control.

"What? They took the doctor away? What for? He saved us during the air raid on Warsaw. He always helped, golden hands, golden heart. Why?" I pressed my lips together. I want to cry, but there are mothers with their children that have come to see me to be cured at the hospital. I am off the three-week shift due to my child's illness.

For a long time we told ourselves that we had not lost everything. All of us, wives of doctors who had been taken away, would meet together to give each other advice about what to do. Frauds would come along and take our money. Someone saw Isaac alive, working in a coal mine, others saw him in France, and in Bergen-Belsen. We wanted to believe, we were willing to pay any price to hear one word from our loved ones. In the end we had to believe that there was no hope left. What had that man said at Mokotowska? People are disappearing without a trace.

After that, others began to vanish. Rysienka disappeared, mother vanished, my sisters, my brother, and their families. Our senses were becoming dull. The ravages of the war took away everything and left nothing behind, not even a flicker of hope.

How my sister Maria died.

Memories of my mother.

I see her to this day, my Mother, a quiet heroine, a grand ghost. A mother, who was pregnant with me, the tenth child, at the age of forty, she allowed her dear husband to leave the house, children, factory, to go study medicine in Zurich. He had dreamed of becoming a doctor, he had studied on his own all throughout his life, and now Mother was happy to replace him at the factory. Without hesitating, she abandoned her job as a midwife to allow her husband to get his degree in medicine. And then, when she was left alone with ten children, she raised us, educated us, while continuing her job as a midwife day and night. Nobody was allowed to call us orphans. "I am a mother and father" she would say full of pride.

She stood barefoot on Leszno street number one, before the hospital building, a former school. The hospital on Czyste, the pride of every doctor in Warsaw, had been moved here. She found herself in the hospital, because, like other doctors, I had injected intramuscular milk, to cause a fever, so that I could have her near me. She waits with others, to continue the journey, onto Niska, straight to the Umschlagplatz. She did not know why I had not returned to the hospital for the night. She did not know, that it was said, the ambulance had taken my ten year old daughter away a day earlier, during my absence. She did not know I had spent a sleepless night on Niska, where earlier the Berson and Bauman Hospital had been transferred to and where the foremost doctor, Dr. Braude-Hellerowa promised to save my child.

My mother's slippers were locked in my medical cabinet. I brought her slippers and distressing news of my daughter's abduction. She looked at me with her blue eyes, which penetrated right through the soul.

Beautiful, a face of alabaster-like skin, light hair, not gray in spite of 78 years. She raised her right hand: "Look, my dear daughter, what is happening. Look! A policeman is pulling an elder woman by her gray hair. 'Enter immediately, or else I will use my baton'." (Lonely, orphaned children, lonely elderly, the homeless, were the first victims.) "I'm not crying over myself, I'm not crying over you or the tragic lot of my dear grandaughter, whom I raised. I am not crying over the lot of my beloved son in law, who was taken away straight from the hospital to his death by the executioners. I am crying over the destiny of the Jewish population!" She seemed gigantic against the background of the Warsaw Ghetto, full of strength and prophetic inspiration.

I had protection. I seated her in a rickshaw, so that she would not have to walk. The personnel walked behind the rickshaw, and behind them were the Ukrainians with their guns ready to shoot.

On Niska Street you could only see the outlines of the hospital. We, doctors, handed bed pans to the sick, we dragged mattresses from one place to another. Why? We did not know ourselves. The nurses washed the floors, as to keep the place somewhat clean, or maybe just to keep themselves busy. There were two or three patients to a bed. Is it dysentery, or typhus, or pneumonia? Soon after there was word that certain doctors were receiving what were known as "life tickets". The wife of the famous surgeon Stanislaw Szenicer, who after divorcing him, remarried and had four children, received such a "life ticket" and this way she saved her four children, but she herself, not wanting to leave the children's nanny, a Polish woman, who went into the ghetto at her own will, went with her and both passed away in Treblinka.

"Maybe I will go to the council, Mother?" I asked. "Maybe it is possible for us to escape this hell?" "Go," she argued without a second thought. "You are young, maybe you can save yourself, and maybe you will manage to pull me out, too." "But we might never see each other again," I replied "I could die on the way." "Go this moment, now, quickly!"

I set gruel for her on the electrical stove, which I had brought home; I took off my bracelet, golden ring, and golden watch. "Maybe you can buy yourself for gold?" It had been awhile since I had given her 20 tablets of Gardenal, but every moment was threatened by a catastrophe. I was afraid to give potassium cyanide, maybe she will take it prematurely, and tomorrow the war will end? I would not have reached a few steps, when a shooting would begin on the street. There were the Ukrainians randomly shooting. I ran to the first gate, I ran to the attic, where I stayed for three days without something to drink or eat. It was there that I met Dr. Swiecowa, whose husband, like mine* (the author's second husband, Dr. Feliks Majnemer) worked in the emergency department.

After three days the shooting stopped. Suddenly someone from downstairs called us by our last names. How our husbands found out about us remained a mystery to us. "Hurry, come downstairs, the ambulance is waiting!" They laid us down on the floor, and we were taken to Nowolipki 20, where in the past, you could find "Linas Hacedek" ("Help for the needy"), and now it was the emergency department.

I saw an empty bed. I had run out of tears. "Bring my mother. Isn't the ambulance constantly on the move? Take her from the hospital, we will be together." The ambulance circled the ghetto without a break. The doctors predominantly stated death by suicide. I begged, threatened with suicide. I cried nonstop. Everyday there was a different story. He tantalized me. Until a week had passed by, he told me the bitter truth. That same day, when I had left the hospital, they had liquidated the hospital with the patients and personnel. I never saw my mother again.

In the Ghetto

In 1942, Hitler declared the work of the doctors in the ghetto was unnecessary. They forced us into physical labor. They rounded up all the surviving doctors in one block on Kurza Street (earlier Kupiecka). There, Feliks, my second husband, and I received a room with a kitchen. The whole family, mine and Feliks's, had already been exterminated. I only had a brother left, Witold, who sent his wife and two daughters to friends on the Aryan side; he himself escaped as a Pole and whilst leaving the ghetto, gave me his number on the Aryan side, as to not lose touch with him, for if a chance occurred he wanted to move us to the Aryan side.

A specialist in internal medicine who was famous before the war lived in our block, Dr. Lichtenberg. I turned to him, when Feliks began to cough and claimed to have pains in the area of his heart. I found him lying down in the kitchen on a bed. The bed was covered by a gray blanket. The kitchen reminded one of a prison cell. Dr. Lichtenberg came to life somewhat, and promised to stop by. He came, examined Feliks, diagnosed him, prescribed treatment, and then looked around him, and saw the door curtains that Feliks had put up to separate the bedroom and the consulting room and said, "Oh how happy you two are together! How jealous I am!"

Dr. Lichtenberg, when he returned from the war in 1939, he found his house on Muranowka 44 in rubble and under that rubble the bodies of his wife and beautiful sixteen year old daughter. His despair had no borders. After a certain amount of time, not able to handle the loneliness, he settled down with a woman with whom he did not connect at any level. After that she took all his fortunes and gold which the doctor kept in a safe in the wall of the house, and she ran away to the Aryan side, leaving him to plunge into depression. A few days later after he had visited us, he committed suicide using potassium cyanide.

In that same block we also met a well-known throat specialist, Dr. Kenigsztajn. I finished medicine with his son and daughter-in-law.

During this time, hide-outs were being built wherever they could be built, as to be able to hide somewhere during raids. Once, by chance, I overheard the neighbors talking about a double roof that had been built in our block and that you could hide there during a round-up. One day when we were going out to work, we were told beforehand not to come down when the Germans were outside. I felt the blood escape to my legs, for a few minutes I stood paralyzed, then I told my husband, "Come, there is a hide-out in the roof, they have to let us in, because we know." There existed an unwritten law, that whoever knew about the hide-out, bought themselves the right to use this hide-out, for if they were not let in, and fell into the hands of the Gestapo, in their despair they could give away the hide-out, with the ones who did not let them in.

The roof was oblique. Those who entered first were able to sit comfortably, the farther away, the less space. We were nearly the last ones. All together, it was around forty people. We closed the opening to the double roof and waited, we held our breaths. Next to us sat a young woman with a newborn. The baby began to cry. We all ordered the mother to cover the child's mouth, as to not let the child give us away with its noise. Dr. Kenigsztajn and his wife were at the beginning of the roof, it was obviously his idea and his money. We heard echoes of shoes with nails in them. The Germans were in the attic. The roof was dominated by silence. The child's noise was suppressed. The Gestapo moved around the attic. It never crossed their minds that on this roof forty people were seated, wanting to survive the war. They left. We waited for ten more minutes, to be sure that the danger was over. We opened the entrance. Suddenly a frozen scream that ran through the blood in everyone's veins sounded in the air. It was the young mother who finally took away her hand, that held her infants mouth, but the child in her hands was dead, she had choked it.

The Germans had caught many doctors; they had forced others into physical labor.

We worked for Wiktor Nuss. He was the boss of the undertaking business "Werterfassung". Wiktor Nuss was a Jew from Poznan, he was tall, 1.90 m, and he worked for the Germans. He wore officers knee boots, he could be spotted for his red face, his podgy neck and the satisfied look on his face, that they were feeding him what was known then as "German butter". He carried a riding whip in his hand, which he waved around and threatened with at all times. During the ghetto uprising, he was the first to be put on trial under the court of the uprising; he was shot on Gesia Street.

At six in the morning there was an assembly. We formed ranks of five, we were told to march in a military manner and sing. Our assignment was to clean out the houses after murdered Jews. We had to separate porcelain, glass, silver, tableware, and cookware. Clothing was to be folded and left on the staircase. Bedding was to be thrown out of the window, on the streets trucks waited to collect everything. All these things were carefully packed and sent to Berlin. The money raised by these things funded for armaments used in the war. That is why a secret propaganda ran through Nuss' business, to sabotage the work done. Someone was always on the lookout whether someone was coming in to check on us. If they came close, we separated into different rooms, as to give the impression of hard work underway, because Nuss threatened to send the unruly to concentration camps. During assemblies he sometimes told us what was happening, that women were coming to work without this and that, but left with something. It was apparent, that we put on various pieces of clothing and underwear, to enrich ourselves with clothing and steal the treasures of the Third Reich.

We began work at six in the morning, and finished at four in the afternoon. We had to march in military steps and sing. One time, I found myself on Gesia Street 27, in my sister Dina's apartment. She had been sent not too long ago to Treblinka, along with her nine year old son.

Dina was a midwife. When they were going to take her, I went to the midwives' union begging for help or advice. They replied, saying they could send a letter by me with assurance that they will do everything to try and take her and her son away from the hands of Hitler. But the promise was given to me, just to have her be deluded with hope of her being saved. The visit with the midwives union left me with a horrible memory, in my presence one of the midwives took potassium cyanide and immediately dropped dead.

I saw two glasses of unfinished tea on the table, on the floor family pictures that had been trodden on, and letters. Among the letters I had found, was a letter from our grandfather written in Hebrew in miniature letters. This letter my grandfather was writing to his son in America. This son, our uncle, sent these letters over the years to my sister, to show how well grandfather knew Hebrew and how beautifully he wrote. In one moment the whole unfortunate life of Dina came to a full stop before my eyes.

At the age of twenty she married a man with no education, a simple man. She was deluded; she said she would teach him, and that she would change him. At that time it was fashionable for members of the intelligentsia to marry with simple people. She wanted to show, with her life as an example, that two people on different levels, but in love, could produce a beautiful and happy life. Mendel did not want to learn, books bored him. At family gatherings, he would be the subject of sneer. His manners at the table were constantly being observed and commented on by brothers and sisters. Dina would take her husband's side, and each of these gatherings ended in arguments.

They lived with the mother-in-law, a poor widow, in Wegrow. There she learned to speak Yiddish; there she bore two sons. In the end she wished to divorce, she could not handle his ordinary manners and in her soul she admitted that her brothers and sisters had been right. She returned to Warsaw. At first she lived with Mother, and not wanting to take away the children's father, she sent her husband to his family in Argentina, so that the children would get used to not having a father. Of course she planned on getting a divorce. It did not happen, soon thereafter she received news that Mendel had died of influenza.

When the war had started, Eli was eighteen years old. Like his father, he distanced himself from learning. He became a chauffer. His boss, a rich Jew, decided to run away to the east. Eli, as his chauffer, had a chance to escape Hitler. He set a condition: he had to take his two year younger brother, Wolf, with him. They went. But when they got to Siedlce and Wolf saw Warsaw in flames, he declared to his brother, that he would not leave his mother alone. He returned. Dina, dismayed, saw her beloved son, and cried: "We survive together, or we die together".

I stood in the middle of the room and cried over my sister's destiny. She died together with her son in Treblinka.

During the time we worked for Nuss, the doctor's block had been liquidated. Most doctors had been sent away to concentration camps, others had separated. We lived in a house on Muranowska 37. Over there, they had built a hide-out, where forty people were hiding. To get to our household, you entered through gate number 37. This apartment was located on the third floor with a front-room, kitchen and two rooms and suite. In the last room the wall had been knocked through, which led to the living room, belonging to number 35. In the apartment on Muranowka 35, one room had been bricked up. In that manner we had a room that did not belong to number thirty-five or thirty-seven.

The wall in the last room, belonging to number 37, was knocked out and that was where the kitchen was situated, slightly bigger than standard sizes. In those times, when more than one family lived in a place, another kitchen was not suspicious at all. It was perfectly normal. In this kitchen was an oven also slightly bigger than standard sizes. The wall behind the oven was movable. You could open and close it, so through this oven we could reach the "open apartment" and back. We never cooked in this kitchen, but there always stood a pot with cooked grits or soup. In this oven no baking was done, but there always stood a pot of food.

Many people slept in the open apartment, to get fresh air. Feliks and I wanting to sleep peacefully, slept always in the hide-out on a camp-bed, stretched with our luggage, in which our "treasures" were to be found. That is what we called the things belonging to our loved ones who were murdered by Hitler. For these things we were able to get a loaf of bread on the Aryan side. For little money, we sold undergarments, furs, suits and dresses. Through holes in the wall, little children crept through, only they could fit through these holes in the wall, which separated the Aryan side from the ghetto. A military policeman, who guarded the wall, often shot at these children, the wall that divided Warsaw into the ghetto on one side and the other side came to be known as the Aryan side. This military policeman, who had a real long Jewish nose, and whom you could bribe, we named, Joseph Hacadyk, which means almost holy in Hebrew. He could not sit down to breakfast, unless he had shot a couple "cockroaches", that is what he called the children because of their black hair. When the trembling bodies stiffened, he could eat his breakfast with appetite, and the families in the ghetto waited in vain for someone to return alive.

In our room took place the segregation of clothing, found in the waste on the street. The majority of the inhabitants in our room did the cleaning, washing and ironing of these things found. They bribed the policeman so they could go out with a group of workers working on the Aryan side for the Germans (washing windows, washing floors, plucking geese stolen from Polish farmers).

Our room was dominated by a symbiosis of people with lice. The lice would get under shirts, into shoes and underneath our tights. We became used to their "pleasant" tickling.

An engineer named Jonas, with his five year old son Jurek, lived together with us. Jurek was intelligent enough, that whenever there was a roundup, he would remind us to stop the wall clock, for the Germans might hear the ticking. Jurek took a liking to use rude language, which I, a widow and married for the second time, did not understand, and when Feliks had to explain this, I had to blush. It could be that Jurek took revenge against his own parents, that they "took" his room full of toys away and put him in a room that was dirty and full of lice.

Engineer Jonas and old Goldberg decided that there must be a tunnel built that would lead us to the Aryan side, even though danger of "szmalcownicy" lurked on that side as well. Engineer Jonas took people whom he had full faith in, because there were many Jewish informers who were at German service, who thought that with betrayal of brothers they will save their own life. The organizer of this whole plan of building a tunnel, was of course Jonas. At first they did not want to let me work with them, for they believed the work was too hard for a woman. But I insisted, in case the time comes when we will have to escape and I, too, will have to use the tunnel, thus I wanted to be a part of this hard work.

We began to dig the tunnel. Jonas and Goldberg secured axes and spades. Each time we worked, the tunnel became wider and deeper. The dug up earth had to be put in bags and taken away far from its source, as to not give our work away. We worked during the nighttime only. It was humid in the tunnel. We had to hunch; you could not straighten yourself up. You worked on your knees, once the tunnel reached a certain depth, you could work while sitting down, once you were tired. Each night we descended like ghosts, not saying a word, so that the neighbors would not hear us. We worked in secret. When the tunnel was deep enough so that you could stand and work in it and when engineer Jonas began to outline the ceiling of the tunnel, at that time we left the ghetto. We bid a hearty farewell to Jonas and his family, and others, who had no one on the Aryan side and could not escape the ghetto. Feliks did not want to leave; he defended himself as well as he could. "I don't believe that they are sending people to their deaths. It's the enemy's propaganda, to break us. I have a sister and brother with their children there. I don't want to believe that they are not alive. I'm not leaving." Engineer Jonas kept on persuading Feliks the whole time: "If I had a brother-in-law, like you yourself, I would not remain in this hell for a moment".

On the ground floor of the house on Muranowska Street 35 there lived a shoemaker, Berezowski. He fixed shoes, but we never believed that he really was a shoemaker. You could tell that he had been a white collar worker before the war. The Germans opposed the intelligent especially, thus everyone preferred to be a blue collar worker. My sister was a teacher, in the ghetto she became a cook. Berezowski had a fourteen year old son with flaxen hair and bright blue eyes. No one would recognize him as a Jew.

He went out with a group of workers everyday to work for the Germans. Following my brother Witold's advice we sent clothing with this boy, so that we would have something to wear when we left the ghetto. After some time the boy was caught and killed.

On April 17, I had my last telephone conversation with Witold. He explained it quickly: "If you are not out of the ghetto by tomorrow, you have no need to come here, for I don't care whether I save my own sister or another Jewish woman. I will give the cards to someone else". I knew my brother's character very well and answered: "Tomorrow we will come out".

Returning home I used diplomacy. "Tomorrow I am going out to the Aryan side, if God wills, we shall meet again after the war." Feliks was terrified. "What, you are leaving without me?" It worked.

The next morning in denim, like all the other workers working for the Germans, we found ourselves on the Aryan side. Joseph Hacadyk was bought for 20 zloty and instead of 20 Jews going out there were 22, only 20 returned. In the factory in Wola, I changed, after bathing beforehand. I put on an elegant black suit and a hat with a veil to hide my Semitic characteristics and I rode freely accompanied by Witold and one Pole onto Radna Street number 10, on the bank of the Vistula, where the caretaker Aleksander Maczynski was waiting in his house as well as a room assigned to us, where his junk was kept.

Feliks was afraid to leave the factory; to him it was still a part of the ghetto, where he still felt safe. Witold came with an alleged policeman with an order to arrest Feliks Majnemer (that was my husband's real last name). The man was a member of a Polish underground organization. Witold turned to the German, who was the director of the factory and who employed many Jews, and asked him to hand over Feliks Majnemer, for he had a warrant to arrest him. The German who knew Witold, answered from his place: "I can give you all the Jews!" When Feliks entered the room terrified after being called up by the director, Witold slapped him twice and shouted: "Not a word, dirty Jew!" He was afraid that Feliks would swing his arm around his neck to thank him.

On the way Witold and the policeman separated and Witold brought Feliks over to me, whom I was already crying over, for I was convinced he had fallen into the hands of the Gestapo.

The House on Radna Street, #10 on the Bank of the Vistula River.

April 19, 1943, two days after leaving the Warsaw Ghetto, my brother, Witold, knocked with the pre-arranged signal on the door to our room, which was on Radna Street number 10. We unlocked the door quietly. None of the neighbors was aware that people lived in this room; it was the caretaker of the house, Aleksander's junk room. This room from two sides adhered to apartments lived in by Poles. In one of them, we later found out, there was a shooting school of the underground organization NSZ (Narodowe Sily Zbrojne), where girls learned how to handle a weapon. Warsaw was beginning to prepare for a fight against the occupants.

"Do you have a hammer?" Witold whispered. Even in this situation he was able to joke around. "Then hammer out the idea of getting your clothes from the ghetto. Look through the hole which Aleksander made for you through the paper on the window. Do you see the bloody glow in the sky? The ghetto is on fire. Apparently the first bombs fell yesterday, lightening the ghetto. There is no way of bringing your things from the ghetto here."

With the eyes of my soul I saw our masked room in the ghetto, in which forty people slept, as well as five-year-old Jurek, the son of engineer Jonas. Will they all perish this horrible way?

After the war we found out, that the first bombs fell actually on the house on Muranowska Street 35/37 and that the mother threw Jurek out of the window of the burning place and that the Germans shot at the children who were thrown out by their own mothers.

Witold did not give much time for contemplation. He said: "We will have to bring in Jews with money as we want to pay Aleksander". And so we lived in a group of five or four men and me alone. In the corner, hidden by a curtain, there stood a bucket to relieve oneself in. Aleksander took the full bucket out every evening, cleaned it and brought it back. Aleksander lived in a small room, in what was called a caretaker's lodge. He was a habitual alcoholic. He had sent his wife and son, whom he loved dearly, far away to a village, so that in case of an attack no one would be able to find them. "I'll stop drinking", he swore. "If I find you drunk, I will shoot you like a dog. You are accountable for five people's lives. And your wife, as I hear, is threatening to leave you if you don't stop drinking", Witold would threaten. And so Aleksander, not knowing Witold was my brother, cowered before him and when he came to sleep off the vodka on our bed, he begged me not to tell Witold.

The boys wore their long johns, as to keep their pants in good condition, in case we were forced to escape. We also had a bottle of foundation, in case the paleness of our face would arouse suspicion that we were from the ghetto.

The lack of nutrition was evident and my husband, Feliks, had hunger bouts from time to time. But not everyone starved. The oldest among us, Stanislaw Topaz, a former factory owner, stuffed himself with ham and beef fillets. These goods were brought to him by his sister-in-law, who like Witold, had what was called "good looks" and did not arouse suspicion that she was Jewish. Stanislaw saw that we were starving but not one time did he offer us even a piece of bread. Also I would have to wake him up at night: "Mr. Stanislaw, wake up sir, you are snoring very loudly. The neighbors could hear it!" He thought I was avenging him. "Not true, I was not snoring ," he replied whispering, "You are just jealous of an old man's ham! Please do not look at me! Your black eyes terrify me at night! Please do not wake me up or I'll scream", he whispered in anger. There was no choice.

We decided that when I heard the snoring I would wake up Seweryn, who was better trusted by Stanislaw and he would wake him up. This way we solved the threat of Stanislaw's snoring to everyone's relief. We connected ourselves with strings. When I hear the snoring, I pull the string attached to Seweryn then he would pull the string attached to Stanislaw's legs.

"Mr. Aleksander", Feliks said one day, "maybe we could start to learn how to read a little? "Alexander was an analphabet. "Ho, ho", Aleksander laughed, "what would the tenants think if they saw Aleksander with a book instead of a shot glass! That would cause a laugh!" But the thought interested him. He was incredibly talented. He learned fast, yet when we were on the right road, the enthusiasm for learning lessened and Aleksander returned to the shot glass. He always thought of his beloved wife who definitely would leave him, if he did not stop drinking.

One time as always when he came to us, he said: "You know that saleswoman from across the street, who you observe through that hole in the paper everyday? They took her to the hospital today, she had poisoned herself. What do they call those pills?" Feliks told him, "Luminal!" "Yes, yes luminal" Aleksander repeated with happiness.

After Aleksander left I scolded my husband that he did not need to tell Alexander the name of those pills. "Who knows", I said "maybe he wants to commit suicide because he cannot stop drinking". Of course the boys laughed at me.

The next day he came with news: "Do you know that they saved her. Today they took her from the hospital back to her house. What, what's the name of those pills?"

Feliks was already mumbling but Seweryn wanted to show off his knowledge of medicine: "Luminal". "Yes, yes luminal", Aleksander repeated. Now I was even more nervous. Who knows what the intentions of such an unhappy victim of alcohol are!

After a few days, the day before Easter, Aleksander came to us to share an egg. He was very hearty. We wished him a merry holiday and with our best humor we bid him good-bye. The next day he did not come to get the bucket. We thought he had gotten too drunk. The boys, terrified, carried out the bucket so that no one would see them. They had to go down three flights of stairs with the dangerous bucket. On the second day of the holiday Witold came to give Aleksander holiday greetings. He knocked on his door for a long time. There was no answer. He looked through the window and saw Aleksander lying in his bed. He was sure that he had drunk in the name of the holiday, he shouted loudly: "Open the door, it's me, Witold. Drunk again, you pig? If you don't get up right now I swear I'll shoot you." His fear for Witold was so great even though he was half conscious, he dragged himself from the bed and tried to open the door with his key but unsuccessfully. He fell onto the floor. Witold in no time broke the window and went inside. On the night table he found an empty packet of luminal. He understood everything. The breaking of the window had alarmed everyone. The women neighbors had already gathered. The presence of Witold surprised no one. He visited Aleksander often. Witold, in an instant took the grave situation in control, not only for the life of Aleksander, but he thought of the five of us that relied on the life of Aleksander. "Would you ladies please wait here?" he turned to the neighbors. "I'm going to find a doctor."

Because of the holidays he could not find a single doctor. Pale as death he ran into our hideout. "Put on your clothes Feliks, paint your face." He spoke in a manner that did not ask for replies. "You will come downstairs with me. Aleksander is saving your life, the time has come for you to save his. Aleksander has poisoned himself with luminal." We became paralyzed. Feliks was pale. "Quickly, quickly, you have to look elegant. Alexander's home is full of neighbors."

Feliks, urged by Witold, in an elegant suit, with a medical suitcase, a green tilted hat (he had received this hat during the occupation from his pre-war friend, the late minister of health, Litwin, who was in contact with Witold and who many times gave money to buy us food), entered Aleksander's lodge together with Witold and ordered everyone to leave the room. It did not cross anyone's mind that this doctor was a Jew hiding in this house. Aleksander, as we found out later, had recognized Feliks but did not betray him.

Feliks worked for hours saving Aleksander's life; he had shots, syringes and medicines with him. Afterwards, being physically exhausted as well as mentally, he calmly entered our hideout. "They did not recognize me" he finally sighed, and undressed. Along with Aleksander, we were saved, the death sentence had yet again been postponed.

And suddenly our quiet peaceful life on Radna Street was over. Witold disappeared. We did not know what this meant. The nights became harder to handle. We felt as if the any moment the house would disappear in the air. As if all the depths of hell had opened. The grating sound of saws, the knocks of hammers, the hum of machines, drills. Was it the scream of metal, or a child's cry? Or was it our sick imaginations? Compelled with hunger and fright we lay there without moving in the darkness. Stanislaw stopped snoring because he did not sleep. "Quiet, quiet", I would whisper and I did not hear, that I myself was whispering quite loudly. "The neighbors will hear", I exclaimed with agitation, "be calm!" Across the street all the windows were lit. The people were gathering, conversations were heard, and you could see they were commenting on accidents. On the paper across the window, secretive shadows were seen. The situation was hard, and difficult to handle, filled with unsteady nerves. During the day there was silence. Through the hole in the paper you could see that every time a person would run across the street they would fall, hit by a bullet. Who was shooting? Who were they shooting at? We found out later, that these weren't people that were running across the street, they were puppets pulled along by strings from each side of the street by the insurgents. In this way, they were able to stand in safety and observe where the bullets came from. The Germans occupied the roofs of Warsaw's University and from there they shot at the banks of the Vistula.

Aleksander, fully recovered, brought us the news. An uprising started! Underneath the city there was a second Warsaw, an underground city. This explained the noises we had heard at night. Streets, hallways and routes have been built among the buildings.

Morning. Is my hearing fooling me? The words of a command in Polish! In occupied Warsaw! My heart stopped beating. I wanted to laugh and cry. A battle was beginning against the horrid Hitler regime. Is this possible? Or is this only a dream? Both of us, Feliks and I had a hard time sitting in the hide-out. We wanted to get out of the hide-out.

"Mr. Aleksander, sir, help us. Could you please find out where a hospital has been set up by insurgents, for we could be of great help? Two doctors cannot just sit here lifelessly when the battles against the occupant commence." Aleksander was scared to let us go. "Just in short time", he would say, "and we will chase those bandits away. No, we will not let them out alive. Those like Witold, will make sure of that."

The director of the hospital set by the insurgents along the bank of the Vistula, was Dr. Adamski. Luckily he still remembered me from my student days and certified that I was in fact a doctor. We received a small room on the terrain of the hospital. Feliks, as always, was able to make the place look nice and cozy. We lived there and all day, as well as at night in most cases, we worked in different wards, we went to homes with the initiation of the RGO. We decided not to be separated, as to not lose each other. He came with me to visit sick children and I would go with him to his sick people.

Walking on the street was impossible. The Germans shot at everyone. We used underground hallways to get to houses, crawling on our stomachs and being pulled up inside.

In the orphanage named after Father Baudouin, an epidemic of dysentery broke out. We visited the orphanage daily, bringing serum. When the epidemic was over, I bid goodbye to the priest, who wanted to pay me. "I come here because of the RGO", I told him, "I do not need money." "But" the priest insisted, "for all those hearts! Your life could have been taken away because of your visits here." In the end we came to an agreement. The priest gave me tins of condensed milk, so that I could distribute them among the sick at the hospital, which did not have a family.

One time, a Soviet doctor came to the hospital, who wanted to take over the ownership of the hospital. He observed the entire hospital. Our wonderful little room impressed him. "I am going to live here starting tomorrow, get out of here." Feliks was angry and was not going to let him do that in any way. "Who does he think he is, coming in and sending out orders? I'm going to Dr. Adamski!" But Sister Maria begged us to let him have the room. Thus we started to linger in the hospital's hallways. There was no time to sleep anyway.

When rumors started flying about the Ukrainians being near the banks of the Vistula, that they were on the other side of the street, we decided to run away to city center, which was in the hands of the insurgents. There were battles over every building. In order to get to the Warsaw city center, we had to get onto the other side of Jerusalem Avenue. The Germans had placed themselves on top of the roof of the National Bank and from there they shot with their machine guns at anyone who attempted to reach the other side. Here we had to separate; the insurgents did not allow two people to cross together, as to lower the number of victims. On the other side Warsaw already belonged to the Polish. We took a deep breath. This way we reached Wspolna Street number 10 where we had friends and where we survived the Warsaw Uprising.

After the Warsaw Uprising.

Through the frozen window I saw a lit oil lamp. A hearty fire glowed in the fireplace. Is that Feliks sitting by the fireplace, or his shadow? His beautiful eyes, without a glisten, stare before him beyond hope. His palms, once upon a time were well-kept palms, they hang helplessly, expressionless, dead. "Let us go to the kitchen" was his greeting. He did not feel like himself. He introduced me as Polish woman, who looked after him during the Warsaw Uprising. Many of these "Warsaw bandits", as the Germans called us, crawled around the neighboring villages of Warsaw. He showed me his kingdom, a niche in the kitchen, a feather bed, what a splendor! "They threw me out, those Krongold friends, after three days. They lived well. They had 'good looks', both of them were doctors and played the violin. They lived together, along with the wife of one of them, with a deaf/mute person. They said: "Your looks are bad, you will give us away. We will lose our jobs. We play in a German dancing casino. Today one man is a wolf to another, go, wherever you want."

We looked at each other the whole night, as if we wanted to remember each dear characteristic of the other. "At five in the morning you have to leave, so that the housemaid won't notice", Feliks said. "Where will you go, little one?"

Only three days ago had we separated, when after midnight mass an administrator came and told us he had heard that we were Jewish. That was when we decided to separate.

We came to Strzeniowki after the Warsaw Uprisings capitulation, October 6, 1944. We brought in forty-year-old Julia on a stretcher, Mrs. Levitoux's daughter, who was injured in the chest on the second day of the uprising, when she was sitting on the balcony in her mother's apartment. After a few days stay in the hospital she was dismissed because she could not get any adequate medical help. I met Julia's mother in the gateway before the house on Wspolna Street number 10, where she lived. We would find ourselves during the lengthy battles, where Feliks's friend lived on Wspolna street.

In between the bombardings, women would place pots, if there was anything to cook on the bricks. In between two bricks, wood was placed and a fire was started. The insurgents killed cats and dogs, for there was nothing to feed the animals, so they were given to the people. And we like many of the others starving, prepared a dog that we had received from the insurgents, and cooked it. Under these circumstances, Mrs. Levitoux confided in me about her worries. Not wanting to give ourselves away as Jews I told her: "I met a medical student here by chance, who seems to be very talented. He is only missing one exam. And I was about to finish nursing school, when the war broke out, maybe we could be of help?"

Feliks recognized it as an abscess in the lungs, he prescribed intravenous injections, which he came about to do himself. "You have nothing to lose", I would tell her. Mrs. Levitoux had a cellar full of trinkets. With all those things you could buy everything. Feliks began to heal Julia, the fever began to fall, her cough became less tiring, her breath less putrid. We received a bowl of delicious soup everyday and a place to sleep in the hallway, which during a bombardment, was the safest place to be.

When the insurgents hung white flags and we were forced to leave Warsaw, Mrs. Levitoux begged us not to leave her alone. It was necessary to carry Julia on a stretcher, her mother, wanting to save whatever she could, put two fur coats and a coat underneath her, which made the stretcher even heavier.

We walked on glass, wires, rubble, that reached the first floor, and Julia would shriek on every bump.

The German orders were to march in the direction of the Mokotowskie Field. There stood nurses from the Red Cross handing out coffee and bread. From there people were also sent on to labor camps. Hundreds of people, elder, younger, priests, civilians, walked with packages in their hands at the mercy of the Germans.

At a certain point, somewhere on the way, a German shouted over to Feliks: "Komm, komm!" We set the stretcher down and awaited his return. I did not expect to see him ever again. After two hours he returned. It turned out that there was an order, that every Polish male leaving Warsaw has to clean rubble for two hours. We moved on. Again a German stopped us. This time wanting to show his good heart towards Felix, he stopped an elderly man and shouted: "Can't you see that this person is staggering, he is in no condition to carry a stretcher?" The elderly man, without a word, took the stretcher and together with him, we carried it on. After ten minutes, when Feliks was sure that the German had disappeared over the horizon, he went up to the elderly man and took the stretcher from him: "Good day, professor. I was your student from the Wilno University." The professor had tears in his eyes, squeezed Feliks's hand and said: "Thank you, sir."

At the Mokotowskie Field we heard through the loudspeakers that we were allowed to dig for potatoes that grew there. But only for fifteen minutes. Whoever stayed longer was shot. Many victims stayed behind.

Mrs. Levitoux bribed a German with a truck. After being paid, he agreed to take us to Strzeniowki, where Mrs. Levitoux's divorced husband, the father of Julia, lived. We were going to live there too and continue looking after Julia.

The German told us to lie on the floor of the truck, so that we could not be seen from the outside, because the Poles were not allowed to leave Warsaw, only when being taken to a labor camp. The truck began to move, Julia on her stretcher, and we tried to stay as low to the floor as we could, so that no one would see us. Suddenly with terror we saw a sign of great size above us with the writing "Gestapo". We stopped breathing. We had heard that Germans took money, only to turn in the people to the Gestapo. The terror did not last long. We heard that the German was unloading guns and was putting them away somewhere. In a moment we were once again on the move and found ourselves on the highway from Warsaw. We sighed. The danger had passed. However, he did not take us to Strzeniowka, as he had promised. He had taken us to the closest village, he knocked on the first house and said: "Spend the night here with these people! I will be back in two hours."

We were not welcome in this household. Only Julia received a glass of tea. We slept on the floor, and at five in the morning we were told to leave. And once again we had to drag the heavy stretcher; at least the road was even. On the way to Strzeniowka, which was still a long way away, we spent the night with Mrs. Levitoux's friends, who welcomed us heartily. The raised tomatoes, but since there was no one to sell them to in Warsaw, they remained on the bushes. Knowing the situation of the Warsaw citizens, they told us to pick as many tomatoes as we could. Of course, after having starved for a couple of weeks, we thought we were in paradise. The results were that for a few weeks we were not able to get rid of diarrhea.

We slept on hay, we had nothing to cover ourselves with, and we were freezing. In this house there was another room, occupied by the gamekeeper and his wife and daughter, Jane. His wife was of a ruddy complexion, healthy looking and an enterprising woman. From the very beginning she began to try to talk me into doing business. I hesitated, explained, that I don't know how to conduct business. I walked barefoot, because the men's ski boots, which I received during the Warsaw Uprising from Dr. Lewenfiszow, who I worked with in the pediatric clinic and whom I ran into at number 10 on Wspolna

Street, were ready to be thrown away. The gamekeeper's wife however was insistent. "What is this; will you live by the cards that the Germans give you?" Then one day she handed me a bottle of oil, she gave me the address of a shoemaker in a faraway village, who asked for a bottle of oil, for the distance from the city was too great for him. I brought the oil to him, he paid for it and this is how it all started. I distributed sewing needles, thimbles, shoe laces, threads, and oil. I took orders and brought them what they asked for. I began picking mushrooms with the gamekeeper's wife, I took orders from the nearest town Nadarzyn and business boomed. We split the profits. She was still not content. Even though Poles were forbidden from entering the forest, we began to saw down trees, the wood brought in good money. Feliks had to cut the firewood.

One day while sawing a tree, three gendarmes appeared out of nowhere. "Kennkarty (identity cards) !" The gamekeeper's wife told them, that we had the kennkarty at home, right next to us, and that her husband is a gamekeeper and invited them into the house. I ran to Feliks to warn him, and to tell him to stop burning grain for coffee in an underground area we had dug up, and not show up until the gendarmes had left. The gamekeeper's wife served vodka and food. Later they brought her their underwear to wash, and thus we could peacefully saw our wood, sometimes even together with them.

During my journeys to villages I met three shoe factory owners, who were able to take some shoes away from Warsaw and added them to my business. Afterwards, when I had to run away, I made sure I always returned the goods; I did not want them to think that I had cheated them.

I walked barefoot from village to village, and one time I noticed I had walked into a military camp. It was too late to turn back. I had walked straight into the lion's lair; I began to make deals with Germans and Ukrainians. They ordered newspapers, matches, cigarettes, socks and underwear.

One time a German asked me if I wanted to buy a five liter bottle of oil. I bought it readily, for I liked the bottle it came in. It would be easier for me to sell oil with it. I had been carrying around oil in regular bottles before. When I returned home, Mr. Szwacki, who was a pharmacist, recognized the fact that I hadn't bought oil, but castor oil, which at the time was worth gold on a scale. I sold castor oil in the pharmacy in Nadarzyn, and from the money I earned I bought my husband warm boots, so he would not have to freeze when chopping the wood for the gamekeeper's wife. I bought a few pots as well as other well needed things, such as a featherbed. After two days I returned to the German, to buy more castor oil. Of course, the German had been sure that he had cheated me, for castor oil tasted horrible. The German, when he saw me coming, hid in the attic, he was sure I had come to demand my money back. A bit in Polish, along with some finger language, I let his neighbor know that I wanted more "oil". "Hans, you can come down, she does not want her money back."

The gamekeeper's wife kept on telling me to marry Felix. "I can see", she told me "that he is interested." I would respond in a careless manner, that during the war everyone pretends to be a bachelor, maybe he has a wife and a pile of children, who knows. The gamekeeper's wife never let herself lose. She tried to talk Feliks into proclaiming his love for me, and when that didn't work, she offered us a bed with a featherbed in her house. "I feel sorry for both of you", she said,"take it anyway, why should both of you freeze in the attic?" The temptation was great, the frost was unpleasant. We accepted the gamekeeper's wife's deal under certain conditions.

"... Unless Feliks will marry me." We lived together with the gamekeeper in one apartment. Christmas was nearing. "I won't go to midnight mass in this paltry overcoat", Feliks announced. "I won't show myself in church looking like this." He had received the overcoat as a present from one of the actors in Warsaw, who was short in height and was hiding, like us from the German bombs on Wspolna Street number 10. I, however, although dressed just as bad, decided to go.

I visited my friend beforehand, who was hiding our mutual friend and gave her a job as a nanny. I wanted her to show me how to behave during midnight mass. My friend could not help me, for she was not a practicing Catholic. But she did give me a beautiful Siamese cat as a present, to give to the gamekeeper's wife. The gamekeeper's wife got tired of the cat quickly and ordered her husband to shoot it and take its fur, I received the meat. Right then, my own pots came in handy, as the gamekeeper's wife thought of it as disgusting to cook cat's meat in her pot.

On the way to my friend's house, I ran into a college friend of mine, who had "good looks". He gave me his address and proposed if I needed any sudden help to stop by.

The following day the police officer of Strzeniowka came. "Gossip reached me that you are Jews, I will not harm you, and if you have money I will find you a hiding place, if not, get out quickly." We spent one more night at the gamekeeper's. In the morning we each took a bundle of bread with us and left Sztrzeniowka.

After 2 kilometers we noticed a German who was setting up his gun. We were certain that we were his targets. But no. He shot at the birds.

Felix went to Zalesie to his friend, Mrs. Maria. I, to the brothers Krongold. We both knew each other's address, in the worst case we could die together.

In Zalesie I did not meet Maria, nor Feliks, for Mrs. Maria Kwiatkowska-Rozanska had left Zalesie. Her mother and brother now lived in her house. I also met there her cousin, Dr. Niedzielska. She gave me Feliks's address and helped me find him in Zlotoklosie. I introduced myself as a Polish woman, who had helped Feliks during the Warsaw uprising. I spent the night in a chair in Mrs. Rozanki's mother's room; Germans were quartered in the neighboring room.

The night went by fast. At five in the morning Feliks opened the door and we bid each other goodbye, maybe forever. He stood in the window and cried. This strong, hard man was crying like a little child. "My little one, how can you go out into the cold and will Mr. Rozanski really meet with you as he had promised me, to find a place for you?"

I walked quickly. I did not know where to go. His sad eyes followed me for awhile. Even when I knew that the Germans had taken him away, I kept on seeing those sad eyes full of tears that still followed me.

Foretelling of the Gypsy.

In the night from January 12 to the 13 in the year of 1945, the Gestapo raided the home in Zlotoklosie, inhabited by Mrs and Mrs. Rozanski. They were looking for "that man with glasses", meaning Feliks, who was hiding in this home. "Open! German police!" A bullet was shot through the window. Until the end of his life Feliks would show this scar on his head, where the bullet had grazed him. Three Gestapo officers and a civilian policeman forcefully entered the home. "Hands up and face the wall!", they ordered. After examining all who were present, they ordered Feliks to take his belongings and shoved him outside. They hit him in the head. His glasses fell. "Finally we have you, Witold!" he heard. He admitted to being Jewish, for he wanted to be finished off as soon as possible. "You are worse than a Jew. You are the eyes and ears of Stalin!"

It turned out that they were arresting him as General Franciszek Jozwiak, "Witold". They put him in a car, a Gestapo officer on each side of him, with guns ready to shoot with. Every trace of him disappeared.

In the meantime I was living in the same village, not faraway from Feliks. I hid as a Polish woman, a refugee from the Warsaw Uprising. I had a place to sleep by a kitchen stove; I spent the whole day distributing various things for business from village to village. I dragged bottles of oil, cigarettes, matches and various delicate fancy goods. I also went to see Feliks on strictly business terms, this way I was able to see him everyday. Talking to him was dangerous, as it could give us away, we even didn't want the Rozanski family to know, that we were married. The day after Feliks was taken away by the Germans, I went out as usual with my "goods", holding a bottle of milk in my hands tightly, as if for sale, but in reality it was meant for Feliks, I noticed Mr. Rozanski, the lawyer hurrying towards me. In his hands he was carrying my black cardigan with a velvet collar. I had left this cardigan at the Rozanski's, as to not lose it. "Felix?" I asked. "Yes", he said." Yesterday the Gestapo came and took him away." He said it in such a calm way, as if that one word did not decide for me life or death. I reached for the potassium cyanide. Each one of us had potassium cyanide on us. But Mr. Rozanski noticed my move, and took the poison away from me. "No", he said."You have to live and avenge his death. Now run away as soon as you can, I fear that Feliks will crack and give away your address." If only I could have only thrown myself on this Rozanski and tear him up with my own hands.

I went out into the world, without looking. I was alone in the world! I walked further, like a machine. I stood, counted my money, until a village family invited me to spend the night. "The front is getting closer", said the hospitable householder, "what good is it for you to be wandering at night? We have enough space and nourishment will be found. Whether from the city or the countryside, we are all Polish brothers."

At one o'clock in the night, the radio broadcasted that the Germans were running away in panic, the Russian army was nearing. Every minute the deaf sound of a rumble could be heard. Shooting and explosions intersected every minute. In the night people would come and speak of Russian soldiers quartering in the countryside. Young women should be hidden from them. My host sent his daughter and me to a village further away, toward his family. There we spent the night. When we returned "home" the next day, we could not believe our eyes. On the bed in the kitchen one next to the other, in uniforms, in boots, you could tell fresh from a battle, slept Russian soldiers. In the living room, the same sight. Together there must have been a little over a dozen. The householder was brewing coffee and preparing their breakfast. Were there any Gestapo officers? I felt a sting in the area of my heart. One, one more day! And we would have survived it together! Happiness and pain, and the urge for revenge coaxed me. Avenge his death, and who knows what he went through before his death. It was common to hear of the Gestapo's methods. Suddenly an idea hit me like lightening. I will go with them on the front! Doctors are needed in a war! Maybe I will die on the front, but I will have avenged the death of my whole family.

I waited, until one of the soldiers had woken up. In broken Russian, I asked where their headquarters was located; I wanted to see the commander. He pointed to some house, which had been designated as the headquarters for the time being. In the house, which was quite wide, three tables had been placed across, making one long table. At the table soldiers were sitting, officers from the lowest to the highest rank. In the honorary place, a colonel or a general with a chest full of medals and honors. The soldiers and officers were asking for a rest in their motherland. One explained, that he had pains in his lungs; a second had received a letter, that his wife had given birth to a son and he would like to see him; a third received a letter that his mother is seriously ill; many others asked for a vacation. The commander with a tough face and stern looks, in his place threw out all the pleas. "In the motherland they are taking care of your mothers, wives and children. And now everyone together, without exceptions we are going to Berlin, to overthrow the dying beast. Everyone to Berlin!" No one dared to oppose. The commander's looks were equivalent to an order. "And you, what do you want?" I was standing in the corner of the room in a ragged dress, in men's skiing boots that were ruined for the most part, in a black elegant jacket with a velvet collar, which did not go at all with my humble appearance. "I am a Jewess", I said with difficulty. Fear had overcome me. Such a great general! A man of life and death! "I have lost my entire family and only yesterday the Gestapo took my husband away. I am a doctor and he was a doctor! I came to ask if you could take me to the front." He looked at me and laughed at me jeeringly. "A doctor! Yesterday you slept with Germans, and today you want to sleep with Russians!" I trembled. I wasn't in any state to respond a word. I turned around and left the house.

When I had walked quite a bit, I heard quickened soldiers footsteps. "Wait! Don't run away!" I stopped. "The commander would like to apologize and would like to take you to the front." I could not believe my own ears. I felt dizzy. I fell. I saw the front, fire, falling Germans and myself with a gun in my hand. On the next day, to be exact at one o'clock in the afternoon, I stood with all my belongings at the designated place. There was no trace left of the Russian army. Had they played a trick on me? I had given myself away before my host family that I am a Jewess. Flee, flee, where my eyes will take me.

Like in a movie the villages, paths and people went by me. Again I walked from one village to another; once again I was selling goods, when one of those buying told me I was returning goods with German money, which were worth nothing. In the meantime I had woken up as if from a trance. I realized that the situation had changed. I returned to the Rozanskis, who were last to see Feliks alive. I entered the niche, where he had lived. It was a niche in the kitchen, designated for a cook, which during Hitler's time seemed like a palace to me. I found Feliks's photographs and a few souvenirs that were dear to me. The Rozanskis told me that people were returning to their cities in hoards, but there was no point to return to Warsaw; after the uprising the Germans burned one house after the other.

The Rozanskis decided to go to Lodz. I could not separate from them. We went, like many others, to Lodz. But before the trip I insisted my long braids, that Feliks had loved, be cut off. In the ghetto, when I was ill with typhus and I asked for a hairdresser to cut my hair, Feliks, who at that time was only my doctor, threw him out the door. Feliks is not alive, I don't want hair. The hairdresser hesitated. "The war is over, what a pity, such beautiful hair!"

It was January 1945. It was enough to enter the first better looking apartment, make keys, close the door and it became your property. Along Piotrkowska Street, in the center, you could take a five-six room apartment, elegantly furnished with everything. You could find apartments left by German doctors, with laboratories, with microscopes and other medical instruments; closets full of clothing and underwear.

I did not want an apartment. I was in no state to live alone. I asked the Rozanskis, if they could take one more room and I became their subtenant. I received a room with a cupboard and a table. I did not need anything more. I went to the PPR. I threw myself into the whirlpool of labor. I began to work in children's hospitals named after Korczak.

This hospital would later become a university clinic under the supervision of Professor Popowski, whom I had worked with before the war in a children's clinic in Warsaw along Litewska Street. I remembered the sad meetings with him in the prosectorium, when the summer dysentery epidemic would kill a newborn. We were at that time compelled to assist in the sections of postponement of our little patients. I was then a young doctor and a strong sensation roused a fact, that such an old doctor, like Popowski, often had tears in his eyes and was used to saying with deep sadness: "Is it not a too high toll on human life?"

In Lodz I worked in the tuberculosis department under the supervision of Dr. Anna Margolis, as well as in the hospital's laboratory. There still was only a small number of doctors. The majority of the doctors had been murdered, others had not yet returned. Many mothers of different nationalities would come by to the sickbay; they would form a long line. Whenever I would be examining a German baby, tears would fill my eyes. In my imagination my daughter, murdered by the Germans, would appear, I would become paralyzed. I made an effort to suppress these unhealthy reflexes, but I could not. In the end I turned to the director of the hospital and asked him to exempt me from the obligation of examining German children. They would be sent to other doctors. In the afternoon I had been through all of Lodz, completing home visits. Sometimes I would return as late as eleven or twelve at night.

I also worked voluntarily. In the hospital I was chosen by my physical co-workers as their representative. I decided who received what type of bonus. Household items, clothing material and dresses, all of these things were assigned as bonuses, for it was hard to buy anything on the market. For some time I was the pediatric assistant secretary. Professor Popowski was the president. I had my own column in a women's magazine named The Health of Our Children.

One time someone came to me, and asked me to appear on the radio and appeal to all the women in Poland that they cooperate with the newly created government.

One day I met my friend from university on the street. Every meeting after that horrid war was a distressing moment. When he found out, that I did not have my own apartment, he would insist that I promise him I'd find myself an apartment. "Soon it will be tough to find an apartment in Lodz", he told me, "People are returning in hoards. A doctor must have a roof over her head." I do not even remember my friend's last name; thanks to him I did find an apartment. Not in the center and lacking a bathroom, but with three rooms and a kitchen in a neighborhood known as Uptown and it was my own apartment.

I killed myself with work, as to not think. Yet at night, when I would be falling asleep, before me marched my sisters, mother and brother, all murdered by Hitler. Sometimes I would hear the silver laughter of Rysienka and I would wake up with a wild heartbreaking sob, realizing that I will never really hear it again. I would read for whole nights, trying to get rid of these nightmares. That is when I wrote a letter to my dead daughter.

Letter from Lodz between the 22nd & 23rd of February, 1945

Today is your birthday, Rysienka, my dear and only daughter. You are not here! Hitler executioners took you away from the hospital, where Feliks, my future husband, worked. Later, like in January 1940, they took away your Daddy from the hospital on Czesta Street from the operating table while he was operating on a patient. I took you away from the hospital where I worked where they took your tonsils so I could have you near me.

Then it was said that it was safer in emergency hospital, so Feliks took you together with his little nephew Edward, and his sister-in-law Maria (the Germans killed the brother as well as his wife and two children) to save all of you. You went together with them into the dark abyss.

What did you think in the hour of death? Did you think that your mother had given you away? That she had just thrown you away? What terrible thoughts could have gone through your light little head, when you saw death before your eyes? What hopeless despair, when you were shoved with Maria and Edward into a wagon!

We were lying in bed with your fake father, we talked about you, but you would nag us: "Why did you not talk to me?" Then we kissed. I brought you food, but the candy, which I had received for you in the hospital; I even forgot to give it to you! Such was the turmoil; we were scared that the boss would find out that I was your mother! That he would throw you out on the street!

I didn't see you again. Only that horrible night in the hospital on Niska Street, not far from the Umschlagplatz. I knew, that there behind that wall, on the Umschlagplatz, you were there, Rysienka! And that hopeless sobbing and the lost hope, which Dr. Braude-Hellerow, the director of the hospital, tried to turn into something positive, that in the morning, when the nurses leave with coffee for the condemned, they would call: "Henryk Szachnerowicz" and they would bring you back to me. And then there was the shooting from the Ukrainians at every attempt to leave the hospital and the animal-like apprehension before death, which I longed for with my whole heart. And then the opening of the gate for a new party of condemned and struggling with Sister Lubilner, who closed the gate so that I could not go out and die together with you. Maybe I could have found you among the thousands of people and it would have been lighter to die together.

And then it was the window on the fourth floor. You could see hoards going in deathly silence to wagons. And among those thousands there was one little girl in a plaid blue dress and red sandals. No, I could not imagine you among those thousands. But I knew you were there, and I, your mother, I stood in the window and watched. I did not howl, I did not shout, I did not have a heart attack, or convulsions – nothing, nothing. They walked five after five. They died in the abyss of wagons, and I, your mother, stood in the window of the hospital, in a white suit, I watched, but I could have jumped from the fourth floor.

Rysienka! Even you cut off golden braids, which I hid from the eyes of the public; in the end they too were lost in the Warsaw Ghetto! Today you would be 13 years old. What a big girl! Today I would be baking cookies and inviting guests over. Remember, what beautiful birthdays you always had? Even in the hospital you told me: "Mommy, I would love to have a birthday again!"

No one will ever call me "mommy" again. How horrible!

Often during the night I would be called for when there were sudden accidents. My friends warned me, not to open the door, when you live alone, they come to plunder and murder. I laughed at these warnings. I hoped to be finally murdered. One afternoon, when I opened my door to my apartment, I caught a glimpse of my neighbor, who, as it turned out, who had studied medicine together with me. This was Marysia Wajsbachowna, who because of her German name went through hardships, as she was a Pole and did not want to profit from what was known as "German butter". From the day that we met, Marysia and her husband, Captain Frankiewicz would not have dinner without me. They knew I had lost my entire family. They would even wait until midnight and strived to calm me down, and Marysia would always tell me, that nothing was for sure, for during war many strange things happen and that maybe someone could still return.

Once, when I was walking from the hospital, I saw an officer from afar, who was standing in the gateway to my house, he was obviously waiting for someone. When I got closer, I nearly fainted due to emotion. It was none other than my own brother Witold, who took Feliks and me away from the ghetto and looked after us the whole time we were on the Aryan side up until the Warsaw uprising, when he disappeared. I had been sure he was dead.

On the 1st of May, which in the year 1945 was especially festive, the health workers protested. One of my friends invited me in his name and his wife's for dinner after the protest. During the dinner a gypsy appeared with a newborn in her arms. She wished to see the lady doctor that came here. Until this day I cannot understand how this gypsy woman had found me. I put on my doctor's apron and received the strange patient. I sent her to the hospital with the suspicion. The gypsy instead of paying for the child's examination proposed to foretell my future with cards. She shuffled the cards for a long time, from one hand to the other; she examined my face, the lines on my hands. Suddenly brilliance appeared in her black eyes. "A handsome blonde from far away is on his way, he will be here soon, in a year you will have a child!" I trembled. How could the gypsy know, that my only wish was to have a child again? To hear the most wonderful words again "mommy"! "Throw salt in every corner of your bedroom along with a piece of bread." She also gave me a ring with a red stone, which I still have today. I was completely bewildered, but I had not believed a single word the gypsy had said.

A couple weeks after the gypsy's reading a feast of Zielone Swieta had come. Holidays were always the hardest thing for me to endure. I got up at five in the morning, I put on my house apron, and a scarf in my hair and I began to dust the furniture in the apartment. Suddenly the bell rang at the door. It must be a sudden accident! "Who's there?" I asked. "Yours" I heard the response. But that "yours" sounded very familiar and close. I was sure that it was one of my friends from university. I opened the door. Before me stood my husband Feliks, alive and whole, in a green rimmed hat, with a suitcase in his hand, as if he was returning from Krynica or Zakopane. He was thin as a skeleton. I felt the blood leave my body. "Feliks, are you alive?" I was only able to spit those words out alone. And he, completely calm, began to push me delicately into the hallway of my apartment. He was afraid I would begin to cry loudly, but he was very discrete. I left him in the bedroom and like a crazy woman I ran to the Frankiewicz's, not paying attention that it was the holidays and five in the morning. Captain Frankiewicz opened the door in his pajamas. He was horrified to see me almost unconscious. I ran through the four rooms. "My husband is alive, he came back from Berlin!" I shouted and returned to Feliks. After an hour, a hot bath, and clean underwear had been prepared for Feliks by the Frankiewicz fmily. They knew that he had returned almost by foot from Berlin.

In the afternoon, when we went out – happily, to speak of our happiness and not to bewitch it – for a walk, the director from the Health Department waved us over. "I have a letter for you." It was a letter sent by the minister of health, announcing the news of Feliks's rescue. That same afternoon a telegram arrived from my friend in Warsaw, from whom Feliks had gotten my address. "Feliks is back from Berlin, in a few days he should be there".

In one moment the whole world turned into happiness. I did not allow myself to think of the past. Feliks is alive. Feliks's treatment by the Nazis is another story in itself. I was afraid to speak of luck, as to not jinx it all. Will the gypsy's foretelling all come true?

During this time I received an official proposal from Professor Popowski. He offered me to be his assistant in the clinic. The dream of my whole life was to be fulfilled. But I was already pregnant and Feliks was against me taking night shifts, which were an obligation even to a professor, because of money, and spots to be a professor's assistant were rare. I opted for a happy family.

On March 24, 1946 I became the happy mother of little Joasia, and ten months later our second daughter, Elzunia, was born.

Memories of Dr. Feliks Mrozowski

During the time that I was in the Warsaw ghetto the death of Dr. Kalksztajn whom I knew personally would stay in my memory permanently. It was in the beginning of Hitler's rule. During this time I was working in a hospital named "Linas Hacedek" ("Help for the Poor"), on Nowolipki street number 20, on the corner of Karmelickiej street. One day I was standing in the window of the hospital and I observed the following scene. I saw two Gestapo officers who were escorting Dr. Kalksztajn. The officers beat him mercilessly and pushed the victim about. At one moment they ordered him to walk before them. When the doctor turned his back on them, the Gestapo officers shot at him. He immediately fell.

Also this work in these places known as 'points of lodging" was hard and hopeless, that it was hard to forget about it. Hitler's army herded the Jews from nearby towns and villages as well as from Germany to what were once schools. These were people who remained without means for living. In one room lived a couple families. They slept on beds of boards and if those ran out – straight on the bare floor. They had no underwear, and slept in their clothing. Lice and worms prevailed in these "points of lodging". We the doctors were in charge of looking after "hygiene" and supervision, so that the clothing of typhus victims was burned.

We were completely helpless over the extreme poverty that dominated this place. One time I turned to Janusz Korczak the owner of an orphanage, asking him to take a few gifted children, which he might be able to save from a likely death. I will never forget the sight that happened before my eyes.

In a large room, in which all the children could be found, stood behind a screen the old doctor's bed. I did not know whether it was like that because of lack of space, or maybe Korczak did not want to leave the children alone, when death was so threatening at every moment for these children. Dr. Korczak replied to me, that he will only take children who cannot cope with life on their own, my plea was not granted. He said: "The gifted ones will cope". Soon the children of the orphanage walked on the streets of the ghetto for the last time. They walked towards death. Dr. Korczak held them by the hands, the youngest child he took in his arms. He walked with them towards death.

Halfway through the year 1942 I stopped working as a doctor. The Germans thought the work of a doctor was unnecessary; we were forced to conduct physical labor. Together with my wife, a doctor, we began to work for Victor Nuss. Our job was to clean apartments and take away belongings of murdered victims, separating their things and organizing them in marked German storage units. These things went to Berlin.

April 17, 1943 we went out with a group of Jews, who worked outside the ghetto for the Germans. The German overseer was bribed and instead of 20 Jews, there came out 22, only 20 returned. Us in denim like everyone else, made it to the factory on Wola street, who's director was a German, many Poles worked there as well as Jews passing as Polish, members of the underground movement. There we could bathe, eat, and change into normal clothing, which were ready for us. My wife was sent further away that same day by her brother Witold with a Polish escort. They took the tram as a pair of lovers and got to Radna street number 10 on the banks of the Vistula River, where the owner of the house, Aleksander Maczynski, had a room ready for us for a certain sum of money.

I was left behind at the factory and was afraid to go out into the city. In the meantime my brother-in-law, Witold, who circled the factory grounds often, went up to the German director and told him he had an arrest warrant for a Jew Feliks Majnemer, since that was my real name. "I could give you up all my Jews" – the German replied. When I entered the room terrified, after being called up by the director, Witold slapped me twice and and – "Not a word, dirty Jew!" for he was afraid that I would swing my arms around his neck to thank him for helping me escape the ghetto. He walked out with me, assisted by a policemen, he too was part of the underground organization. When we neared the banks of the river, Witold bid the policeman goodbye and walked me to Radna street 10, where my wife was already mourning me, having waited twenty-four hours for me, she had been convinced that the Germans had finished me off. Together with my wife and three other Jews, we stayed there for half a year until the Warsaw uprising broke out. During my stay on Radna street Dr. Franciszek Litwin (the late minister of health) transferred some money, intended for purchasing provisions for us, my brother in law would appropriate the provisions for us. Behind the wall of our hide-out, two apartments occupied by Poles, who thought the room in which we lived was the owner's storage room for junk. In one of these apartments there was a shooting school for girls of NSZ.

Dr. Litwin was to help us join the group of partisans known as the Folk Army, but the train which we came in was five minutes late and the partisan who was waiting on us, disappeared. We should have returned to Warsaw to the river bank. On the way back in Minsk Mazowiecki there was a search. They were looking for smugglers. Before we had left the village, night fell and we were lucky enough (I was accompanied by a Polish lady who was assigned to me, my wife was accompanied by a Polish man – both members of the underground organization) to be able to spend the night with the railway man. Here we listened to many warnings on the subject of Jews, who disguised themselves as Poles, yet the railway man did not think that such a couple is sleeping in his guest bed.

During our stay on Radna street, our protector Maczynski an alcoholic, he attempted suicide, when he was afraid his wife would leave him due to his alcoholism, but I saved him.

When the Warsaw uprising broke-out, we came out of hiding and began to work in the underground hospital, where the sick and wounded were brought to. After the electrical plant burned down and the fall of the river bank we made our way back into midtown. There, along Wspolna street, we hid during the bombardment of the capital together with the Poles.

On Wspolna street, we met Mrs. Levitoux, whose forty-year-old daughter was wounded in the chest in the first days of the Warsaw uprising. She was checked out of the hospital as not being able to be cured. Mrs. Levitoux having nothing to lose and finding out that I am a medical student (my disguise), asked me, whether I could examine her daughter. I recognized a wound on the lungs and prescribed intravenous injections, which I decided to administer myself. Mrs. Levitoux, the owner of an apartment along Wspolna street (I do not remember the number), had a cellar full of trinkets, with which she could buy the most expensive medicine. Noticing the improvement in her daughter's health, after the fall of the uprising in October, she bribed a German and he rode us out, along with a stretcher, on which we carried the sick, to the outskirts of Warsaw. He did this for a few bottles of cognac disregarding the Germans ban that all the "Warsaw bandits" should gather next to the polytechnic school. He took us to Wlochy, and from there by foot we found ourselves in a village named Strzeniowka under Nadarzyn, old Sochaczew.

In Strzeniowka lived Mr. Szwacki, the divorced husband of Mrs. Levitoux, the father of the sick one. He immediately gave up his room to the daughter and mother, and he himself went up to the attic, where we were placed as well. In the meantime Mrs. Levitoux knew the truth and that we are both doctors.

In the neighboring room, in the same house lived a gamekeeper with his wife and four year old daughter. They did not know we were Jews and married, they offered us a bed and a featherbed, with the terrible frost in mind (we lived in the attic on the bare floor, without any covers), yet with a certain uneasiness we took the offer. My wife had documents under the name Paulina Wojcik, I – Feliks Mrozowski.

December 24, 1944, when my wife went to midnight mass with the neighbors, the village administrator came to me and told me that word had gotten to him that we were Jews. Feeling a friendly gesture towards us, I immediately admitted that I was a Jew, in the meantime my wife returned from midnight mass and stubbornly insisted that she was Polish. The administrator asked us if we had any money, then he could find us a place where we could hide, if not, we had to leave, from his side nothing bad could happen to us.

December 25 we made it to Zalesie. I had intentions to go to my friend Maria Kwiatkowska-Rozanska, my wife to two brothers Krongold, Jews, who disguised themselves as Poles. These were our friends from university, both of them doctors and violinists; they played at the officer's casino.

In Zalesia at Kwiatkowski I did not stay. I stopped by her cousin, Dr. Stanislaw Niedzielski. I was heartily received; they fed me, bathed me and looked after me for a few days, gave me clean underwear and helped me find Maria. She lived in Zlotoklosie, Grojec county. The Niedzielskis unfavorably directed me to Maria's brother, Pulko-Lukaszewicz, and claimed that he worked with the Germans. In spite of this, I lived with the Rozanki's from December 31, 1944.

January 12, 1945 at ten o'clock in the evening a knock was heard on the door. My host's got up terrified. We heard a loud shout: "Polizei, aufmachen!" Two series of automatic machine gun shots went through the window. The skin on my head was lightly grazed by one of the bullets. Five armed Gestapo officers stormed into the apartment, as well as three civilians. They did not look for me in the kitchen, where they had seen me before through the curtains in the window; they had assumed I had run away, they began to fervently search the whole house with flashlights in their hands. They shouted: "Wo ist der Mann mit der Brille?" In the beginning I forced myself to hide, later though, regarding the situation as hopeless, I came out of my hiding and ran into one of the civilians, who slapped me and escorted me to the kitchen wall, where the rest of the household had been gathered with raised hands. Three uniformed Gestapo officers conducted a search, during which all my belongings were taken, including my handkerchief and glasses. After this I was positioned facing the wall with my arms raised.

They started the general search in the house, which lasted about two hours. The room I had lived in was inspected thoroughly. After the search, the household was questioned in the next room. I gave them my identity: "Feliks Mrozowski" and that I was in Zlotoklosie only a few days looking for a job. I had found myself at the Rozanski's randomly; I did not give away the fact that I had known Maria for a long time. From the very beginning I was suspicious about their behavior.

At a certain moment the Germans took a straw basket, filled it with my belongings and threw me my jacket and hat and ordered me to follow them. It was midnight. Right after leaving the house a tall dark brown-haired man approached me in a black jacket, with a small fur collar and blinded me with a flash light, telling his companion, average height blonde haired in civil clothing, who was also present in the apartment during the search: "Yes, it's him, finally we have you Witold". I immediately answered that they were mistaken, for I wasn't Witold. "We definitely know that you are Witold, the head Gestapo officer would not be here and the many other highly ranked officers if that were the case. "They ordered me to walk ahead, to my left walked the head Gestapo officer holding me by my jacket sleeve, to my right was some civilian officer, and behind me a bunch of bandits, about fifteen of them. I expected a gunshot to my head at any moment. I remembered that I had two false identifications on me with the names – Feliks

Mrozowski and Zygmunt Majewski, my real name was Majnemer. I anticipated a quick ending. But the end did not come. We found ourselves half an hour away from home, where they took me from, near the train station. There were three cars nearby. I was ordered to sit in one of them, I had two civilian officers with revolvers in their hands sitting on both sides of me. The head Gestapo officer sat in front. The rest of the company got into the remaining cars, and we drove off.

After an hour of driving we stopped before a house, which turned out to be the headquaters of the Gestapo in Sochaczew. I was taken to the room, here they recorded my identification before civilian officers, who had arrived with me in the car. I gave myself away as a Jew before the head Gestapo officer, that my real name is Majnemer, that I am a doctor. To which one of the civilian officers said in Russian to another: "See, I told you so "(he was certain that he recognized a Jew". Hearing the conversation in Russian I shuddered, then I became suspicious, that I had become a victim of Maria's family. Her brother, Pulko-Lukaszewicz, he was running away from the returning to Kijow Red Army. He arrived from Kijow and lived with the Rozanski's in Warsaw. Maria also had a son-in-law, Czerwinski, who worked for the Germans.

A volksdeutch from Lodz named Honig interrogated me. After recording personal data I was taken to a single cell, situated on the first floor across from the office and I was told that it was for the best that I did not speak with anyone. On Saturday, January 13, I was given a loaf of bread along with some jam. Around ten o'clock the chief Gestapo officer showed up and took me to his private apartment, situated in that same building on the second floor. He was exceptionally polite, he introduced me to the other officer, and a normal friendly conversation followed. He asked me, if I had slept well, if I had any needs, offered me tea, proposed vodka. I asked for my glasses and handkerchief, which I received immediately. He asked me about my specialization and in what way I had managed to escape the ghetto, where I had stayed up until the Warsaw uprising and about the time my wife and I were on the Aryan side. Our first conversation lasted for two hours and no political subjects were brought up. They escorted me back to my cell, where I ate the soup and meat they had given me.

That evening, they took me again to their place to talk. The evening conversation was already carried out in a different manner. He asked me if I knew who Rola-Zymierski is, what the difference was between the People's Army and the People's Guard. He considered my answers naive. He lost his temper quite a few times and he told me that the information given to him by the Gestapo points out that I am very familiar with the underground movement, which I did not want to talk about. He said that he had been very kind to me, yet I am lying to him. He asked me how I had survived, when I was in hiding for eighteen months on the Aryan side. When I answered that the patients sent me food, he lost his temper and screamed: "You were in touch with Rola, you had a radio and you directed people to the east! You don't want to admit to the fact that you were a paid communist agent". The other officer present picked up a heavy ashtray and aimed at me. The chief Gestapo officer shouted: "Erich, calm yourself, it's a waste of nerves!" the chief Gestapo officer spoke to me again: "You knew that the ghetto was to be burned, otherwise you wouldn't have left on April 17, when you started a fight with us in the ghetto." He then threw my two false documents on the table, found during the search. The beating started, from which I barely came out alive.

The next day in the morning, Paul Schwarzwald, the chief Gestapo officer called me up again, and made it clear secretly, that Rola-Zymierski is a Jew, who has a jewelry store on Zlota street. He knows exactly because of his people, who are errorless, that I am an affiliate of the underground Polish organization PPR, that the hold-up in the national bank and the disappearance of 5 million was all my doing. Finally he told me that his patience was running out and that my life was in my own hands. Such people like me are needed by them. If I tell them everything about myself and my activities they will give me a passport and I will find myself free in Switzerland. At this the conversation ended. In 2, 3 hours later a civilian policeman with a round face and of average height walked into my cell and asked: "How are you Witold?" "I am not Witold," I answered. He took me to the office, situated opposite my cell, he spoke fluently in Polish. The conversation was frequently mixed up with beating. He asked me about Dr. Lande and an architect whose last name I forget. He made me suffer for over an hour and took me back to my cell half conscious.

In the evening that same day the chief Gestapo officer called me in yet again. The conversation was filled with threats. My mumbling did not help, since I had been observed by them for two years. He gave me a deadline until tomorrow. The following day, January 15, a Monday, the chief Gestapo officer appeared with the same civilian policemen from yesterday. I barely entered the office, they gave me a pen "Pelican" and I was asked if I recognized it. "Of course I recognize it," I answered. I was ordered to show them how to place the ink in the pen. I tried to unscrew the top of the pen, how I usually would, unsuccessfully. I assumed that the pen had stopped working due to it having not been used in a long time, but the German lost his temper, and attacked me, beat me mercilessly, and to my surprise, he showed me that you unscrew the pen at the bottom and that it was empty inside. Until this day the pen incident has been a secret to me. Meanwhile the chief officer came and asked me, what's new "Witold". He heard prepared naivety in my answer yet again. They threatened me, that they will wait no more, they're giving me until four o'clock and they will find a way to make me tell them everything and stop me from being so secretive about the underground organization. They know that Rola-Zymierski did not take any action without inquiring me that I, as an intelligent member of the PPR, directed the whole movement on the green border, that I myself had the intentions to get to the east, but in the last minute they had caught me. This is not the first time they've had an encounter like this before. In the beginning no one admits, soon they all sing like a bird. They made it clear that they had many different ways to get me to talk, they advised me to make-up my mind before noon.

At four o'clock they called me into the chief Gestapo officers and he asked, if I would reveal everything. I answered, that I had nothing else to add. In the meantime he called for another Gestapo officer and they told me that they will not wait any longer. They tied my hands together with string, took me to the attic with special machines in this Sochaczew Gestapo torture room. They fixed my body to poles, so that I was not able to move. Then they threw me over two chairs. I was hanging over these chairs. One of the workers stood before me and poured water over my head. I felt like I was drowning. When I was close to suffocating or fainting, the torture was paused, only to be picked up again. All this time civil Honig buzzed around the attic, talking in Polish, he shouted: "I cannot watch your suffering, Witold, acknowledge your identity, who you are, and you will find yourself free." Finally, half conscious, they took me away from the chairs and they placed me in the same position in the corner of the cell. When taking his leave, the chief Gestapo officer added: "Tomorrow you will be finished with". The guards were instructed to give me my food in this uncomfortable position, seeing next to me a comfortable bed, which I longed for, I did something that only a strong will could do. With tied hands I pushed away the pole and hauled myself onto the bed. I had a safety pin on me and knowing the anatomy of the heart I pierced it through my body. Regardless, my heart kept beating. I must have missed the area due to my tied hands. In the morning I returned the pole to its original place and again I was seated in the position in the corner where they had left me. That night I was aware of movement, which dominated the whole building.

On Tuesday, January 16, two Gestapo officers entered my cell and shouted: "What are you counting on you dog? Soon they will shoot you off!" After two hours had gone by a fully uniformed SS officer stormed into my cell. Picked me up the stick form under my knees and elbows, threw a jacket over me and a hat and ordered me to follow him. I found myself on the street before the Gestapo headquarters. I was told to get into the car, my hands were tied. In the car, the chief Gestapo officer was sitting along with his SS-man mate and Honig who learned to speak Polish.

The city was overwhelmed with traffic. Having been cut off from the world for five days, I did not know what to think of this. But by overhearing pieces of conversation on the street I assumed that the Red Army was nearing and that there was an evacuation underway in Sochaczew. In the car they drove me around to multiple prisons that kept on being evacuated. And so from Sochaczew I ended up in Lowicz. In Lowicz the prison keeper wanted to save my life. Zlotoklosy was already free; they were preparing to evacuate the prisoners from Lowicz. This is when the prison keeper came up to me and said: "I know that you are a Jew, I wish to save you". He escorted me to another cell and locked it. He believed that the Germans would forget me in the light of panic. In the morning I heard footsteps. The Germans were knocking into the closed door, they were knocking into it so hard, so that they broke the door. They did not want to lose "Witold".

From Lowicz they took me to Kutno, then Konin, Poznan, Leszno, Sagan, Muskau, Frankfurt on the Oder and finally on February 2, 1945 I found myself in Berlin. Only here at the headquarters of the criminal police, lead by the chief Gestapo officer from Sochaczew, did I officially find out that I had been accused of communism. Here, a long conversation took place about me with the chief of the criminal police division. My identity was taken down. Upon his farewell, the chief Gestapo officer from Sochaczew told me to clean my muddy shoes with the hat which was taken off my head.

I was put up in Zellengefangnis, Berlin, Lehrterstrasse 3, I was kept in the political prisoners section. I was the only Pole, the rest were German, who took part in the last attempt against Hitler. While in prison I was given the job of taking care of menial services. I walked from cell to cell picking up buckets of waste, which I had to empty out and return clean. Since I was always hungry, I noticed that along with the excrements were fruit peelings, for the Germans had family in Berlin, who would send those packages full of nourishment. I told the prisoners to separate the peelings of pears, apples and oranges for they were clogging up the toilet, and to put them on top of the lid of the bucket. Eating clean fruit peelings I was able to protect myself from a vitamin deficiency.

In Berlin I found out from the judge that I had signed a document where I admit to being "Witold" – Franciszek Jozwiak. Not a surprise, during examination in Lowicz and in Frankfurt I had signed papers, not having read them, for I was pretty terrified due to the torture I underwent. During that whole time, day by day, they promised me: "Morgen fruh bist Du erschossen".

During my stay in Haftanstalt Zellengefangnis on Lehrterstrasse 3 I went out as usual to pick up a bucket from a cell of a certain someone and I saw a portrait, which I had seen in the office of one of my medical professors in Vilna. It turned out that it was the portrait of professor Bonhofer, a famous psychiatrist, who was the father-in-law of the prisoner.

It so happened that the German prisoner became ill. Since the illness was getting worse, and the prison knew I was a doctor, I was called upon to examine the prisoner. Having had great experience in the ghetto I immediately recognized it as typhus. The Germans were irritated and did not want to believe that a German could fall ill to typhus. A bacterial examination confirmed my observations. From then on I was the unofficial doctor of the prison. During a time of alarm, I used to stay in my cell but now I had the rights to enter the shelter with everyone else. As the unofficial doctor I was able to receive a better diet.

On the day of April 25, 1945 at six o'clock in the evening, on par with the remaining living German prisoners a count of 46 (in the last days many prisoners had been taken away to an unknown destination) I received a Entlassungsbescheinigung (release certificate), even though a striking terror about to happen surrounded Berlin, the Hausvater (father of the house) of the prison ordered all of us to fold our blankets and return them to him.

I came out having nowhere to go. In the meantime pastor Friedrich Leon invited me to his house. I lived with professor Bonhofer, who when I became better acquainted with, offered me a job at his well-know clinic. The professor lived in Charlottenburg, Marienallee 43. I longed to return to my country and find my wife as the rest of my family had perished.

May 2, 1945 I had found the road back to my country. I remember a few last names of the political prisoners: Teodor Bensch, Max Jochintke, Josef Sliwinski, Dr. Eberhardt Pleve, pastor Friedrich Leon, who saved me from the American bombings by giving me a place to stay in his home.

The names of my Nazi torturers: the chief Gestapo officer in Sochaczew Paul Schwarzwald, SS-man Rudolf Honig, the co-tenant of the head Gestapo officer Erich Schneider. My cell number was 222 in section BN 79/45, where I stayed under the name, Majnemer.

Victor Hochberg's Story

Victor Hochberg, now known as "Witold Gora", was born in 1900 in Warsaw, Poland. He was the son of Woolf Hochberg, who had a medical degree, and Rachel Hochberg, a midwife. There were nine siblings in the family. His mother supported the family while the father studied for his medical degree. The father also worked in a shoe factory and died in 1909.

In 1915, while attending public school in Warsaw, there was a takeover of the school building by the German army, resulting in a large protest demonstration by the students. Five boys were arrested, including young Victor, who was participating in the protest. He was taken with the other four to a prison near Stetin, Germany (the Stouer Works Factory). For four and one-half months, his mother did not know where he was, until he was finally allowed to send a postcard saying only "I am alive and alright".

Elder Germans in this "prison factory" took pity on young Victor and helped him. After six months in the prison, he had gained their trust and was allowed to live nearby Stetin. Seven months later he and 60 others escaped to Berlin, where he and some other men rented a room. He learned some skills, got work permits, and worked in Berlin, earning some money to send home, but he had no passport.

In 1918, this time as an organizer, he was a participant in demonstrations and a hunger strike to get Germany to end the war. He helped organize 4,000 factory workers. During this demonstration, a policeman from the factory approached him with a pistol at point-blank range. Victor grabbed the gun and deflected the bullet, which entered Victor's chest and exited behind his right shoulder. A German friend jumped the policeman and hit him with a club. The policeman, Victor, and four others were put in a special area of a hospital reserved for dying patients. Only the dying were given this kind of semi-privacy. Four men died in nine days in this room during the time Victor was hospitalized, and Victor was the only one who lived. He stayed in the hospital for weeks, and then purposely delayed his release by falsifying thermometer readings, with the assistance of other communist friends to keep him from having to return to the prison.

Victor was a member of a communist organization called "Spartacus" at this time. When he left the hospital, the war was still going on, but his work card had the stamp of "Revolutionary" on it, so he found little work, except for odd jobs at night.

During this time period, Russia and Germany were holding peace talks. The First Russian Communist Embassy in the world was in Berlin. All its clerks were workers who spoke only Russian. The only member of the intelligentsia was Ambassador Joffe. Spartacus sent Victor to the Russian embassy to meet Russian diplomats because of his knowledge of the Russian language as well as German and Polish. He got a job as secretary to the Russian military ambassador to Germany. The Russians could only speak Russian. Because Victor had learned German in the prison and already knew Russian, he worked for almost four months in the embassy. During the peace conference, the Russians demanded a return of their prisoners of war in Germany. The Germans who wanted free use of the Russian workers as long as possible, acted ignorant of any knowledge of the whereabouts of the prisoners of war. Victor, however, knew where the prisoners were and how they cold be found, and he set up a network through the German members of Spartacus to learn where all of them were located.

Victor told the Russian Ambassador all he knew for use at the peace conference table, which infuriated the Germans. He was therefore given forty-eight hours to leave Germany by Berlin Commandant Von Kessel. In other words, he was deported to Poland without diplomatic status and this would be the first time he had seen his family since his initial imprisonment at age fifteen.

At the time of his return to Poland, there was a severe depression. He lived a while with one of his sisters, Mania, (Dan's grandmother) and acted as a caretaker for her school.

Victor married in 1921, to a close friend of another sister, Dyna. He had been drafted into the Polish Army on February 1, 1920. There was still a war on at the time between Russia and Poland. Poland was carved up by Russia and Germany.

In 1924, Victor drove a taxi, and performed other odd jobs. He traveled a lot during the 1920's, and he and his wife lived in an attic, which was extremely cold in the winter, and burning hot in the summer. During the 1920's, Victor learned a great deal about forgery and falsification of papers, talents which he had learned while serving in prison, which he needed because he had no diplomatic status and lived under various aliases. Until 1923, he had no passport whatsoever and used the name "Shaia Berger". On several occasions during his life, his survival was miraculous. In 1920, he went to Warsaw without legal status, and if he had been caught at any time, he would have been shot. He was confronted by an elite guard of soldiers, but managed to escape. He lived under various assumed names for four years. During a railroad workers strike in Warsaw, he was able to help the government which then got him a more legal status again. But this did not last long and he was constantly arrested and he had a record against him. In 1938, a clerk in the office of records asked him to tell the truth about his entire past and seek to be reinstated. He had been arrested in 1932 for writing leaflets for communist organizations in his apartment.

After being in the reserves, he was called up by the Polish Army in 1939. When the Germans invaded Poland in 1939, he fought for 29 days, but then he was taken by the Germans to a German prison camp in the Polish corridor at Soldau for 23 days. Somehow he managed to escape this prison camp and made his way back to Warsaw and his family. When Germany created the Warsaw Ghetto, he lived within its borders with his wife and two daughters. He understood, with his great knowledge of the Germans, what was coming. First, he got his daughter, Basia, out of the ghetto by taking her to the wall and telling her that it was better that she try and take a chance on escaping than a sure death inside the walls. He eventually arranged for her to live with a non-Jewish family. Because he had false Aryan papers, he was able to go in and out of the ghetto at will. By now he had changed his name from Hochberg to Gora. In April, 1943, he finally took his wife out of the ghetto and left their home there, which greatly saddened Victor and his wife. He found places for her to live as well as for his other daughter, Danka. Once he posed as a German SS officer and went into the ghetto and arrested his sister's husband in order to get him out of the ghetto.

Victor understood the German mind very well and knew that they always followed a leader, and that they were very rigid and disciplined and would follow orders. He lived in Warsaw proper, and tried to avoid people who would betray him. And as a communist, he had many friends in the underground. At one time he stayed with a sergeant of police who was a communist. Danka was able to get a job in a factory and Basia worked as a maid, and was a smuggler. She moved from one family to another.

Because he had learned forgery, and he was able to steal blank papers, he was able to create false documents for others. At that time, to be caught with one set of blank papers or with one extra set of identity papers would result in an instant execution on the spot. Victor would carry fifty of such documents at a time. He never sold them for money. His instinct told him that if he ever did, he would die. Certain Polish citizens would turn Jews in or blackmail them for money, but no one ever turned him in because they knew he was always hungry and that he had no money and that he never took money for the lives that he saved. He personally took seventy people out of the ghetto and created false documents for 900 others.

At one time during the war, he worked in a technical bureau. He stole things from the Germans, but he always felt this was okay because they had stolen so much from the Jews. Victor also worked in a large laundry in the ghetto. Janus Korshak, a famous doctor and head of an orphanage there wanted to see him. The children of the orphanage had no clean clothes and he would bring them to Victor after the plant was closed during the middle of the night. During the daytime, the laundry did work for the German officers. Once they came in and told Victor that they were going to throw them out. He told them that if he was shot, the boiler would explode and bluffed them away. He saw Dr. Korshak leading the children of the orphanage to the Umshlagplatz, the train station. There was no German escort with them at Korshak's request, so the children would remain calm. They were, of course, all murdered in Treblinka. (Note 1: Read about Victor in biography of Korshak by Lifton. Note 2: Victor's sister's two children were in the orphanage at one time after their mother died.)

In 1947, Victor was injured by shrapnel during a disturbance in Warsaw. In 1968, when there was again a government purge of Jews in positions of government, Victor was serving as a president of a cooperative of engineers. All of his co-workers stated that if Victor was fired, then they would all also quit their jobs. Victor continued to serve in the Polish Army until 1957.

Victor and his family remained in Poland after the war, never wanting to leave because their roots are in Poland and so much of the family is buried there. After his wife died, and until his death in 1994, Victor visited Israel for almost four months each year. He became very close to Leona's friend, Danka Zdunska, as well as her family.

During one of his visits to Tel Aviv, Victor was on his way to the market when he was approached on the street by an elderly man who called him by name. Victor did not recognize the man who proclaimed that Victor had saved his life for which he was very grateful. He said that Victor had procured a false identity card for him which allowed him to survive in Warsaw. The gentleman was on his way to his grandson's bris and took Victor with him to be the baby's godfather. Victor returned to the worried Danka's apartment several hours later – without the milk from the market.